ART TOWNS
CALIFORNIA

These 2,245 nonskid panels fabricated from triple-layer glass lend the Sundial Bridge in Redding a sense of weightlessness.

ART TOWNS
CALIFORNIA

Communities Celebrating Creativity—
Festivals, Galleries, Museums, Dining & Lodging

John Villani

The Countryman Press
Woodstock, Vermont

ISBN 978-0-88150-696-9

Cover photo of *Turn of the Century Beach Life* (1976) mural by artist Jane Golden in Santa Monica provided courtesy of Ambient Images

Interior photos by the author unless otherwise specified

Book design and composition by Hespenheide Design

Published by The Countryman Press, P.O. Box 748, Woodstock, Vermont 05091

Distributed by W. W. Norton & Company, Inc., 500 Fifth Avenue, New York, NY 10110

Manufactured in the United States of America

10 9 8 7 6 5 4 3 2 1

For Zoe

Acknowledgments

For their advice, patience, and friendship
my sincere gratitude is extended to
Sheri, Vince, Helene, Mike, Della, Serge,
Joy, Alvin, MBJ, and Marita.

Contents

Introduction

S omewhere along the insanely twisted ribbon of Highway 128's blacktop a subconscious voice backed my leaden foot off the rented Dodge's gas pedal. The radio, which had been drilling Santana's "Soul Sacrifice" into my eardrums, was switched silent as my left hand started flicking the window controls. Within milliseconds or perhaps even nanoseconds the Dodge filled with an intoxicating ambrosia swirling mossy redwood scents with whatever funkiness was wafting skyward from the dense forest's earthen floor.

No sooner had I filled my lungs with this life force than yet another olfactory tsunami powered its presence throughout the sedan's upholstered recesses. As familiar as my childhood memories were of summer mornings spent adjusting the halyards and rudder of a fiberglass sailboat skipping along the surface of the Long Island Sound, there was no mistaking the Pacific Ocean's crisp and clean aroma.

A few sharp turns later I was tooling north on the PCH, the famed Pacific Coast Highway, whose oceanside meanderings have imprinted their spectacular curves and soaring bridges on the memory banks of the world's movie-watching public. The coast's fog blanket had rolled out to sea, leaving in its stead a spectacularly uninterrupted sky whose crystal clarity offered no resistance to the powerful rays of mid-August's sun. Within minutes Mendocino's breathtaking setting atop the coast's Headlands bluffs angled into view, challenging my corneal receptors with rich ocean blues framed by the eggshell whites of Main Street's storefronts. "This," I said to myself, "is the kind of place you have to see in person and burn into your memory."

Traveling throughout California in researching this book has not only been a test of driving capabilities, it's also been an education in appreciating the state's astounding range of natural assets. Routes such as Highway 128's meander through the vineyards of Anderson Valley followed by an afternoon of gallery visits in Mendocino are repeated all along the coastline and Sierra Nevada, serving as destination points for journeys into California's thriving culture of creativity.

From the sentry point of Crescent City on the state's northwest boundary to the windswept Algodones Dunes serrating its southeast flank, can any other place on the North American continent come close to equaling California's man-made and creator-given diversity? It's the only place I'm aware of that has the capacity to be all things to all of its devotees at all times, which partly explains why the audiences at California's televised sports events seem to always look so healthy and happy.

California's culture of creativity began with its Indigenous tribal people, whose communities traded ceremonial objects from South America to the Arctic and Asia. By 1769, when Padre Junipero Serra established the first of what grew to be a string of 21 Mission churches between San Diego and Santa Rosa, prodigious amounts of devotional art were being commissioned from Spanish and Mexican craftsmen to fill those churches. Today, Padre Serra's Mission churches endure as a legacy of the state's European and Mexican colonial roots. Their distinct architectural flourishes have evolved into the design vernacular known as Spanish Mission Revival and its cousins, Mediterranean style and Tuscan style.

Whether it results from nature's inspiration or an artistic inner vision, the power of creativity is evident throughout all corners of the state's nearly 164,000 square miles. Even the smallest communities have a venue or two exhibiting locally created paintings, and more often than not there's a community theatre in a neighboring town, perhaps sharing a performance venue with a dance academy's productions, or even a chamber music group from the nearby community college, the members of which are also part of a summer Shakespeare production in the town park, and on it goes. What makes California so noteworthy is the widespread prevalence of these community-focused arts dynamics. Other parts of the country feel fortunate to have community-based art scenes that are few and far between, while in California those elements are part of the expectations most residents link to a desirable quality of life.

This first edition of *Art Towns California* is intended as a survey of 27 of these types of communities. Some are better known than others, some are also known as college towns, a few got their start as art colonies during the early 1900s, while a couple served as quiet retreats for Hollywood actors, directors, and producers. Each community's profile includes suggestions for dining and overnighting, with at least one if not several bed and breakfast inns listed for each Art Town. The listings for art venues and art events are intended as useful samplings of what's readily accessible in each community, as well as suggesting prominent performances or festivals ideal for planning a visit.

Any suggestions for new communities to include in upcoming editions of *Art Towns California* are welcomed, as are your picks for dining, bars, java joints, and taco wagons. If you are planning a conference and would like to have me speak to your group about what it takes to succeed as an art town just send me an e-mail describing what your organization has in mind. Visit the www.arttowns.com Web site for more insights into Art Towns across the nation. Or just send me an e-mail with your feedback: arttowns@gmail.com.

John Villani
Santa Fe, NM
May 2008

Arcata

I mbued with a progressive spirit that's reflected in everything from the fashion statements parading along its tidy sidewalks to the variety of organic coffees served in the Northtown neighborhood's Muddy's Hot Cup, the college town of Arcata has a decidedly left-leaning sensibility. Strangely enough, right in the middle of Arcata's manicured town plaza there's a life-size bronze monument of William McKinley, the Republican, Ohio-born 25th American President who never set foot in Humboldt County prior to his assassination in the summer of 1901. In an Art Town with Arcata's 17,000-resident collective conscience it would seem far more appropriate to reposition this memorial celebrating the dodgy Spanish-American War's chief advocate to a less prominent, though equally inviting traffic circle, and in its place have the sculpture crew at Unauthorized Art create an even larger bronze memorial to Jerry Garcia or William Burroughs or Bobby Kennedy, or any public figure whose politics would mesh with the Arcata City Council's.

Arcata's progressive form of political activism has vaulted it into the national spotlight for initiatives such as its 1989 Nuclear Weapons-Free Zone Act, and a 2006 resolution calling for President Bush's resignation. To some these efforts are indulgences brought on by the community's isolation from mainstream society. But to others the community's activism serves as a social petrie dish whose debates, initiatives, and dialogues are the precursors of evolving issues and trends poised to ripple across the national political landscape. While the local tradition of engagement on hot button topics is central to Arcata's civic identity, so has the community's support for all aspects of creativity become interwoven with the experience of living here. Many

Oysters are objets d'art in the eyes of the 15,000 bivalve lovers slurping their way through the annual Arcata Bay Oyster Festival.

communities make a point of describing themselves as "arts friendly" or "arts supportive" but in Arcata's case there's no need for these qualifiers because the presence and impact of art and artists on community life is tangible, pervasive, and acknowledged. For artists who can tolerate Humboldt County's overcast skies and dampness this is a great place to live and work.

Arcata's mid-1800s founding was the result of a Gold Rush era mining boom in the nearby Trinity Mountains. Engineers were brought in to build an east-west rail line connecting Arcata to Korbel, while others designed the grid of streets that now serve as its business district and oldest residential neighborhoods. A centrally located public gathering space was included in those plans, which is how Arcata got its plaza. As rail and road infrastructure improved throughout the rest of the century the lumber industry stepped into the void left by the 1850s mining bust. Today's number of Humboldt County lumber mills is comparatively miniscule to then, and shifting economic tides have allowed communities along the North Coast to reclaim their riverfronts and baysides after removing old mills and remediating their soil contamination issues. Arcata's waterfront on Humboldt Bay has been turned into the 154-acre Arcata Marsh & Wildlife Sanctuary, while its west reaches along Samoa Peninsula extend to the protected sand dunes and the expanses of Mad River Beach State Park, and even toward Clam Beach a bit further north.

From its headwaters in Six Rivers National Forest the Mad River flows past the community of Blue Lake before it cuts across Arcata's north end on its way to the Pacific. Dell'Arte International, one of the most respected training grounds for practitioners of "physical theatre" is based here. It offers year-round instruction leading as far as an MFA degree, or perhaps even a place in its resident professional touring company. The company offers numerous education initiatives throughout Humboldt County schools including a Mobile Mask Project, summer youth theatre camp, theatre training for area educators, and volunteer service in local nonprofit agencies. Blue Lake performances of the Dell'Arte Company are held in its 125-seat Carlo Theatre, though the company's touring productions are showcased internationally and throughout North America. Dell'Arte's outdoor performance venue, the 400-seat Rooney Ampitheatre, is the main venue for its annual Mad River Festival, a five-week presentation that runs from mid-June to late July and combines a summer workshop intensive with performances by touring companies performing physical theatre, puppetry, music, and storytelling. There's also a parade, ampitheatre concerts, and an evening cabaret.

Since its opening in 2007 the Arcata Playhouse has filled an important void in the local arts scene by providing a community arts center venue dedicated to performance. Located in the Old Creamery building and home to Four on the Floor Theatre as well as Shoebox Puppets, the venue hosts a broad range of theatre and concerts, including some of Dell'Arte productions, independently promoted concerts, Shake the Bard Theatre Company's presentations of Shakespeare classics, and touring artist presentations from the Humboldt Folklife Society. During the summer months two of Arcata's most popular gatherings come courtesy of Humboldt Folklife Society. The largest of these, July's week-long Humboldt Folklife Festival, features musicians from across Humboldt County performing in Eureka, Arcata, and Blue Lake venues, while mid-August's Buddy Brown Blues Festival schedules a full day's worth of music and a half dozen bands onstage in Blue Lake's Perigot Park. The City of Arcata's nearly 2000 acres of forestland holdings include its 793-acre Community Forest and Redwood Park, which during late July and early August serves as the backdrop for an annual Shakespeare production from Shake the Bard Theatre. The central location of Arcata Plaza makes it the logical place to hold recurring popular events such as the Saturday Farmers Market organized by the North Coast Growers Association from April through November, and annual

The Arcata Theatre, a 1937 masterpiece of Art Deco streamlining, will be restored to its former glory . . . someday.

bashes like the Arcata Bay Oyster Festival's mid-June celebration of locally-raised Pacific and Kumomoto oysters, a one-day soiree that attracts upwards of 18,000 slurping, shucking, bivalve lovers. Just two blocks from Arcata Plaza is the field of dreams that's home to the Humboldt Crabs, whose two-month summer season features games with the likes of the Sonoma Seals, Maxim Yankees, and the Morgan Hill Mudcats.

Humboldt State University (HSU) offers an extensive range of performances through its Department of Theatre, Film & Dance in campus venues that include the 862-seat Van Duzer Theatre, Gist Hall Theatre, and the Studio Theatre. While the Van Duzer Theatre also serves as the main venue for university-produced events such as March's weeklong Humboldt Film Festival, its most prominent role is serving as the home of Center Arts, the August through May performing arts series whose global reach brings some of the world's leading musicians, dancers, theatre companies, and comedians into Arcata. HSU's Art Department operates two exhibition venues, the on-campus Reese Bullen Gallery, and Old Town Eureka venue named the First Street Gallery. The Bullen Gallery's exhibitions provide a forum for exhibiting the work of HSU art students and recent graduates, as well as artists from the region whose work is selected for a themed show. First Street Gallery, whose exhibitions include HSU faculty as well as students, takes a decidedly regional and national perspective when formulating its slate of contemporary art shows.

Making contact with the creative spirit of this Art Town is as simple as deciding on a visit during one of the monthly second Friday walkabouts known as Arts! Arcata. Most of the creative community at least occasionally prowls from one of the 40 or so Arts! Arcata venues to another, sipping the usual wine and nibbling on the usual cheese while surveying the unusual art being made by their Arcata compañeros and compañeras. Atypical sites such as the Arcata Plaza location of Simply Macintosh, the G Street offices of Umpqua Community Bank, and Grandma B's Fudge Shop get involved as monthly venues for local artists. Working environments such as the 9,000 square foot foundry and artists' studio complex of Unauthorized Art on Alder Grove Road, and the Fire Arts Center's studio and foundry for fused glass and ceramics on South G Street provide a glimpse into their facilities during Arts! Arcata's 6 PM to 9 PM opening receptions. Jacoby's Storehouse, a restored, four-level 1898 commercial building bordering Arcata Plaza, houses several dining spots as well as Arcata Bay Arts, which exhibits the work of local art students during Arts! Arcata. Nearby, the Arcata Artisans Cooperative Gallery exhibits work from more than 30 accomplished, painters, photographers, jewelers, ceramists, and sculptors and is a perfect Arts! Arcata starting point. Humboldt State

Humboldt State University's theatre department has consistently led the way in developing Humboldt County's diverse and accomplished community of actors and technicians. Innovative efforts such as its triennial New Play Season, which solicits nationwide for new works to produce on its Arcata stage, help maintain its record of success.

University's downtown Arcata off-campus exhibition venue is the HSU Sculpture Garden, a compact space on Ninth Street that's immediately adjacent to the Meridian Fine Art Gallery, a commercial art gallery and publisher of limited edition fine art prints whose represented artists include Jim McVicker, Tina Rousselot, Joseph Wilhelm, Michael Hays, Shawn Gould, and Jesse Corning.

Venues

Reese Bullen Gallery
Humboldt State University, Arcata, CA 95521
707.826.5814 / www.humboldt.edu
▲ Dedicated to the memory of the HSU professor who started Arcata's development as an Art Town, this on-campus exhibition space complements two additional, off campus HSU venues; Eureka's First Street Gallery and Arcata's HSU Sculpture Courtyard.

Arcata Artisans Cooperative Gallery
883 H Street, Arcata, CA 95521
707.825.9133 / www.arcataartisans.com
▲ Located on Arcata Plaza, this artist-owned gallery represents the work of more than 30 local talents in a range of media.

Fire Arts Center
520 South G Street, Arcata, CA 95521
707.826.1445 / www.fireartsarcata.com
▲ Specialized education programs and a ceramic arts studio.

Meridian Fine Art
833 Ninth Street, Arcata, CA 95521
707.826.7184 / www.meridianfineart.com
▲ Fine art printers and a gallery exhibiting work by many of the region's top painters and printmakers.

HSU Department of Theatre, Film & Dance
HSU Theatre Arts Building, Arcata, CA 95521
707.826.3566 / www.humboldt.edu
▲ Presenting a wide range of productions throughout the academic year.

Shake the Bard Theatre Company
707.498.1826 / www.shakethebard.com
▲ Arcata's popular, homegrown Shakespeare company presents classics in the Arcata Playhouse as well as summer Shakespeare in Redwood Park.

Dell'Arte International
131 H Street, Blue Lake, CA 95525
707.668.5663 / www.dellarte.com
▲ This training center for talented practitioners of physical theatre serves as a performing arts venue for music and stagecrafts.

Events

Humboldt Folklife Festival
Assorted Venues
707.822.5394 / www.humboldtfolklife.org
▲ One of summer's highlights is the weeklong showcase of Humboldt County music talent participating in the festival's numerous concerts.

Arts! Arcata
Downtown Arcata
707.822.4500 / www.artsarcata.com
▲ This monthly showcase of visual arts coordinates opening receptions at more than 40 downtown Arcata venues.

Arcata Bay Oyster Festival
Arcata Plaza
707.822.4500 / www.oysterfestival.com
▲ The Humboldt Bay's five commercial oyster farms provide the thousands of bivalves savored in this June event.

Slumber

Hotel Arcata
708 Ninth Street, Arcata, CA 95521
707.826.0217 / www.hotelarcata.com
▲ This historic hotel on Arcata Plaza has a Japanese restaurant and elegance to spare.

Cat's Cradle Bed and Breakfast
815 Park Place, Arcata, CA 95521
707.822.2287 / www.catscradlebnb.com
▲ Four-room B&B in a quiet neighborhood.

Quality Inn
3535 Janes Road, Arcata, CA 95521
707.822.0409 / www.arcataqualityinn.com
▲ Convenient to Highway 101, free high speed Internet, and a pool.

Best Western Arcata Inn
4827 Valley West Boulevard, Arcata, CA 95521
707.826.0313 / www.bestwestern.com
▲ High speed Internet, indoor/outdoor pool, and a convenient location.

Sustenance

Humboldt Brews
856 Tenth Street, Arcata, CA 95521
707.826.2739 / www.humboldtbrews.com
▲ Arcata's employee-owned brewpub serves up awesome fish and chips to accompany its legendary brews.

Abruzzi Restaurant
791 Eighth Street, Arcata, CA 95521
707.826.2345 / www.abruzzicatering.com
▲ Romantic spot in the Jacoby's Storehouse, serving regional Italian pastas.

Mosgo's
2461 Alliance Road, Arcata, CA 95521
707.826.1195 / www.mosgos.org
▲ Live music and serious coffees.

———————————•———————————

A s co-director of Arcata Playhouse, located inside a former dairy
processing facility in downtown Arcata, Jackie Dandeneau oversees the operations of a 140-seat facility that presents everything from
children's theatre to Shakespeare.

"We're located in the old Humboldt Creamery building, with New
World Ballet, and Redwood Raks Dance Studio. The whole area
started out as the Pacific Arts Center, which lasted about 15 years. It's
now a place for performance and music, and we've been in there since
the beginning of 2007 as both a producing and a presenting organization. Four on the Floor Productions, which does original work, is the
resident company of the Arcata Playhouse. We bring in family acts,
music acts, and a variety of artists of all types who are traveling along
the coast between Seattle and San Francisco.

"My husband and I come from a background in physical theatre,
the kind of work that's outside the mainstream, so we're willing to be
more flexible when it comes to deciding which performers will be able
to use our facility and the terms they work under. Our presenting program runs strongly in the independent folk artist category. We're living
in a vibrant, active community that's very open to creative expressions
from around the world, and there's no understating the infectious
impact of the creativity taught and practiced at Dell'Arte on this community's sense of itself as a center for artistic achievement. In the next
few years we will guide the playhouse in the direction of being a community arts center for theatre and music."

———————————•———————————

W hen it comes to the Middle Eastern performing arts form
known as Belly Dance, the region's leading performer and
educator is Arcata's Shoshanna. From her Redwood Raks Dance Studio
in the Old Creamery she oversees the Ya Habibi Dance Company as
well as the Redwood Coast Bellydance Festival.

"There's something about the character of this area, with its college town identity and growing community of creative people who
decided this was the right place for them, all of these elements con-

tributed to Humboldt County being home to dance professionals. Dance performances are part of this community's traditions and we're called upon to perform at different events from political rallies to more serious occasions like memorial services and benefits.

"I've taught at Humboldt State for 10 years, forming a Middle Eastern dance club and eventually bringing the idea of a studio into the community as a semiprofessional group. Having a great space for rehearsals and performances has helped grow the dance company in a very positive way. We don't really get much support for what we do from local government, nor do we ask for it. Most of the events where we dance are organized and supported by individuals, organizations, or nonprofits like the Chamber of Commerce, and that keeps us really busy."

Cambria

California's central coast is one of nature's wonders. Sawtoothing south from Monterey Bay to the Channel Islands off Santa Barbara, the coastline's nearly 250 miles of beaches, bays, bluffs, and cliffs are the continent's front porch on the Pacific Ocean. Along most of those miles the ribbon of blacktop known as the Pacific Coast Highway provides travelers with their only access through the central coast communities, rewarding those who endure its challenging curves and steep grades with a steady flow of vistas whose dramatic beauty can only begin to be described as breathtaking.

In the 1920s William Randolph Hearst, whose family holdings controlled 250,000 acres near San Simeon Bay, used his vast wealth to create one of the world's most spectacular residences, known today as Hearst Castle and operated as a State Historical Monument. In the ensuing decades a lively community of artists settled in just south of San Simeon in the town of Cambria. Today this community is widely known for both its range of art galleries and for the hundreds of talented painters, sculptors, and fine craftspeople who call this Art Town of 6,300 full-time residents home. Cambria's remoteness places it beyond the range of many conveniences other Californians take for granted, so someone in need of retail therapy will need to gas up for a 70-mile roundtrip drive into San Luis Obispo or navigate 65 miles of switchbacks into Paso

An ideal way to get a sense for who's-who in Cambria's diverse and talented arts scene is the January staging of the Cambria Art & Wine Festival, a weekend-long affair whose events celebrate regional viniculture as well as local creativity. Artists are paired with chefs and winemakers for a series of exhibitions, demonstrations, tastings, raffles, and general merrymaking.

Moonstone Beach, where barking sea lions scare the bejeezus out of unsuspecting beachcombers.

Robles for a cruise through the shelves at Chelsea Bookshop. In a community like Cambria most artists are on a first-name basis with the local drivers for FedEx and UPS, who bring art supplies in, and haul out completed works of art.

In the 130 years since its founding, Cambria has evolved from a mining and maritime economy to one based on tourism and agriculture. The town is administered as an unincorporated community within the north boundary of San Luis Obispo County. Its year-round temperate climate and unspoiled natural beauty have proven to be as irresistible to artists in search of subject matter inspiration as it is for the California sea otters who thrive in these ocean waters. To live in Cambria is to know when and where one can stand on the shore and observe the northbound, February to June migration of gray whales. It also means having access to beaches favored by elephant seals, the hiking trails of San Simeon State Park, and daily walks along Moonstone Beach Drive. With its mild climate the Cambria area has always been supportive of its farmers and ranchers, many of whom can be found year-round in the Veterans Memorial Hall parking lot on Friday afternoons, selling everything from goat cheese to baskets of oversized raspberries at the weekly Cambria Farmers' Market.

The community's first gallery, Greystone Manor, was opened in the early 1950s by Julia Morgan, the San Francisco architect who for 28 years oversaw the construction of Hearst Castle. Cambria's reputation as a desirable community for on-the-move artists started gaining momentum in the late 1950s following the public opening of Hearst

Looks quaint, doesn't it? Wrong. The schoolhouse home of Cambria's Allied Arts Association is a serious gallery with a region-wide impact.

Castle as a state park. The steady flow of castle-bound tourists along Highway 1 boosted the local economy to such an extent that Cambria built a highway bypass around its congested Main Street, which today is home to the Schoolhouse Gallery of the Allied Arts Association. This nonprofit organization, which also oversees the Cambria Film Society and its monthly screenings of mainstream and classic films at the Theatre in the Old Grammar School on third Thursdays, uses its gallery in what once was the Santa Rosa school for year-round exhibitions whose themes and featured artists shift from month to month. During Pinedorado Days, an annual celebration marking the end of summer, the art association organizes a large exhibition featuring nearly 100 works of art by more than 50 of its member artists. Art in the Pines, the annual juried exhibition of work by association members, is paralleled by the decidedly contemporary art aesthetic of the association's 927/924 Show, which encourages members to experiment with materials and media. Taking on the task of converting a warren of classroom spaces in a former education facility into the Theatre in the Old Grammar School (TOGS) presented the association with considerably more challenges than it had anticipated, primarily in terms of the project's funding. But today, with the 97-seat TOGS playhouse in full operation, the association's partner in this venture, Houselights Theatre, uses the venue to present stage productions such as *Menopause the Musical, All in the Timing*, and *The Best Christmas Pageant Ever.*

In addition to attending workshops organized by Allied Arts Association, local artists can hone their skills through the professional-level programs offered at Camp Ocean Pines. This retreat and conference center presents adult education workshops in forums such as Native American flute performance, the craft of storytelling, and in the workshop offerings of its Annual California Sculptors Symposium. The weeklong April sculpture intensive attracts more than 60 artists working in clay, stone, metal, and wood for the opportunity to engage in one-on-one instructional dialogues with a teaching faculty that includes some of California's most prominent sculptors. The symposium's culminating event, Sculpture by the Sea, attracts artists from all corners of San Luis Obispo County to the Camp Ocean

Equidistant from both Los Angeles and San Francisco, Cambria's gallery district feasts on day-tripping urban tourists.

Pines campus for a public celebration and exhibition.

For Cambria visitors one of the most striking qualities of the community is its concentration of art galleries, whose street level presence exceeds two dozen venues. During busy weekends the sidewalks connecting Cambria's tidy grid of commercial enterprises can become quite crowded, a transitory condition local residents seem to handle with good-natured bemusement. Among the prominent art spaces are Melanee Sylvester Gallery, representing the contemporary impressionism of its namesake artist and owner; Seekers Glass Gallery, where as many as 250 glass artists are represented; Vault Gallery, whose distinctly contemporary emphasis groups together a national roster of talents; Artifacts Gallery, representing well-known talents mainly from outside the region; and Terry DeLapp Gallery, representing one of the West's most acclaimed landscape painters. Many of Cambria's businesses that are not specifically engaged in the art scene nonetheless show their support for the community's wealth of talents by displaying local artists' work on their walls. Included among these alternative exhibition venues are the Heritage Oaks Bank, Willows Bend Antiques, Teresabelle, and the Rainbow Bean coffeehouse.

One of the most unique performance spaces in the state is the Cambria West Village home of the Pewter Plough Playhouse. In all ways this compact and incredibly atmospheric venue fits the concept of what a "jewelbox" theatre truly is. Established in 1976 by Jim and Olga Buckley, the venue combines elements of a lobby piano bar serving wines, brews, and desserts, under the same roof with a 61-seat theatre. In addition to its year-round presentation of plays this organization also networks to the community at large through its monthly Readers' Theatre, a free, workshop-style dramatization of local as well as Broadway scripts being considered for the playhouse's mainstage. Those productions making it into the Pewter Plough Playhouse season become part of a slate of five or six plays that include musicals, dramas, and comedies. And as for the theatre's 61 seats, each is individually named for one of the greatest of Hollywood's stars. So if you ever felt like elbowing up to the representational likes of Spencer Tracy or Julie Andrews, don't pass up the opportunity to enjoy a glass of zinfandel followed by one of the Pewter Plough Playhouse's productions.

Venues

Allied Arts Association Schoolhouse Gallery
880 Main Street, Cambria, CA 93428
805.927.8190 / www.artistsofcambria.com
▲ Membership organization with year-round exhibitions, workshops, and performances.

Camp Ocean Pines
1473 Randall Drive, Cambria, CA 93428
805.927.0245 / www.campoceanpines.org
▲ Secluded facility offering adult art education workshops.

Houselights Theatre
1350 Main Street, Cambria, CA 93428
805.927.4667 / www.houselightstheatre.org
▲ Cambria's newest stage company presents its plays in what once had been the Cambria Union Grammar School.

The Pewter Plough Playhouse
824 Main Street, Cambria, CA 93428
805.927.3877 / www.pewterploughplayhouse.org
▲ Serving up a year-round slate of compelling works, along with a piano bar and an openness to new works.

Terry DeLapp Gallery
POB 718, Cambria, CA 93428
805.927.9416 / www.terrydelapp.com
▲ Considered the leading talent in a community overflowing with artists.

Seekers Glass Gallery
4090 Burton Drive, Cambria, CA 93428
805-927-4352 / www.seekersglass.com
▲ One of the nation's most prominent venues for fine art glass, representing more than 250 artists.

The Melanee Sylvester Gallery
724 Main Street, Cambria, CA 93428
805.927.5450 / www.melaneesylvester.com
▲ Contemporary California Impressionism.

The Vault Gallery
2289 Main Street, Cambria, CA 93428
805.927.0300 / www.vaultgallery.com
▲ Contemporary art exhibited in a former bank building.

Events

Sculpture by the Sea
Camp Ocean Pines, Cambria, CA 93428
805.927.0245 / www.campoceanpines.org
▲ Large sculpture exhibition and soiree capping off the annual California Sculptors Symposium.

Cambria Art & Wine Festival
Chamber of Commerce, Cambria, CA 93428
805.927.3624 / www.seecambria.com
▲ Three January days and nights of art, wine, and great food.

Pinedorado Art Show
Allied Arts Association, Cambria, CA 93428
805.927.8190 / www.artistsofcambria.com
▲ The year's largest Cambria art exhibition features work from more than 50 artists.

Slumber

Castle Inn by the Sea
6620 Moonstone Beach Drive, Cambria, CA 93428
805.927.8605 / www.cambriacastleinn.com

▲ This comfortable, 31-room inn is located within walking distance of town. Its Moonstone Beach views, large swimming pool, waterfront access, and affordable rates keep guests coming back for repeat visits.

Bluebird Inn
1880 Main Street, Cambria, CA 93428
805.927.4634 / www.bluebirdmotel.com
▲ Cambria's creekside retreat is a hop, skip, and jump from the art galleries. Its ten comfortable rooms look out onto lush gardens and the Santa Rosa Creek, whose rushing waters provide a relaxing background for weekending visitors.

Little Sur Inn
6190 Moonstone Beach Drive, Cambria, CA 93428
866.478.7466 / www.littlesurinn.com
▲ This 17-room, boutique inn features stunning views, fireplaces, the sound of crashing waves lulling guests to sleep, and plentiful parking.

Fireside Inn Best Western
6700 Moonstone Drive, Cambria, CA 93428
888.910.7100 / www.bestwesternfiresideinn.com
▲ A great location, moderate rates, heated swimming pool, free wi-fi, fireplaces, and ocean breezes, plus traditional coastal charm.

Patrick House Bed & Breakfast Inn
2990 Burton Drive, Cambria, CA 93428
805.927.3812 / www.jpatrickhouse.com
▲ This log home in a wooded setting has eight guest rooms, and a convenient location to downtown's galleries and restaurants.

The Pickford House Bed & Breakfast
2555 MacLeod Way, Cambria, CA 93428
805.927.8619 / www.thepickfordhouse.com
▲ With each of its eight guest rooms named in honor of one of the legendary Hollywood stars who were regulars at Hearst Castle's lavish soirees, the Pickford House is tailor-made to enhance visits to the great residence.

Fog's End
2735 Main Street, Cambria, CA 93428
805.927.7465 / www.fogsend.com
▲ Surrounded by eight acres of forest, this three-room inn offers seclusion, a pool table, bocce court, and horseshoe pits.

Sustenance

Moonstone Beach Bar & Grill
6550 Moonstone Beach Drive, Cambria, CA 93428
805.927.3859 / www.moonstonebeach.com
▲ Spectacular views and wonderful seafood make this a must-see on any Cambria itinerary.

Wild Ginger
2380 Main Street, Cambria, CA 93428
805.927.1001 / www.wildgingercambria.com
▲ Art-filled setting featuring Asian fusion cuisine with a Thai twist.

Robin's Restaurant
4095 Burton Drive, Cambria, CA 93428
805.927.5007 / www.robinsrestaurant.com
▲ Contemporary California with international highlights.

---

*A*s president of the Allied Arts Association, musician Jeff Mar oversees the affairs of one of California's most highly respected local arts agencies, whose activities include the operation of the Old Schoolhouse Gallery, performances slated at the Theatre at the Old Grammar School, and concerts at numerous Cambria venues.

"My wife and I bought property here in the late 70s and eventually built a home that we visited so often it just made sense to leave Los Angeles, retire, and move to Cambria. Once we got here we both got more interested in art. Her name is Shirley Kirkes Mar and her specialty is figurative painting, while in my case I got involved in a certain amount of local performing. This community has met our expectations and then some. I traded a 90-minute commute in LA for a few minutes' drive to the frame shop we own, while Shirley has started a dance studio where she teaches tap dancing, just a few doors down from the frame shop.

"So for both of us life revolves around either doing our individual art, running our business, or teaching someone about our art. I don't know if you can call that kind of life a retirement, but we're enjoying every minute of it, even though we're as busy as ever. Allied Arts Association is a multidisciplinary organization whose members include visual artists, writers, and performing artists, most of whom come from urban areas where they've had successful careers. We've taken on the development of a performance space in our old *schoolhouse, which has allowed us to bring an entire group of theatre people into our association."*

Clarence Weiss honed his painting skills on the streets of Paris, where he lived and supported himself as a plein air painter who created and sold his work on the sidewalks of the world's most romantic city.

"In many ways being an artist in Cambria has a close connection to the experience of being an artist in Paris. There's a kind of feeling here of living in a town with lots of other artists and people who appreciate art, and then wherever you go around here all you see are great places to paint. For someone like myself whose work is usually done outdoors there's really not much more you could wish for. I'm a member of a group called the Wednesday Irregulars who meet once a week to go out as a group and paint in the canyons, or in the farm country, and of course along the coast.

"If I lived in a different part of the country I'd have to find a way to sell my work in galleries. But here I can just set some paintings out in my front yard and in the driveway, and I'll have better luck selling that way that I would in almost any art gallery in the area. I put up a few signs around town and that seems enough to bring people to my door. Cambria is a place with a long reputation as a place filled with artists, and visitors seem to enjoy wandering around here, looking for things to buy. Those of us living here know that we're lucky to be in this place."

Carmel

One doesn't need to amble very far along a Carmel sidewalk before coming across an art gallery or even a shaded courtyard cluster of several galleries. Famed for the ingenious ways this community of 4,000 residents has somehow loaded nearly 100 art galleries and more than 60 courtyards into the pedestrian-friendly confines of its picture-perfect downtown, Carmel (whose one square mile core is also referred to as Carmel-by-the-Sea) offers its visitors and residents one of the nation's densest art gallery scenes. In no small measure the continued success of Carmel in the increasingly competitive pursuit of cultural tourism's cashflow can be attributed to both the beauty of its location and to the picture frame perfection of Carmel's residential and commercial streets.

The 1906 earthquake that devastated San Francisco's infrastructure also forced many of its best known artists and authors to relocate in communities where they could stay in contact with their art dealers and patrons, as well as find the type of work space suited to their creative needs. Some of the most prominent of these figures, including the likes of Jack London, Upton Sinclair, Ansel Adams, and Mary Austin, unpacked their bags 120 miles south of the Golden Gate in Carmel's tranquil cottages. For creative inspiration they could hike amongst the towering redwoods covering hillsides on three sides of the community. Even in today's Carmel the leisure options haven't drastically changed. In this part of the state, grabbing a bottle of merlot, tossing some brie and a baguette into a picnic basket, and bicycling a few blocks down Ocean Avenue to the white sands of Carmel Beach City Park is a familiar rite of geographic affirmation. After all, it's impossible to resist the lure of this idyllic crescent on Carmel Bay with

Carmel-by-the-Sea's one square mile of shoppers' paradise is one of the prettiest art districts in North America.

the sight of iridescent blue Pacific waters to its west and the verdant fairways of Pebble Beach Golf Course to its north. Before there was anything resembling a golf course on the Monterey Peninsula, and even before an earthquake filled Carmel's cottages with authors, painters, and poets, a number of artists had already discovered that the peninsula's stunning landscape and abundant sunshine were ideal precursors for creating art.

The region's natural assets have exerted their influence over many Carmel visitors and residents, including Padre Junipero Serra. He resided at the Carmel church he established in 1771 as Mission San Carlos Borroméo de Carmelo, even choosing to have his remains interred under its altar. Visiting the Mission's grounds is a Carmel rite of passage, and not only for taking in the structure's elegant, Spanish-Moorish architecture. Walking along the mile-long route separating what today is known as the Carmel Mission Basilica and National Shrine of Blessed Junipero Serra from the crowds along Ocean Avenue's gallery district also delivers an up-close look at some of the coastline's most attractive homes.

While Carmel's galleries are filled with a myriad of painted representations of the regional landscape, there's a certain hit-or-miss quality in respect to what's occupying those gallery walls. This matter of inconsistency isn't an issue when it comes to the images displayed in

Carmel's photography galleries, as the community's long-standing ties to top-level professional photographers has established this Art Town as an internationally renowned home base and commercial market for photographers. For some visitors their initial contact point with the region's photography traditions takes place along the route of Highway 1 as it rambles southward from Carmel toward the majestic landscape of Big Sur. Just past the third mile marker along this 26 mile drive is the Highlands Inn–Park Hyatt Carmel, a 48-room, four-star hotel that's home to rotating exhibitions organized by the Ansel Adams Gallery of

M ajor art festivals thrive on consistency, so when the organizers of the Carmel Art Festival decided to skip past 2008 and instead present their 15th annual festival in 2009, citing "economic facts that are out of the control of the festival's planners," shock waves were felt throughout the Monterey Peninsula's creative community. If everything goes as planned, the festival will slide back into view in mid-May 2009.

Yosemite National Park. These exhibitions typically include a selection of images captured by Adams during the 22 years he resided in Carmel. While many of Carmel galleries include photographers in their rosters of represented artists, an in-town modernist building on a quiet side street that's home to the Weston Gallery is an American fine art photography shrine. Edward Weston first moved to Carmel in 1929, returning in 1938 to the Wildcat Hill home he resided in until his 1958

If you've got a spare $75,000 burning through your pocket the folks at Weston Gallery have a Paul Strand image they'd like to show you.

"In the Land of the Blind, the one-eyed man is King." (Desiderius Erasmus, 1466–1536). Long live the Carmel Art Association (1927–2008, and counting).

passing. His work as well as that of family members Brett Weston and Cole Weston are all represented here, in addition to images from the likes of Irving Penn, Alfred Stieglitz, Imogen Cunningham, Diane Arbus, and Paul Strand. Nearby, the Sunset Cultural Center is the site of the Center for Photographic Art, which boasts both Ansel Adams and Brett Weston among its founders, and today offers workshops and exhibitions through its affiliation with the Arts Council for Monterey County. From the Center it's a short walk to Photography West Gallery, which in addition to the work of Ansel Adams and Brett Weston also represents significant contemporary figures such as Paul Caponigro, Christopher Burkett, and Olivia Parker. Robert Knight Gallery on Dolores Street is another notable photography venue, with its space filled by the landscape and wildlife images captured by Mr. Knight on his adventuresome travels.

The enduring appeal that Carmel, Big Sur, and the Monterey Peninsula extend over the region's artists is reflected in its long-standing tradition of plein air painting. Art dealers such as the Trotter Galleries, George Stern Fine Art, Masterpiece Gallery, Roger Budney Fine Art, and William A. Karges Fine Art all include early California and Carmel artists in their inventories, while Galerie Plein Aire represents a group of contemporary artists who, like their predecessors, are inspired by the region's natural beauty. The downtown space of the Carmel Art Association is home to a large group of experienced local talents. More than 120 of the region's best belong to the association, which since 1927 has connected local artists with the year-round stream of art buyers venturing into Carmel from across the globe.

Just because its attention-grabbing gallery scene enjoys such a high level of day-to-day activity doesn't mean Carmel's performing arts side is wandering the beaches in search of seashells. Case in point is the year-round programming of the Pacific Repertory Theatre, which makes full use of three venues in its season of productions. Its downtown Carmel Circle Theatre is part of the company's 300-seat mainstage Golden Bough Theatre. During the most weather-favorable months of the year Pacific Rep switches its focus outdoors to the Forest Theatre, an open-air relic in a typically sedate Carmel residential neighborhood. The two productions presented at the Forest hew closely to Carmel's enduring theatrical traditions. First up in August and September is *The Wizard of Oz*, followed by two early October weeks of the Carmel Shake-Speare Festival. There are nearly 100 years of local summer stage history behind Carmel's love for its Shake-Speare Festival, which makes tickets quite hard to come by. Another production wraps up the festival, though its staging in late October takes place in the comfortable confines of the Golden Bough Theatre. Like other well-managed stage companies, Pacific Rep stays connected to its ticket-buying public through a myriad of community outreach and education-focused initiatives, including its 10-week, winter and fall School of Dramatic Arts sessions for budding local talents. Carmel's 718-seat Sunset Center is the venue used by local and out of town presenters for events such as pop and classical music performances, and concerts by the Monterey Symphony. Other performers using Sunset Center include Chamber Music Monterey Bay, the Carmel Music Society, Performance Carmel, and the annual Carmel Bach Festival. Considered one of the top North American festival stagings of Bach's work, the Carmel Bach Festival's three weeks of more than 50 performances run from mid-July into early August and make full use of a variety of additional local venues such as the Carmel Mission Basilica, All Saints Church, and the terrace of Sunset Center.

Venues

Carmel Mission Basilica
3080 Rio Road, Carmel, CA 93923
831.624.1271 / www.carmelmission.org
▲ Includes the Mora Chapel Gallery and a Mission store.

Carmel Art Association
Dolores Street, Carmel, CA 93923
831.624.6176 / www.carmelart.org
▲ Interesting art in an ideal setting makes this art space worth a visit.

Weston Gallery
6th Avenue, Carmel, CA 93923
831.624.4453 / www.westongallery.com
▲ One of the nation's leading photography galleries.

James J. Rieser Fine Art
Dolores Street, Carmel, CA 93923
831.620.0530 / www.rieserfineart.com
▲ Outstanding selection of California impressionist art.

Galerie Plein Aire
Dolores Street, Carmel, CA 93923
831.625.5686 / www.galeriepleinaire.com
▲ A contemporary take on California impressionism.

Pacific Repertory Theatre
Golden Bough Theater, Carmel, CA 93923
831.622.0700 / www.pacrep.org
▲ Carmel's year-round professional stage organization presents its productions in three local venues.

Sunset Center
San Carlos Street, Carmel, CA 93923
831.620.2040 / www.sunsetcenter.org
▲ Large venue hosting year-round presentations of classical, chamber, world beat, and orchestral music.

Events

Carmel Bach Festival
Sunset Center Theater, Carmel, CA 93923
831.624.1521 / www.bachfestival.org
▲ Three weeks of innovative performances throughout Carmel have made this July and August event something to celebrate.

Carmel Art Festival
Carmel Gallery Alliance, Carmel, CA 93923
831.642.2503 / www.carmelartfestival.org
▲ Annual event featuring plein air painting, sculpture in the park, kids art shows, etc.

Carmel Shake-Speare Festival
Pacific Repertory Theatre, Carmel, CA 93923
831.622.0700 / www.pacrep.org

▲ Early October's two-week run of the festival's Forest Theatre production brings out Carmel's zaniest persona.

Slumber

The Pine Inn
Ocean Avenue, Carmel, CA 93923
831.624.3851 / www.pineinn.com
▲ This historic hotel just a stone's throw from the beach has been a Carmel favorite since 1903, offering European charm and free wi-fi.

The Green Lantern Inn Bed & Breakfast
Casanova Street, Carmel, CA 93923
831.624.4392 / www.greenlanterninn.com
▲ Gorgeous property with 18 guest rooms and six cottages in a quiet neighborhood setting, with gardens, lawns, and easy access to the galleries.

The Inn at Spanish Bay
2700 17-Mile Drive, Pebble Beach, CA 93953
831.647.7500 / www.pebblebeach.com
▲ Tennis, golf, massages, yoga, and fantastic views make a splurge at Spanish Bay irresistible.

Acacia Lodge
20 Via Contenta, Carmel Valley, CA 93924
831.659.5361 / www.countrygardeninns.com
▲ With its 19 rooms and hillside location in nearby Carmel Valley, the Acacia Lodge experiences sunny and warm weather on days when Carmel's oceanside location is blanketed in fog. Free wi-fi, swimming pool, and jacuzzi.

Cobblestone Inn
Junipero between 7th & 8th Streets, Carmel, CA 93953
831.625.5222 / www.cobblestoneinncarmel.com
▲ This conveniently located, English-style retreat in downtown Carmel features quaint charm and in-room fireplaces.

Sea View Inn
Camino Real between 11th & 12th, Carmel, CA 95953
831.624.8778 / www.seaviewinncarmel.com
▲ A nine-room retreat near the beach, the Sea View Inn's unpretentious environment suits casual travelers' needs for relaxing quiet.

Vagabond's House Inn
Dolores between 4th & 5th, Carmel, CA 95953
831.624.7738 / www.vagabondhouseinn.com
▲ This pet-friendly inn features an in-town location, 14 rooms of classic country charm, and attractive gardens.

Sustenance

Caffe Cardinale
Ocean Avenue, Carmel, CA 93923
831.626.2095 / www.carmelcoffee.com
▲ Art-filled and exceedingly eclectic environment with superb espresso and even better people watching.

Flaherty's Seafood Grill & Oyster Bar
Sixth Street, Carmel, CA 93923
831.624.0311 / www.carmelsbest.com
▲ The best to spend a rainy afternoon in Carmel is simple: oysters and pinot grigio at Flaherty's.

L'Escargot
Mission Street, Carmel, CA 93923
831.620.1942 / www.escargotcarmel.com
▲ Loaded with European charm and serving a bistro-style menu.

A*rtist, teacher, art historian, and ethnologist, as well as past president of the Carmel Art Association, Dick Crispo spent most of his childhood years growing up in Carmel. Still a resident of the Monterey Peninsula, his work has been the subject of more than 70 one-artist exhibitions.*

"My work is usually created in impasto style, with an abstract technique based on the land or the sea. I paint things as far as I want to take them in either abstract or realistic style, then move onto something else. I've also done a lot of social commentary work earlier in my career. I've been painting in this area since 1969 and exhibited my first painting in Carmel when I was 11 years old. My work has been shown in both local galleries and galleries outside the area ever since then.

"When I was in art school Carmel had all of three art galleries. Today we're up to 120 galleries crammed into one square mile of what's known as Carmel-by-the-Sea. And while the rents are horren-

dous, the art association owns its own building so it's not going any-where. The community has eight or nine galleries representing historic work from Carmel, but the Carmel Art Association exhibits its mem-bers' work, which ranges all across the various styles and techniques. Since we're not stuck with a $12,000 or even a $20,000 monthly overhead, the art association can sell its paintings for prices that are very reasonable, no matter what place you're comparing us to."

A s director of the Carmel Art Association, Susan Klusmire over-sees the operations of the nation's second-oldest community art group and its representation of more than 120 member artists.

"Because of our diverse art offerings we have benefited from an enormous client base that has been built up over the past 81 years. Our collectors and walk-in customers are about half local and from other parts of central California, with the rest coming from all around the U.S. and a handful from outside the country. Our Web site has also proven to be an important resource for marketing the work of our members. We regularly advertise in local newspapers and arts publica-tions and do some advertising on television and radio.

"While new artists have always found their way to the Monterey Peninsula, recently it has become more difficult for artists to survive in this area as the cost of housing has increased tremendously from one end of the county to another. This in turn has the peculiar result of shaking up the process by which the Carmel Art Association juries in its new members. Our residency rule clearly states that a member must reside no greater distance than 35 miles outside the one square mile limits of Carmel-by-the-Sea. There are several potential solutions being discussed, though the one people talk about the most is a long-range plan to retrofit some of the housing facilities on the grounds of the decommissioned Fort Ord military base and convert them into an "Artists' Habitat," which would not only be a great benefit to local artists but would also locate a new generation of painters and sculp-tors within 35 miles of the Carmel Art Association."

Catalina Island

Fifty years after the *Niña, Pinta,* and *Santa Maria* set their anchors into Caribbean sands along what today is the Dominican Republic's coastline, a Spanish galleon visited the deep waters off Catalina Island. The island's Pimungan residents, members of a Native American culture that called Catalina Island and the nearby Channel Islands their homelands, greeted the sailors and exchanged gifts with the ship's captain.

Fast forward a handful of centuries to the Catalina Island of today and one finds that while the principals have changed this central tenent of island living has stayed the same. Most visitors still arrive by boat, looking for objects created by the island residents, thus repeating a dynamic that now keeps local artists and craftspeople busy year-round.

If you enjoy looking at photographs of Hollywood celebrities in their leisure moments, be sure to stop in at the Catalina Island Museum, located on Catalina Casino's ground floor. On this compact museum's walls is a collection of dozens of black-and-white shots featuring movie stars at play on Catalina, doing what comes naturally in this quiet island refuge.

The island's proximity to the mainland has inspired a steady flow of would-be settlers ever since the Spaniards named it Santa Catalina. In the 1800s smugglers set up warehouses in secluded island coves for safekeeping their contraband, while miners searching for gold and silver probed the island's hillsides . . . usually in vain. Sheepherders, squatters, and shipwrecked fishermen came and went, but toward the beginning of the 1900s, when summer-long colonies of tents began popping up along the island's coastline, Catalina's fate as a destination for Southern

Don't expect slot machines inside the Catalina Casino, where you're far more likely to find ballroom dancers, jazz musicians, and gents in tuxedos.

Californians in need of rest and relaxation was sealed. Viewed from the mainland Catalina Island is easy to spot, with its dark green hillsides rising out of the Pacific Ocean waters just 22 miles west of Dana Point. Beachgoers from Santa Monica to Oceanside now use the island as a reference point on the horizon, providing a simple way to estimate the distance of their daily walks.

Though vacationers provided a welcomed boost to the island's limited economic base, things started taking a pronounced turn for the better in 1911 when Hollywood directors such as D. W. Griffith determined Catalina to be an ideal place for creating the outdoor settings needed by film industry crews for productions ranging from Biblical dramas (*Ten Commandments* and *Ben Hur*) to pirate thrillers (*Mutiny on the Bounty* and *The Black Pirate*). Demand for on-location island shoots became steady enough that specialized technical crews made Catalina their full-time residence, providing the island with its first wave of permanent, creative field professionals. One film crew even brought a few bison to the island, using them in the filming of a movie based on a Zane Grey novel about American Indians. But after the 1924 production wrapped its island work the beasts were turned loose, planting the seeds of what today has become a herd of nearly 200 North American

Hollywood's brightest stars made Catalina Island their favorite playground during the pre-WWII years.

Bison whose impact on Catalina's fragile ecology is overseen by the Catalina Island Conservancy.

During those same years Catalina's popularity, which combined the glamour of a steady stream of Hollywood stars with the attraction of an island environment loaded with secluded beaches and superb fishing, started drawing a great deal of interest from landlubbers in search of intriguing day trips. It certainly didn't hurt that the Chicago Cubs used Catalina as their spring training site from 1922 to 1942, building a ballpark whose dimensions duplicated the insane geometry of Wrigley Field (but minus the fantastic Sports Corner Grill in Wrigleyville). This ditzy sidebar in American sports history can be traced back to 1919 when team owner William Wrigley Jr. became one of Catalina Island's owners, occupying the Georgian colonial mansion that today is home to the Inn on Mt. Ada. The family's commitment to Catalina Island was expressed in a number of civic-minded gestures, including the 1934 redevelopment of Avalon in the style of a Mediterranean village by scion Phillip K. Wrigley, and the building of Chimes Tower in 1925, a project funded by Ada Wrigley.

The Roaring '20s generation of rich and famous pegged Catalina Island as their playground of choice. Novelist Zane Grey built his hillside home on an Avalon side street in 1926, and local residents learned how to comfortably stroll Avalon's waterfront Crescent Avenue and not get hysterical when the likes of Charlie Chaplin, Humphrey Bogart, Clark Gable, Johnny Weismuller, or Cecil B. DeMille passed by. It soon became obvious that in a place like Catalina Island, whose commercial center of Avalon was attracting tens of thousands of summer season visitors willing to endure the two-hour steamer ride from Long Beach's gritty docks to Avalon's sun-bleached Mediterranean-style splendor, a large facility capable of presenting top performing arts talents would be an instant hit with locals and visitors.

Into the picture stepped William Wrigley Jr., whose combination of enormous wealth and sophisticated design tastes resulted in the 1929 opening of the Catalina Casino, an architectural masterpiece whose Art Deco splendor continues to define the far end of Avalon's harbor. The structure is also home to the Page Organ, an American masterpiece that is one of two such organs in existence. Designed as a multipurpose facility capable of serving as a venue for music, film, and theatre presentations, the Catalina Casino's height is equivalent to that of a medium-size office building, though its rounded form has also attracted comparisons to a massive wedding cake. Tiffany chandeliers are suspended from the ballroom's 50-ft. ceiling, and today this carefully restored treasure serves as the focal point for Avalon's sur-

Catalina Islanders have shared their favorite barstools with yachtmen from across the Pacific.

prisingly strong arts scene, housing the Casino Art Gallery, the Avalon Theatre, the Avalon Ballroom, and the Catalina Island Museum.

The Catalina Art Association, which operates the Casino Art Gallery on the ground floor of Catalina Casino, makes the best of a site that practically defines what is meant by the phrase "a difficult space." With its rounded walls, the Casino Art Gallery has a configuration some might regard as quaint, while others would consider it challenging. On the other hand, the location gets unparalleled foot traffic, which results in steady sales and a generally high level of skill reflected in the association members' exhibited work. The association's annual Catalina Art Festival, which takes place in September, has since 1959 gathered the island's best talents along with artists from throughout Southern California in a weekend-long, outdoor exhibition.

Several commercial gallery spaces provide visitors with year-round opportunities to connect with the island's visual arts community. Perico Gallery is stocked with a selection of island-theme posters and prints, while the nearby Ruth Mayer Fine Art is loaded with originals created by Ms. Mayer herself, who if she's not sitting behind the gallery's front desk can usually be found at her other namesake gallery on South Coast Highway in downtown Laguna Beach. The island's newest art space, Catalina Artists' Market, is part of the El Encanto Marketplace and is a satellite of the Catalina Artists' Market and Gallery inside the nearby Metropole Marketplace.

While the Avalon Theatre offers Hollywood's latest cinematic creations to island audiences, the Avalon Ballroom serves as an important venue for the island's performing arts presenters. Among the largest of Catalina's annual music events is the Catalina Island JazzTrax Festival, a two-week onslaught of top jazz talents from across the globe performing in dozens of concerts on the ballroom's stage and other island venues. Catalina Island Performing Arts Foundation, which operates KISL 88.7, the island's NPR affiliate, is also the originator of programs such as the Catalina Theatre Festival, a summer youth art camp, and artist residency programs in local schools.

Venues

Avalon Ballroom & Theatre
1 Casino Way, Avalon, CA 90704
310.510.0179 / www.visitcatalinaisland.com
▲ Restored to their 1929 Art Deco splendor these two venues inside Catalina Casino provide a glittering testimonial to the generosity of their patron, the Wrigley family of chewing gum and Chicago Cubs fame.

Catalina Art Association / Casino Art Gallery
1 Casino Way, Avalon, CA 90704
310.510.0808 / www.catalinaartassociation.org
▲ It's impossible to miss walking straight through this modest art space's door, which is located on the ground floor of the Catalina Casino.

Ruth Mayer Fine Art
116 Sumner Avenue, Avalon, CA 90704
310.510.8318 / www.ruthmayer.com
▲ With galleries both here and in Laguna Beach, Ruth Mayer paints a wide range of subjects in a broad spectrum of styles.

Catalina Artists Market
205 Crescent Avenue and 101 Marilla Avenue, Avalon, CA 90704
310.510.3544 / www.catalinaartistsmarket.com

▲ Representing many of the island's artists, these two exhibition spaces are ideal contact points for visitors wondering who's who in the local visual arts community.

Events

Outdoor Art Market
101 Marilla Avenue, Avalon, CA 90704
310-510-7469 / www.kisl.org
▲ Monthly event in the El Encanto Marketplace courtyard featuring painters, jugglers, poets, and the like.

Catalina Arts Festival
Downtown Avalon streets
310.510.0808 / www.catalinaartassociation.org
▲ September annual outdoor event organized by the Catalina Art Association.

Catalina Island JazzTrax Festival
Catalina Ballroom and other venues, Avalon, CA 90704
760.323.5770 / www.jazztrax.com
▲ This annual celebration of jazz musical genius takes place during two weeks in October.

Slumber

Hotel Villa Portofino
111 Crescent Avenue, Avalon, CA 90704
310.510.0555 / www.hotelvillaportofino.com
▲ The island's harborside hotel has elegant rooms filled with art, perfect views, Ristorante Villa Portofino's northern Italian cuisine, free wi-fi, a sundeck, and European service.

Zane Grey Pueblo Hotel
199 Chimes Tower Road, Avalon, CA 90704
310.510.0966 / www.zanegreypueblohotel.com
▲ Perched on a hillside overlooking Avalon harbor, this gorgeous, 16-room inn with a pool makes it easy to see why America's greatest Westerns novelist chose Catalina Island to fire his imagination.

The Inn on Mt. Ada
398 Wrigley Road, Avalon, CA 90704
310.510.2030 / www.innonmtada.com
▲ This Georgian mansion was once the estate of the Wrigley family, whose influence over Catalina Island has met the test of time. The inn's elegant rooms (there are six guest rooms) and spectacular

grounds retain their 1921 appeal, and its commanding view from 350 feet above the harbor make this a wonderful place for breakfast or lunch.

Seaport Village Inn
119 Maiden Lane, Avalon, CA 90704
800.222-8256 / www.catalinacatalina.com
▲ This 43-room inn has a family-friendly atmosphere with great views of the harbor, affordable rates, and free shuttle service to the ferry dock.

The Avalon Hotel
124 Whittley Avenue, Avalon, CA 90704
310.510.7070 / www.theavalonhotel.com
▲ This boutique hotel traces its architectural pedigree back to the 1920s, updated with nice touches such as flat screen televisions, free high-speed Internet, local art, and a half dozen comfortable rooms.

Sustenance

Avalon Seafood
Green Pier #20, Avalon, CA 90704
310.510.0197
Open Daily
▲ This outdoor cafe on Green Pier has eye-popping views of Avalon's harbor.

Steve's Steakhouse
417 Crescent Avenue, Avalon, CA 90704
310.510.0333 / www.stevessteakhouse.com
Open Daily
▲ This spin-off of the Casino Dock Cafe has a friendly vibe and a reasonably priced wine list.

Mi Casita
111 Claressa Avenue, Avalon, CA 90704
310.510.1772 / www.catalinahotspots.com
Open Daily
▲ The island's best choice for margaritas has harbor views and a cantina vibe.

Chi Chi Club
105 Summer Avenue, Avalon, CA 90704
310.510.9211 /

▲ The loudest bar in Avalon has live music, pool tables, and a retro Polynesian style that keeps locals coming back for more.

Luau Larry's

509 Crescent Avenue, Avalon, CA 90704

310.510.1919 / www.luaularrys.com

▲ From cheeseburgers in paradise on Wednesdays to the weekend's mai tai madness, this Hawaii-themed hangout never fails to entertain.

Marlin Club

108 Catalina Avenue, Avalon, CA 90704

310.510.0044 / www.marlinclub.com

▲ Catalina Island's oldest bar, "Where the Young Surrender and the Old Grow Tender," is the right place at the right time for the right price . . . anytime.

In 1996 Catalina Island art collector Roy Rose helped establish the Society for the Advancement of Plein Air Painting, as part of an effort to inform art viewers about the challenges and value of plein air painting, and to encourage younger artists to adopt the technique in their own creative expressions. In 2003 the society published the comprehensive, 256-page "Enchanted Isle: A History of Plein Air Painting in Santa Catalina Island," detailing the achievements of nearly 100 artists who fell under the island's spell.

"Catalina Island has that wonderful combination of natural beauty, inspired architecture, and perfect weather that you find in many of the best examples of plein air painting. And it doesn't matter if different artists are painting the same scene or if an individual artist is returning to paint something for the second or third time because the natural conditions on the island are changing all the time.

"We still organize annual exhibitions of plein air painting on the island but we've moved away from the kind of large events at the casino with maybe 35 artists and 500 visitors and have scaled down to where we will feature 8 to 10 artists in the dining area at the country club, where the artists can still sell lots of paintings. We're a volunteer group and our intention is to maintain the best context for displaying this kind of art."

As the Catalina Art Association's gallery manager, island resident Porschia Denning exhibits the work of many Catalina Island artists.

"I moved to the island eight years ago from London, mainly for the climate and the opportunity to do art. The Catalina Art Association's gallery is a long-standing island art presence that's developed a great reputation with visitors. With our location in the casino we're typically one of the first places people walk toward once they get here, so stepping inside the gallery is just part of many people's island exploring. We have a great space with high ceilings, good lighting in a somewhat small space but we have plenty of room for our 90 members' art.

"The association is very welcoming of new members, and we've started accepting musicians recently so that's led to weekly jam sessions in the evening where anyone who feels inspired to play guitar, drums, or whatever they can walk in here with is invited to join in the fun. Typically it takes place from 6 to 9 PM on Thursdays.

"Artists in the association can submit any sort of images they want, though the ones that seem to sell best have something to do with the lifestyle or natural beauty of the island. We just work with the artists to rotate art on and off the walls, with most of the art selling in the $300 to $1,000 range. We get visitors from all over the world, and especially now with cruise ships coming here we're seeing lots of Japanese and Korean tourists."

Chico

This progressive college town bordering the Sierra Nevada foothills has defined itself as an arts-supportive environment celebrating all facets of creativity. In Chico the combined impacts of innovative arts events, inspired art exhibitions, affordable performances, and open-minded networks of creative field professionals have enhanced the quality of life for all of its 80,000 residents.

From the visitor perspective Chico's bustling downtown and accessible art scene bear surprising similarities to the dynamics defining San Luis Obispo's alluring texture. Historically and architecturally these Art Towns aren't even distant cousins, but in several meaningful ways their parallels form key components of what attracts return visitors and even convinces some to return as full-time residents. Both places enjoy the benefits of having a university presence, reflected here by the 17,000 students attending California State University, Chico. Both communities also have exceptionally attractive public parks in their midst, and in Chico's case that refers to the pastoral ambiance of lower Bidwell Park's meandering presence along parts of downtown's commercial grid. And in much the same way that downtown SLO bursts to life during its Thursday evening Farmers' Market on Higuera Street, the popularity of this community's Saturday morning Chico Certified Farmer's Market and the Thursday Night Market on Broadway both enhance the Chico version of an Art Town experience throughout the year.

Because the upper Sacramento Valley lacked convenient anchorage for Padre Junipero Serra's Spanish galleons, westernized civilization and the religious conversion of Chico's original inhabitants was forestalled until the mid-1800s Gold Rush. But starting with the Feather River's 1848 mining boom, and General John Bidwell's subsequent

Sculptor Donna Billick's Our Hands *monumental terrazzo tile work is installed outside the entrance to downtown Chico's Municipal Center Building.*

purchase of 28,000 acres bordering Chico Creek, the region's indigenous Maidu population was rapidly displaced by the blacksmiths, preachers, and bartenders who provided the necessary services in a frontier outpost. Decades later in a large gesture of civic mindedness uncharacteristic of the era's wealthy, the General's family gave 1,900 of those acres to the city as a park. With the help of additional bequests and purchases, today's expanse of what's known as Bidwell Park includes 3,670 acres, making Chico home to one of the nation's largest municipal parks. By comparison, NYC's Central Park covers 843 acres, Los Angeles's Griffith Park includes 4,107 acres, and Rock Creek Park in Washington DC tops out at 1,754 acres. During the 1930s Bidwell Park served as the setting for several Hollywood classics, including standing in for Sherwood Forest in the *Adventures of Robin Hood* and working as Tara's body double in *Gone With the Wind*.

Though the Sierra Nevada's foothills encroach upon Chico's east boundary, the region's landscape is otherwise flat. Laced with mountain-fed rivers and streams the valley provides a picture-perfect environment for growing water-dependent crops such as rice, fruits, and nuts. It comes as no surprise, then, that one of the community's most popular public celebrations is the recently established, four-day California Nut Festival, whose late February staging is timed to parallel the nearby blossoming of hundreds of acres of almond trees.

Venues throughout Chico are pressed into service for the festival's nutty events, which include exhibitions of jewelry crafted in the shape of nuts, gallery exhibitions of nut-inspired two- and three-dimensional art, and competitions involving culinary artisanship in pursuit of baking perfect pecan pies.

Downtown's presence of the CSU Chico campus places the university's multitude of visual art exhibitions and performing arts events within a short stroll of the business district's restaurants and wine bars. Laxson Auditorium, located inside the university's historic Central Campus, serves as the 1,200-seat venue for Chico Performances, whose late August through May season of local as well as touring international talents in dance, music, theatre, and comedy showcases the likes of George Winston, the Shaolin Warriors, Youssou N'Dour, Chico Community Ballet, Lila Downs, the Theatre Department's Spring Musical, and Bill Cosby. The school's Performing Arts Center holds three venues including a 450-seat main stage, a black box stage, and a recital hall, all of which are used for performances presented by the theatre arts and music departments. The region's most prominent classical music organization, North State Symphony, is largely populated by faculty and students from CSU Chico's music department, which also provides the talent for campus choral groups and jazz bands. On its visual arts side CSU Chico exhibitions take place in the Humanities Center Gallery, whose exhibitions draw from northern California's contemporary art scene with an emphasis on students, graduates, and faculty; the student-centered University Art Gallery in Taylor Hall, whose range of interests include survey exhibitions as well as artists from the campus arts community and the northern California region; and the Janet Turner Print Museum. Named in honor of the Millard Sheets protégée whose two-decade efforts during the 1960s and 70s ultimately leveraged a fine arts program into the academic catalog, this collecting and exhibiting institution produces both a Summer Arts Academy and a National Print Competition, while its exhibition spaces in Laxson Auditorium and Ayres Hall serve as venues for touring shows as well as shows drawn

When the organizers of Artoberfest, a community-wide and monthlong series of exhibitions, concerts, performances, and art fairs, decided to have fun with the concept of the Palio di Sienna, a centuries-old horse race around the Piazza del Campo in the Italian town of Sienna, they came up with a winning formula. Instead of having various Terzieri (neighborhoods) represented by four-legged thoroughbreds, the Palio di Chico uses the leg power of humans to carry sculptures of race horses around the Downtown City Plaza.

A delightfully inventive blending of exhibition space, education facility, coffee shop, and gift store have reincarnated a classic train depot as the Chico Art Center.

from the museum's permanent collection. The Chico Museum, whose downtown presence occupies a former Carnegie Library building, is an occasional exhibition venue for works from the Turner Museum's collection.

The range of exhibitions, classes, and activities at the Chico Art Center, whose exhibition space and education studios are wedged into the old Southern Pacific Railroad depot, serve the off-campus community as its center of creative action. Local as well as noted regional talents are showcased in the center's year-round shows, which include the annual National Juried Exhibition. Local arts community figures, including musicians as well as painters, poets, and fine craftsmen, are the focal point of the center's monthly Artist Lecture Series on Final Fridays. In addition to the lattes served in the Empire Coffee Car, a restored, 1947 Pullman masterpiece, the art center's hands-down crowd-pleaser is its annual Open Studios Art Tour. Its October staging spreads across three weekends and includes most of the area's leading talents as well as members of the evolving arts community in neighboring Oroville. More than 100 artists open their work environments during the tour weekends. Chico Art Center serves as both the distribution point for maps outlining the self-guided tour's stops and as the exhibition venue for representative works of art from each of the tour's participating talents. The city's Art in Public Places program has installed three-dimensional works along several of the community's thoroughfares, funded the painting of dozens of murals around the city, and rotates locally-created art exhibited in the Municipal Building. Among its best known works are the "Our Hands" sculpture in downtown, the "Ancestor Gates" sculptures in East 20th Street Park, and "The Silver Plow" installation on Park Avenue.

A mix of artist-owned collaborative spaces and commercial art businesses comprise the majority of exhibiting venues included in downtown Chico's monthly Art First Saturdays, which run from 5 to 8 PM 12 times annually. The longstanding 1078 Gallery has weathered more than 25 years of downtown's ups and downs by providing a non-profit environment for exhibitions by local and regional contemporary art talents, as well as serving as a venue for performances, literary readings, and workshops. A youthful vibe prevails at 24hr Drive By Gallery, which exhibits the work of its six member artists as well as that of emerging local talents. Avenue 9 Gallery exhibits the work of local artists, offers instruction in specialized art skills, and serves as a venue for new media electronic exhibitions. CRUX Artist Collective, a Park Avenue facility housing studios for a dozen artists, is known for showing art by emerging talents. Satava Art Glass Studio's handblown

Chico's public art program has installed dozens of murals, tile works, and art benches throughout the community.

lamps, sculptures, glassware, and ornaments are some of the best-known creative concepts produced in Chico. Represented by galleries from Cape Cod (Chatham Art and Jewelry) to Maui (Bella Vetri), a national arts audience is well familiar with the work of founder Richard Satava and glassblower Jim Radey. Chico's performing arts productions are presented by organizations such as Chico Cabaret, which uses a converted retail storefront for its year-round raves of classical farce and contemporary gut-busters. Chico Theatre Company presents musicals for family audiences, while downtown's the Blue Room Theatre has developed a solid reputation for its adept handling of all stage material, be it Broadway favorites or freshly workshopped experiments in stagecraft. Blue Room's performance space in a former Masonic Hall attracts enthusiastic audiences for the company's season of eight productions staged from December through June. In the same community-conscious spirit seen in companies such as Sonoma County Repertory Theatre in Sebastapol, Blue Room offers young talents an opportunity to develop their skills through the classes and youth productions presented by its Blue Moon Young Company.

Venues

Janet Turner Print Museum
400 W. 1st Street, Chico, CA 95928
530.898.4476 / www.janetturner.org
▲ From its quarters on the mezzanine of Laxson Auditorium, the Janet Turner Museum organizes exhibitions of work from its own collection at several campus venues and also serves as a destination exhibition site for touring shows.

Chico Art Center
450 Orange Street, Chico, CA 95928
530.895.8726 / www.chicoartcenter.com
▲ Once a Southern Pacific depot, the art center uses its gallery, classrooms, coffee shop, and expertise to organize and present a full spectrum of events and services.

1078 Gallery
820 Broadway, Chico, CA 95928
530.343.1973 / www.1078gallery.org
▲ Considered one of the best exhibition venues for Chico artists, 1078 has mastered the balancing act that defines what it means to be a nonprofit venue for several creative art forms.

Chico Theatre Company

530.894.3282 / www.chicotheatrecompany

▲ By emphasizing family fare and childrens' theatre productions in its year-round offerings this stage company has carved out a prominent niche in a competitive market.

Events

Chico Certified Farmers Market

2nd Street & Wall Street Intersection

530.893.3276 / www.northvalley.net/farmersmarket

▲ From 5-lb bags of locally grown almonds to liters of extra virgin olive oil, this market on Saturday morning, rain or shine, opens a window into the region's culinary culture.

Artoberfest

530.896.7214 / www.artoberfest.org

▲ A monthlong compilation of events, exhibitions, and performances from local and regional talents.

Open Studios Art Tour
Chico, Paradise, and Oroville

530.895.8726 / www.chicoartcenter.com

▲ With more than 100 self-guided stops in three communities, Chico's annual studio tour is a three-weekend bash.

Slumber

Vagabond Inn

630 Main Street, Chico, CA 95928

530.895.1323 / www.vagabondinn.com

▲ Located close to the downtown galleries, with free wi-fi, swimming pool, and affordable rates.

The Grateful Bed

1462 Arcadian Avenue, Chico, CA 95928

530.342.2464 / www.thegratefulbed.net

▲ Sweet dreams of sugar magnolias will be truckin' through your sleep cycle in this four-room, neighborhood inn close by Enloe Hospital.

Hotel Diamond

220 W. 4th Street, Chico, CA 95928

530.893.3100 / www.hoteldiamondchico.com

▲ Chico's best lodgings are the Hotel Diamond's niche, and this remodeled, 1904 facility with 43 guest rooms plus a street-level jazz club lives up to the promise.

Heritage Inn Express
725 Broadway, Chico, CA 95928
866.909.1191 / www.heritagehotelgroup.com
▲ Great rates plus a pool, happy hour reception, and nearby restaurants.

Sustenance

Peet's Coffee & Tea
145 Main Street, Chico, CA 95928
530.894.6716 / www.peets.com
▲ From Denver to Seattle, this java haven has positioned itself as Starbucks' classy competitor.

Sierra Nevada Brewing Company
1075 E. 20th Street, Chico, CA 95928
530.893.3520 / www.sierranevada.com
▲ From Hood River to Santa Fe, Art Towns and breweries are hotbeds of creativity. But when it comes to having an impact on the local cultural scene, the awesome concerts presented on its Big Room stage and the superb food served in its Taproom & Restaurant place Sierra Nevada Brewing at the top of all the rest.

The Black Crow Grill & Taproom
209 Salem Street, Chico, CA 95928
530.892.1392 / www.theblackcrow.com
▲ This lively downtown restaurant has an engaging atmosphere, well-chosen wine list, and great prices.

From her backyard studio in a quiet Chico neighborhood, artist Chunhong Chang paints ethereal, soothing images capturing the essential beauty of atmospheres, wildlife, flowers, and fruits. Her synthesis of traditional Chinese symbology with structured elements of Western still life painting tradition infuses her work with romantic genius.

"I've lived in Chico almost twelve years now, having met my husband here and we are now raising our two daughters here. Chico is a really nice, livable community with liberal political traditions and a great university. Living here you don't feel as if you are lacking for intellectual stimulation. We certainly have lots of artistic activity, and more artists are coming to live here from other parts of California.

"I'm very pleased to be living here in Chico and making my living as an artist. Of course an artist can only sell so much work in a community of this size, so the challenge is finding other galleries to represent you, and mine are in San Francisco, Seattle, and New York. I belong to a group of artists who live here and meet once a month to exchange information. For the way a community does business, on both the public and private levels, people in Chico seem to know how to get things done right.

"As a parent I'm very pleased with the education my children are receiving here. There are advanced classes in the schools and up 'til recently there were lots of art education programs at all levels, but those are being cut back, which is a problem."

As one of California's leading masters of contemporary glass art, Chico's Richard Satava has also mastered the dicey balancing act of pursuing fine art experimentation while managing the day-to-day operations of a successful glass art production studio. Because of his leadership Chico is now home to more than a dozen glass artists and several hot glass studios.

"When I started here in 1977 the town was half the size it is now and for artists to survive they had to make their living by selling out of town. But as the size of the community changed so was there a change in the kinds of people living here and in the ways local people thought about buying art. Today not only are local people well informed about the art created here but people from outside Chico are aware of the kind of art transformation that's taken place in Chico and they're coming to us instead of us having to go find the buyers.

"I think the community has done a good job promoting itself to prospective visitors as an art center and having that kind of support only makes the advertising I do on my own that much more effective. We're at the point in Chico where we are now starting an annual art glass event, Chico Glass Fest, and the credit for that has to go to the program at Chico State University and the influence of Dr. Manuel Esteban, who served as President of CSU and took a personal interest in reviving the glass art program."

Encinitas

The enviable lifestyle shared throughout this North San Diego County community of nearly 60,000 residents is partly the result of assets such as the 11 Pacific Coast beaches dotting Encinitas's 6 miles of coastline. It's also the result of a widespread awareness that the downtown's well-preserved collection of historic buildings infuses this Art Town with a manageable, familiar, and pedestrian-friendly scale ideally suited to Encinitas's bicycle riding, surfboard carrying take-on style. And as for the presence and impact of local creativity there's an abundance of signals testifying to the variety of art talents calling this place home, from the hand painted banners flying from Encinatas streetlights to the monthly gatherings of spoken word artists whose meetings are timed to coincide with the presence of a full moon.

The best way to appreciate all of Encinitas's creativity assets is to consider this place in context with its neighboring communities of Leucadia, Cardiff, Solana Beach, and Del Mar. To local residents these smaller towns and some of the surrounding area are viewed as a single region named San Dieguito, whose boundaries stretch along the coastline before turning eastward to include Rancho Santa Fe. This dramatic landscape was once home to Native tribes such as the San Dieguitos and the LaJollas before Spanish settlers designated the place as Encina Cañada in admiration of its oak-covered hillsides. Today, connected by the historic Coast Highway 101 (called the Pacific Coast Highway in other parts of the state), which replaced the Camino Real once traveled by Franciscan missionaries, development pressures have brought changes to the San Dieguito communities, though not to the scale that's overwhelmed many Southern California towns. Most important, the natural attributes that characterized the local lifestyle for more than 100 years, from the rural nature of the Olivenhain district's riding trails to the towering eucalyptus trees framing the Coast Highway's route through Leucadia, have largely been protected from change.

Residents of small, arts-friendly places such as Encinitas tend to purchase art directly from the studios of local individuals whose talents they admire. And with the Art Town gem of La Jolla located just south of Del Mar, traveling art collectors tend to be more focused on dashing through Museum of Contemporary Art San Diego's (MCASD) latest exhibitions than they are willing to sift through the spread out San Dieguito area's art spaces. Encinitas is home to two

Full Moon Poets may schedule their readings to coordinate with the rise of a full moon, but its twice-annual Poetry Slams at the historic La Paloma Theatre in downtown Encinitas take place in summer and winter without lunar cycle cues. (Photo courtesy of Jim Babwe)

nonprofit art spaces as well as several outdoor art fairs, while the area's commercial galleries have clustered along Cedros Avenue in neighboring Solana Beach. There, in the Cedros Design District's dozens of design shops, furniture stores, cafes, and jewelry shops, several art galleries are making a go of things by networking with the district's daily influx of decorators, project managers, architects, and wandering tourists. Trios Gallery represents a strong group of local and national fine crafts artists, while Susan Street Fine Art Gallery emphasizes paintings from its roster of more than 30 artists, and Judy Moffson Gallery represents its namesake artists' paintings. To get an unhurried look at each of the district's galleries stop in during one of its Third Thursday Art Walks from 5:30 to 7:30 PM, or check out the more than two dozen members of the Del Mar Art Center's gallery in the Del Mar Plaza.

Leucadia's end of San Dieguito projects the vibe of a classic Southern California surfing haven and is home to one of the area's must-do annual events, LeucadiART Walk, whose staging on a late August Sunday afternoon features double-decker shuttle buses, live entertainment in both Leucadia Roadside Park and on the grounds of the Leucadia Post Office, and nearly 50 artists' booths set up alongside the west side of Coast Highway 101 as it ambles north toward Carlsbad. The annual Encinitas Streetfair and November's Fall Festival feature hundreds of artist booths crammed onto downtown's streets, with Streetfair stretched out across two days while Fall Festival is limited to a single Sunday.

San Dieguito Art Guild operates one of Encinitas's two noncommercial exhibition spaces in addition to its year-round schedule of member shows in venues such as Encinitas City Hall. This influential group includes more than 100 artists working in a range of media. The guild's Off-Track Gallery in downtown Encinitas rotates its exhibitions monthly throughout the year. Its popular Mother's Day Weekend Art Studio & Garden Tour directs its self-guided participants toward eight tour sites across its two-day, mid-May run. The community's other noncommercial exhibition space once hung its rotating exhibitions of contemporary art on the walls of an Encinitas storefront but has recently elected to display those same shows on the virtual walls of an online gallery existing only in cyberspace. 101 Artists' Colony has a long record of achievement as the community's leading advocate for the interests of its artists. In addition to its changing exhibitions the 101 Artists', Colony presents performances of dance, music, spoken word, and literature, as well as a summer art camp for local youth. 101 Artists' Colony kicks the year off to an arts-aware start through its annual Arts Alive Banner Project, which organizes 101 of the community's many artists and convinces each of them to paint both sides of

Encinitas is widely known for its flower growing industry, which takes full advantage of the area's year-round, temperate climate to grow and ship an amazing variety of local flowers to destinations worldwide. All are on display year round in the 35-acre Quail Botanical Gardens, a sculpted and manicured oasis that's home to 4000 varieties of plants set amongst themed environments replicating everything from a tropical rainforest to a dense bamboo forest and desert cactus groves.

The art-filled environment of the 101 Artists' Colony has been turned into condos, but Encinitas talents like the Steve Mendoza Band, pictured here onstage at 101 Artists' Colony, keep Encinitas nightspots filled with hip-shakin' music lovers. (Photo courtesy of Jim Babwe)

a canvas banner measuring either 18" x 50", or 30" x 84". From mid-February to mid-May those banners are hung from streetlight poles throughout the San Dieguito communities, elevating public awareness of the area's creative talents and generating interest in the auctioning of the banners during a Sunday afternoon gala in the Cardiff Towne Center Courtyard.

Another of the community's popular arts events organized by 101 Artists' Colony is the twice-yearly Spoken Word Poetry Slam staged in downtown Encinitas's 400-seat Paloma Theatre. These free-to-the-public performances take place during summer and winter and are supported by the monthly readings and workshops of Full Moon Poets, a local organization whose more than 30 members schedule their monthly meetings of the Full Moon Poetry Circle to coincide with the appearance of the full moon.

The most prominent San Dieguito performing arts organization is the North Coast Repertory Theatre (NCRT). Its 194-seat playhouse in Solana Beach is home to a professional theatre company presenting adult audience material as well as a Theatre School Season of childrens' productions and a summer theatre camp. NCRT's mainstage season programs are at the same levels found throughout San Diego's professional theatre community, with its year-round schedule of productions built around challenging works, many of which receive their West Coast and San Diego premieres on NCRT's stage.

Venues

La Paloma Theatre
471 S. Coast Highway 101, Encinitas, CA 92024
760.346.7469 / www.lapalomatheatre.com
▲ This 400-seat entertainment venue has kept Encinitas inside the film, music, poetry, and drama loops since it opened in 1928. If there's not a concert or poetry slam taking place on La Paloma's stage it will invariably be screening a first-run Hollywood favorite.

North Coast Repertory Theatre
987 Lomas Santa Fe Drive, Solana Beach, CA 92075
858.481.1055 / www.northcoastrep.org
▲ Year-round, professional theatre company whose stage is kept busy with mainstage productions of new and recent works that deliver challenging material to audiences expecting excellence.

Cappella Gloriana Chamber Choir
619.291.3055 / www.cappella-gloriana.org
▲ Popular, 17-voice choir that uses St. Andrews Episcopal Church in Encinitas for its performances.

101 Artists' Colony
www.101artistscolony.com
▲ Encinitas's most active community arts organization may only exist in cyberspace, but its programs, events, and occasional exhibitions have helped guide the smart growth of Encinitas's art scene across multiple creative forms.

San Dieguito Art Guild / Off Track Gallery
500 Second Street, Encinitas, CA 92024
760.942.3636 / www.offtrackgallery.com
▲ Since 1965 this local arts group has provided Encinitas's artists with education and exhibition opportunities.

Del Mar Art Center
1555 Camino Del Mar, Del Mar, CA 92014
858.481.1678 / www.dmacgallery.com
▲ Monthly exhibitions and workshops for member artists.

Events

Arts Alive Banner Auction
Downtown Encinitas Main Street Association
760.943.1950 / www.encinitas101.com
▲ This mid-February to mid-May display of 101 banners on area streetlights culminates in a fund-raising auction benefiting local art education programs.

Full Moon Poetry Circle Poetry Slams
760.944.6027 / www.fullmoonpoets.com
▲ Twice annually the best and brightest stars in the San Diego spoken word scene gather at La Paloma Theatre to compete before enthusiastic audiences.

LeucadiART Walk
320 N. Coast Highway 101, Encinitas, CA 92024
760.436.2320 / www.leucadia101.com
▲ This late August event along the ecalyptus-bordered route through Leucadia showcases local visual and performing artists.

Slumber

Black Orchid Bed & Breakfast
653 Requeza Street, Encinitas, CA 92024
760.753.0584 / www.bedbreakfastsandiego.com
▲ New Orleans style runs throughout this seven-bedroom mansion and infuses its atmosphere with a decided sense of the Big Easy's lagniappe culture.

Ocean Inn
1444 N. Coast Highway 101, Leucadia, CA 92024
760.436.1988 / www.oceaninnhotel.com
▲ Great location and kitchenettes make this an affordable favorite for surfers, families, and vacationers.

Howard Johnson–Encinitas
607 Leucadia Boulevard, Encinitas, CA 92024
760.944.3800 / www.howardjohnsonencinitas.com
▲ Free wi-fi and a pool give this Ho-Jo's an advantage with business travelers.

Leucadia Beach Inn
1322 North Coast Highway, Leucadia, CA 92024
760.943.7461 / www.leucadiabeachmotel.com

▲ This classic, 1920s-style "motor inn" is a charming and fully renovated throwback to days gone by. Featuring Spanish Mission style, tile floors, and an easy walk to the beach, plus bargain rates and a pet-friendly policy.

Hotel Villa Mar
960 South Coast Highway, Encinitas, CA 92024
760.753.1267 /
▲ Recently renovated, this 15-room motel is quite affordable and offers rooms with kitchenettes.

Portofino Beach Inn
186 North Coast Highway, Encinitas, CA 92024
760.944.0301 / www.portofinobeachinn.com
▲ A short walk from this centrally located facility leads to Moonlight Beach. Affordable rates, plus a spa room, and easy parking.

Days Inn
133 Encinitas Boulevard, Encinitas, CA 92024
760.944.0260 / www.daysinn.com
▲ This 124-room hotel offers free wi-fi, a pool, and easy access to Interstate 5.

Sustenance

Java Depot
243 N. Coast Highway 101, Solana Beach, CA 92075
858.792.4545 /
▲ Art exhibits, great pastries, and freshly roasted coffee keep the Java Depot at the top of local lists.

Firefly Grill & Wine Bar
251 N. El Camino Real, Encinitas, CA 92024
760.635.1066 / www.fireflygrillandwinebar.com
▲ Superb menu and wine list make the Firefly a sociable center for Encinitas foodies. Don't pass up its special winemaker dinners.

Kaito Restaurant
1476 Encinitas Boulevard, Encinitas, CA 92024
760.634.2746 / www.kaitorestauurant.net
▲ Chef Kazuo serves up Encinitas's best Tokyo style favorites.

101 Diner
552 South Coast Highway, Encinitas, CA 92024
760.753.2123 /

▲ This popular breakfast spot serves legendary pancakes and omelets, but you've got to arrive early to get a parking space. Come back later in the day for its chili burgers and root beer floats at reasonable prices.

Beachside Bar & Grill
806 South Coast Highway, Encinitas, CA 92024
760.942.0738 /
▲ A wide selection of draft brews, a huge patio, and outdoor fire pits have made this friendly joint with a diverse menu an Encinitas social spot.

Trattoria I Trulli
830 South Coast Highway, Encinitas, CA 92024
760.943.6800 / www.itrulli.com
▲ This friendly spot in Encinitas' business district is a spinoff of downtown San Diego's Sogno DiVino and offers an extensive wine list in addition to its classic Italian specialties.

---

*O*n most days, Trish Dugger, who serves as the official Poet Laureate of Encinitas, can be spotted walking along the community's quiet streets, softly reciting poetry to herself as she logs in another of the two-mile jaunts that clear her mind and keep her ready for the rigors of the poetry slam circuit. At 78 years young, she's a creative force to be reckoned with.

"Having a poet laureate in Encinitas has raised the community's awareness of the entire arts community that lives around here, and when you consider that the poetry slams at La Paloma Theatre bring big business into town what we've created here is an arts community that cares deeply about poetry. I got my performing start in 2000 and had been involved in poetry groups for a few years before that. The size of San Diego County's poetry community surprises lots of people just finding out about it for the first time, and a lot of the driving force behind that poetry community is centered in this spirited, encouraging, and accepting arts community of Encinitas.

"I'd like to see the community's visual artists have access to a centrally located and easily accessible place to exhibit their work. That would help all of the local individuals who care about the arts, from younger people who are just starting out to the experienced artists who live here but have no place to show Encinitas what they're up to in their studios."

Arts organizer Danny Salzhandler has played an important role in the development of the Encinitas art scene. Everything from the 101 Artists' Colony online art gallery to the Full Moon Poets to the community's highly regarded art banners project are reflections of the many ways his dedication has helped shape the creative voice of Encinitas.

"It's really the artists themselves who have come together to make things happen, either working in small groups or large groups they've just needed to pull together as a way to advance their own financial interests as well as just do their art. I see more of that kind of cooperation as being one of the most important developments in this town. There's always the possibility that in dealing with public art you'll have differences of opinion about the best ways to get things done. But in the process of rethinking Encinitas as a viable, attractive, and well-known arts district it's important that the artists become key players in whatever process is taking place around the downtown because the presence of local art and artists is what makes us different from all the other places around us. Once you do get locally created art at the center of any retail art district's plans the real magic starts happening.

"We're located in between Laguna Beach and La Jolla, so with Highway 101 cutting right through the center of town we've got an incredible opportunity to use the presence of public art along with the development of several art galleries in high visibility places as attractive reasons for getting art buyers to consider Encinitas as a prime place to find real, authentic, Southern California art."

Escondido

he rolling hills and verdant valleys of North San Diego County are home to one of the most sublime climates found anywhere on the continent. With a year-round range of temperatures that typically bottom out in the low 50s and push past 90 in the hottest part of summer, it should come as no surprise that anything resembling a seed will grow with a Jack-and-the-Beanstalk vengeance in the region's loamy soil. For centuries the Pala and Barona Indian cultures enjoyed whatever nature offered, until Spanish colonists moved into the neighborhood and introduced sheepherding and Christianity to the area's original residents. By the early 1800s the Spanish had passed a series of edicts appropriating what historically had been Indian lands, dividing the countryside in huge ranchos for the well-connected. One of those parcels went to Juan Bautista Alvarado in the form of 12,633 acres known as Rincon del Diablo (Devil's Corner), a swath of land that today is known as the Escondido Valley.

First through the use of hand-dug *acequias* or *zanjas*, and later through the application of modern irrigation technology, the valley's miles of flatlands soon bloomed with avocado groves, citrus trees, lush vineyards, and family farms. Agriculture's impact on today's Escondido Valley's economy is one of the region's many economic drivers, and it's impossible not to notice the vast farms bordering this community's fringes. Escondido's residents enjoy easy access to the 3.5 miles of alluring Pacific beaches at Oceanside, just a 20-mile drive west, and to the cultural and entertainment amenities of urban San Diego beckoning from 30 miles southward. And for backup, both Dodger Stadium and Cinderella's Castle are just a two-hour drive in the opposite direction.

Escondido is a medium-size community with major league arts programming offered through its centrally located California Center for the Arts.

Escondido's lifestyle embodies many of the qualities that make Southern California famous. The community remains one of the more affordable housing markets in the region, with average home values in the range of $400,000. Its neighborhoods, such as the 900 Victorian and Craftsman homes included in the Old Escondido Historic District, are surprisingly attractive and located close to the community's wealth of parklands, lakes, hiking trails, and recreation facilities. One of those public facilities, Kit Carson Park, is named after the legendary sheriff of Taos, New Mexico, in honor of his leadership in the 1847 Battle of San Pasqual on nearby Mule Hill. So it only seems appropriate that today the park is home to a significant piece of public art in the form of Niki de Saint Phalle's fantastic and colorful, nine-figure "Queen Califa's Magical Circle," which is one of nearly two dozen conspicuously located works of art installed throughout Escondido as part of its public art initiative.

There's an eminently walkable downtown business district whose main artery, Grand Avenue, is lined by an enjoyable mix of art galleries, restaurants, pubs, antiques stores, and specialty stores selling everything from appliances to newspapers. Key components of the local art infrastructure such as 10 North, the Escondido Art Association Gallery, and several artist-owned studio/gallery operations occupy street-level spaces along both the East and West ends of Grand Avenue inside the multiple-block area known as the Escondido Arts District. Altogether there are more than two dozen sites operating as studios, galleries, or combinations of business with gallery interests in Escondido's downtown. The majority of them participate in the monthly 2nd Saturdays ArtWalk that keeps the Grand Avenue and adjacent East Valley Parkway art venues open from

4:30 to 8 PM for coordinated exhibition openings and the "de rigeur" wine and cheese socializing.

One of the best places to draw a bead on the expertise and depth of Escondido's art scene is the rotating exhibits offered by the Escondido Art Partnership's city-operated EAP/Escondido Municipal Gallery. Unencumbered by commercial restrictions, the gallery provides an ideal forum for diverse survey exhibitions covering the many facets of talent living and working in the North San Diego County region. The gallery's forward-looking approach to contemporary work and experiments by emerging, as well as mid-career, artists is especially noteworthy. Any Art Town worth its visual arts reputation also supports its performing arts sector, and in Escondido's case that measure is met through both the street-level West Grand Avenue presence of the 70-seat Theatrx performance company, and the East Grand Avenue presence of the Patio Playhouse Community & Youtheatre. Theatrx is an offbeat and very community-focused theatre/drama effort led by Stephen Store, presenting musicals, comedies, and even blues bands on a year-round basis. Patio Playhouse takes a more education-focused approach though its main stage productions and youth performances, offering a season schedule that covers musicals, comedies, and drama.

When it was first planned, the California Center for the Arts was envisioned as the heart of a broadly funded effort to develop Escondido from its former identity as an agriculture-based community into the North San Diego County cultural counterpart to the museums and performance facilities found in downtown San Diego's Balboa Park. Escondido's ambitions were sidelined, however, as city and county entities worked through the process of allocating their resources for what eventually evolved into Escondido's arts scene.

What really sets Escondido apart from other Art Towns is its pair of influential and well-funded art facilities whose far-reaching and year-round programs draw thousands of culturally-attuned visitors into the Escondido Arts District. Along West Grand Avenue, in a two-level structure once occupied by retail businesses, one of Southern California's leading cultural institutions, the Mingei International Museum, has added its dynamic, year-round programs to Escondido's cultural scene. This 21,000 square-foot satellite location of the museum's main facility in downtown San Diego's historic Balboa Park has added a globally-informed sheen to the local art experience through its exhibitions of art, craft, and design objects from across the continents. The Mingei's constant stream of changing exhibitions is supported by a multitude of programs offering the community a

Innovation and inclusion are the hallmarks of downtown's Escondido Arts Partnership (EAP) municipal gallery.

tsunami of artist demonstrations, workshops, lectures, dance performances, music, youth education classes, a comprehensive reference library, and even school outreach initiatives.

Just to the north of the arts district, across the busy thoroughfare of East Valley Parkway, is the 12-acre campus of the California Center for the Arts, a showcase facility whose complex of buildings includes a 1,523-seat Concert Hall, the 406-seat Center Theatre, numerous rehearsal studios, and the 10,000 square-foot Art Museum. Since opening its doors in 1994 the museum's spacious galleries and sculpture garden have provided an ideal environment for exhibitions of large-scale contemporary art. During its early years the Art Museum has hosted exhibitions of work by local, regional, and international artists, informing Escondido's fine arts audience with creations from the likes of Bruce Nauman, Dale Chihuly, Therman Statom, and Gerhard Richter. The museum's year-round slate of public events includes monthly Gallery Talks by leading members of the regional arts community as well as presentations by talents featured in the museum's changing exhibitions. The center's theatres are kept active throughout the year by a combination of full-scale touring productions that bring mainstage spectaculars ranging from Julio Iglesias concerts to multidate Broadway plays to downtown Escondido, and a busy slate of productions from the center itself as well as a range of concerts, plays, and events produced by local organizations such as Center Stage Productions and the Arts Off Broadway Community Theatre.

Venues

California Center for the Arts
340 North Escondido Boulevard, Escondido, CA 92025
760.893.4138 / www.artcenter.org
$5 admission / Closed Monday
▲ Multidisciplinary art campus presenting a full range of performing arts and music. Also home to a 10,000 square foot art museum whose exhibitions showcase contemporary work.

Mingei International Museum
155 West Grand Avenue, Escondido, CA 92025
760.735.3355 / www.mingei.org
$6 admission / Closed Sunday and Monday
▲ This satellite branch of downtown San Diego's famous Mingei presents year-round exhibitions and programs emphasizing international folk art, crafts, and design.

Escondido Art Association Gallery
121 West Grand Avenue, Escondido, CA 92025
760.489.0338 / www.escondidoartists.org
Closed Sunday and Monday
▲ Escondido's oldest arts organization exhibits the work of its members in a series of rotating monthly shows.

Escondido Arts Partnership / Escondido Municipal Gallery
142 West Grand Avenue, Escondido, CA 92025
760.480.4101 / www.escondidoarts.org
Closed Sunday and Monday
▲ Downtown headquarters for the community's arts renaissance, presenting intriguing exhibitions and a monthly Art Connection speakers program on the same dates as the 2nd Saturdays ArtWalk.

Theatrx
155 East Grand Avenue, Escondido, CA 92025
760.735.2491 / www.theatrx.com
▲ Downtown performance space presenting theatre, music, and lots of local color.

10 North Artists Group
115 W. Grand Avenue, Escondido, CA 92025
760.480.9000 / 10north.blogspot.com
Closed Sunday and Monday
▲ Contemporary art gallery and artist studio complex featuring work by its 10 resident artists.

Distinction Art
317 East Grand Avenue, Escondido, CA 92025
760.781.5779 / www.distinctionart.com
Closed Sunday to Tuesday
▲ Contemporary gallery and studio complex for
14 resident artists.

Events

Escondido Street Faire
760.745.8877 / www.downtownescondido.com
▲ For one weekend in October and May downtown's Grand
Avenue gets jammed with hundreds of vendors selling everything
imaginable.

2nd Saturdays ArtWalk
Grand Avenue and East Valley Parkway, Escondido, CA 92025
760.745.8877 / www.downtownescondido.com
▲ This monthly event from 5 PM to 8 PM year round on the second
Saturday of the month features exhibitions and opening receptions
in more than two dozen downtown Escondido arts venues.

Festival Escondido
760.745.8877 / www.festivalescondido.com
▲ Mid-October, daylong celebration tying together the community's culinary, visual arts, music, and theatre talent.

Escondido Renaissance Faire
Felicita Park, Escondido, CA 92025
www.goldcoastfestivals.org
$15 admission
▲ For two consecutive weekends in early April this county park
becomes a haven for jousters, jesters, and jugglers.

Slumber

Best Western Escondido
1700 Seven Oaks Road, Escondido, CA 92026
760.740.1700 / www.bestwestern.com
▲ Close to the Escondido Arts District, with a pool.

Welk Resort San Diego
8860 Lawrence Welk Drive, Escondido, CA 92026
760.749.3000 / www.welksandiego.com

▲ Thirty-six fairways on two golf courses, large fitness center, the 339-seat Welk Resort Theatre's live entertainment, lovely grounds, and swing bands on Friday nights.

Zosa Gardens Bed & Breakfast
9381 West Lilac Road, Escondido, CA 92026
760.723.9093 / www.zosagardens.com
▲ Spanish-style hacienda on 22 acres with pool and tennis court.

Sustenance

Stone Brewing World Bistro & Gardens
1999 Citricado Parkway, Escondido, CA 92029
760.471.4999 / www.stonebrew.com
▲ Fresh brews, wonderful foods, and a friendly atmosphere make Stone Brewing worth the drive and the inevitable wait.

Blue Mug Coffee & Tea
122 South Kalmia Street, Escondido, CA 92025
760.796.7540 / www.bluemugcoffee.com
▲ Escondido Art District's favorite java fix.

150 Grand Cafe
150 West Grand Avenue, Escondido, CA 92025
760.738.6868 / www.150grand.com
▲ Chef Scott Clark has networked local farmers and ranchers into all corners of his contemporary American cuisine menu.

A Delight of France Bakery and Bistro
126 West Grand Avenue, Escondido, CA 92025
760.746.2644 / www.delightoffrance.com
▲ With its walls exhibiting local art and its pastry chef creating perfect éclairs, this downtown Escondido bastion of French cuisine is a locals' favorite.

Bistro 221 Restaurant & Martini Bar
221 East Grand Avenue, Escondido, CA 92025
760.737.7398 / www.bistro221.8m.com
▲ Live jazz on weekends and a sidewalk patio make this downtown Escondido establishment one of the top places to relax and enjoy the view.

Vincent's on Grand
113 West Grand Avenue, Escondido, CA 92025
760.737.3835 / www.vincentsongrand.com

▲ Chef Vincent Sirinos brings the traditions of his Besancon, France, heritage to the menu of this downtown Escondido name-sake restaurant, which offers a fantastic wine list to accompany its innovative menu.

A Taste of Florence
340 East Grand Avenue, Escondido, CA 92025
760.745.0691 / www.atasteofflorence.com
▲ Fantastic pizzas, patio dining, 50 percent discounts on Wednesday's wine list, and Bistecca a la Florentina make chef Eric Edney's downtown Escondido restaurant a winner.

A s executive director of the Escondido Arts Partnership, Wendy Wilson-Gibson oversees a dynamic and influential organization whose wide range of events, exhibitions, and educational offerings are considered to have played a key role in the success story of downtown Escondido's revitalization.

"We're the city's nonprofit agency for promoting the arts in down-town Escondido. Contemporary art has a big presence in our galleries, which tend to cover a wide range of the art spectrum including social realism and the types of work more widely associated with galleries in Los Angeles. Escondido has had a lot of residential growth in the past few years, especially when prices on the coast were skyrocketing and artists became hard-pressed to find any kind of living and studio space that was affordable. Artists moving here are welcome to exhibit their art at the gallery we maintain in the Escondido Arts Partnership building, which is always looking for new voices from the community.

"Downtown's become very conscious of the ways visitors and local residents now expect to find themselves dining, shopping, or strolling inside an environment expressing the creativity of local artists. It's a small town at heart, the kind of place where artists help each other out, especially the artists who are still learning their techniques. Our downtown branch of the Mingei Museum has been very successful at drawing the cultural community from across Southern California into Escondido for its great exhibitions and programs."

Mixed-media sculptor Renee Richetts maintains her home and studio in a quiet, rural setting just a few miles removed from the arts activity along Grand Avenue in downtown Escondido.

"The first thoughts that come to mind when people discuss public art usually connect with paintings or some other two-dimensional work. But in Escondido the idea takes on an entire new meaning because of our major performing arts venue, a strongly supported public sculpture program, two theatre companies, and an important contemporary art museum. The city of Escondido has stood behind its commitment to support the arts through forums like the Municipal Gallery and the Center for the Performing Arts. Our 2nd Saturdays ArtWalk has been expanding its reach through events like an annual Fashion Week and by signing up alternative exhibition venues to display local artists' work.

"Escondido gets lots of visitors coming into town specifically for arts or cultural events, especially since 2003 when they unveiled Niki de Saint Phalle's sculpture installation. "Queen Califia's Magic Circle" is the only large scale public sculpture environment she created in North America, and she only did three other installations of this type during her lifetime, and people come from across the world to see it. Once those visitors get here they're impressed with our friendly and supportive arts community. If you're an artist looking for a new place to call home my best advice is to come into town for an ArtWalk weekend, check out the different venues around downtown, get engaged in a few conversations with the artists you'll meet, and decide if Escondido's right for you."

Eureka

I t seems reasonable to assert that Eureka defines the southern frontier of the Pacific Northwest. Certainly from the standpoint of architecture alone the tidy streets and quiet neighborhoods where Eureka's 27,000 residents live bear far more resemblance to the Victorian era vernacular found nearly 700 miles north in the Art Town of Port Townsend, Washington, than to the Spanish Mission Revival ambiance of Monterey, less than 400 miles south. If there's a shred of truth revealed by axioms like the one concerning absence and fondness, then someone should spread the axiomatic wisdom that remoteness frees creative impulses, and point toward Eureka when challenged for proof. If challenged further they could pull out a continental map and draw an Art Town arc stretching from the Buffalo Bar in Silver City, New Mexico, to Tom's Burned Down Tavern on Madeline Island, Wisconsin. Needless to say, any such conversation would best take place in the friendly confines of the Fourth Street headquarters of Lost Coast Brewery in downtown Eureka and would best be understood while quaffing a pint of brewmaster Barbara Groom's legendary 8-Ball Stout, rumored to be the penultimate test of any man's knee strength. Afterward the most rewarding way to clear out those cobwebs would be to take a neighborhood walking tour of the elaborate murals that Eureka artist Duane Flatmo has painted on a number of downtown's walls. All providing further proof that Humboldt County's largest town is by all measures an exceptionally creative community.

Founded in the years preceding the Civil War, Humboldt County was the ancestral homeland of American Indians from the Yurok, Hupa, and Karuk tribes. Natural resources have been the region's economic underpinning, with mining, fishing, and forestry taking turns at the top rungs of Humboldt County's economic ladder. Towering redwoods dominate the landscape, and frequent rains keep its dozens of rivers and streams in prime condition for Humbold's legions of fly fishing enthusiasts. When weather conditions line up correctly anyone who can break away for a few hours of beach time will head either to the sandy shores of Samoa Spit, the narrow land strip sheltering Humboldt Bay from Pacific Ocean waves, or drive a half hour north to the broad beaches of Mad River County Park, where dogs can get their fill of chasing seagulls and fetching frisbees. Dayhiking along the Headwaters Forest Reserve's trails just south of Eureka is a popular form of exercise, while the drive along Humboldt Redwoods State Park's 32 mile long Avenue of the Giants is an unforgettable adventure in neck-spinning amazement.

The Carson Mansion was built in 1884 by the region's wealthiest family and remains one of the best surviving examples of no-holds-barred Victorian era architecture.

While most Art Towns are home to either an art museum or a community art center, they don't always exhibit the level of community-wide support that allows the existence of both. Eureka is one of those exceptions, and its Morris Graves Museum of Art is located in the meticulously restored environment of a 1904 Carnegie Library, while its Ink People Center for the Arts runs a multitude of classes, community programs, exhibitions, and special events from a warren of converted classrooms inside what once was an elementary school. The museum, which also serves as the Humboldt Art Council's home, is organized around its seven exhibition galleries and sculpture garden, as well as its permanent collection of contemporary art that includes major paintings and works on paper by Morris Graves, who lived in Humboldt County from 1964 until his passing in 2001. Among the other leading artists included in the museum's collection are Thomas Hart Benton, Richard Avedon, and Guy Anderson. Through the museum's outreach initiative there are year-round education and instruction workshops targeted toward Humboldt County's younger arts audience, as well as a range of free programs such as Second Saturday family art days, First Thursday Film Nights, First Saturday Arts Alive! music nights, and live jazz music on Fourth Saturdays and Third Sundays. The museum exhibits national, regional, and local artists and rotates works from its permanent collection in one or more of its galleries. The Ink People Center for the Arts has supported Eureka's evolution as an Art Town on many levels since its 1979 founding. It offers a full range of art education programs for all age groups, exhibits the creations of local and regional artists in its Brenda Tuxford Galleries, coordinates a region-wide Alternative Galleries initiative rotating local art on the walls of business offices and government buildings, provides Eureka with an important creativity resource that squarely addresses the sensibilities of its residents, coordinates the community's public art program, and serves as a community access technology center, to name just a few of its services.

As the core sections of Old Town Eureka become increasingly expensive places to run a business, some artists are taking a short hike down Second Street in search of affordable studio rentals. The C Street cluster of studios concentrates more than a dozen working environments between Second and Third Streets, including S Studios, Buhne Art Studios, and Accident Studio/Gallery.

Old Town Eureka, whose collection of historic buildings leads to the waterfront's First Street Plaza, is home to most Eureka galleries including the exceptional First Street Gallery operated by the creatively-thinking art department of Humboldt State University in nearby Arcata. Off-campus ventures in the form of serious galleries representing work from a college or university's students, faculty, and visiting artists are few and far between, and this is one of the best anywhere, not only making HSU's First Street Gallery an influential presence in the downtown art scene, but giving its art students an important leg up in the challenge of transitioning from academic life to the competitive environment of today's contemporary art world. In addition to the neighborhood's significant community of working artist studios on the upper levels of commercial buildings, some of the other nearby exhibition spaces in Eureka's attractive Old Town include the Truchas Gallery inside Los Bagels on Second Street, the American Indian Art & Gift Shop on F Street,

Old Town Eureka is the heart and soul of the community's creative, entrepreneurial spirit.

E2 Gallery on Third Street, Kronos Fine Art Gallery in the historic Grove Building on Third Street, Cody-Pettit Gallery on Fourth Street, Old Town Art Gallery on F Street, Art of Wine on Second Street, Piante Gallery on Second Street, Many Hands Gallery on Second Street, C Street Hall Gallery on C Street, and Jennifer Kincaid Gallery on Third Street.

Downtown Eureka's performing arts sector underwent a major change in 2007 when the Spanish Colonial Revival showcase formerly known as the State Theater underwent a top-to-bottom renovation and reopened as the Arkley Center for the Performing Arts. Everything about this majestic theatre's restoration, from its acoustical tuning to the contours of its 770 seats, to the backstage facilities serving artistic and production needs, has been done the right way. North Coast Dance moved its operations to the Arkley, as did the Eureka Symphony. During its initial season of presentations the Arkley struck a mainstream note, leaving outside presenters an open opportunity to develop niche audiences. For now, just having the dance company and orchestra on solid, long-term footing in the Arkley is reason enough to anticipate expansion of Eureka's performance and music sectors. North Coast Repertory Theatre's (NCRT) 139-seat playhouse in Old Town Eureka has also undergone a slew of recent renovations and upgrades, providing an improved audience and backstage experience for its season of six Main Stage productions and Second Stage readings. NCRT's productions strike a balance between musicals, Broadway hits, new takes on theatre classics, and comedies.

The monthly staging of Arts Alive! provides an ideal opportunity for surveying the strength and diversity of Eureka's art scene. Held from 6 PM to 9 PM on the month's first Saturday, Arts Alive! is a rain or shine gathering of the county's artists, arts supporters, and weekend fun seekers. From exhibition opening receptions at the Morris Graves Museum of Art on 7th Street to fair weather live music performances on the First Street Plaza and the nearby Boardwalk, as many as 80 venues take part in Arts Alive! by not only keeping their doors open late one night a month but by also featuring the work of local artists on their walls. Among the range of businesses that have caught the Arts Alive! fever are Smug's Pizza, Alirose Boutique, Eureka Books, and Bella Baskets. Other events that mobilize the local arts community are the Humboldt Artisans Craft & Music Fest in early December, the weekly Artists in the Park gathering on summer Sundays, and the two June weekends of the North Coast Open Studios self-guided tour through more than 150 artists' studios spread across more than 110 miles of Humboldt County landscape.

Venues

Morris Graves Museum of Art
636 F Street, Eureka, CA 95501
707.442.0278 / www.humboldtarts.org
Admission by donation / Closed Monday and Tuesday
▲ The museum's seven galleries and sculpture garden offer interesting exhibitions and a full slate of programs.

The Ink People Center for the Arts
411 12th Street, Eureka, CA 95501
707.442.8413 / www.inkpeople.com
Closed Sunday and Monday
▲ Changing exhibitions every month, Tuesday night writers critiques, classes, demonstrations, and creativity for the entire community.

Arkley Center for the Performing Arts
412 G Street, Eureka, CA 95501
707.442.1956 / www.arkleycenter.com

▲ Restored to all of its original glory, and enhanced by state-of-the-art features, the Arkley PAC gives Eureka the venue of its dreams.

North Coast Repertory Theatre
300 Fifth Street, Eureka, CA 95501
707.442.6278 / www.ncrt.net
▲ Eureka's oldest performance group stages its season of six plays throughout the year.

The Cody–Pettit Gallery
527 Fourth Street, Eureka, CA 95501
707.444.3995 / www.williamfcodygallery.com
▲ Representing a strong group of regional talents in a setting that balances antiques, art, and artifacts.

Kronos Fine Art Gallery
317 Third Street, Eurcka, CA 95501
707.443.1991 / www.kronosartgallery.com
▲ The type of exhibition venue that attracts artists from across the region.

Jennifer Kincaid Gallery
905 Third Street, Eureka, CA 95501
707.443.1855 / www.jenniferkincaid.com
▲ The namesake gallcry of a talented painter, along with the work of a few regional painters.

First Street Gallery
422 First Street, Eureka, CA 95501
707.443.6363 / www.humboldt.edu
▲ Sophisticated environment for intriguing exhibitions, and an anchor of downtown's art scene.

Events

Arts Alive!
Humboldt Arts Council, Eureka, CA 95501
707.442.9054 / www.humboldtarts.org
▲ The first Saturday of each month turns out hundreds of art-loving locals for Old Town Eureka's three-hour splurge of opening receptions, art talk, and networking.

North Coast Open Studios
707.834.6460 / www.northcoastopenstudios.org

▲ The first two weekends in June are the best time for connecting with Humboldt County artists with more than 150 of them taking part in this once-yearly, self-guided event.

Blues by the Bay
Halvorsen Park, Eureka, CA 95501
707.445.3378 / www.bluesbythebay.org
▲ Two-day outdoor concert series in late August featuring top touring musicians from across the nation.

Slumber

Red Lion Hotel
1929 Fourth Street, Eureka, CA 95501
707.445.0844 /www.redlion.com
▲ 175 room hotel with fitness center, pool, and restaurant.

Hotel Carter
301 L Street, Eureka, CA 95501
707.444.8062 / www.carterhouse.com
▲ Offers lodging in both a restored Victorian masterpiece or a modern hotel, both set in a quiet Eureka neighborhood.

Old Town Bed and Breakfast Inn
1521 Third Street, Eureka, CA 95501
707.443.5235 / www.oldtownbnb.com
▲ This restored and spacious home was built in 1871 and features five elegant guest rooms.

Sustenance

Avalon
611 Third Street, Eureka, CA 95501
707.445.0500 / www.avaloneureka.com
▲ Rotating monthly art exhibitions, live jazz, and a menu emphasizing locally grown produce and meats, and one of the best wine lists in the county.

Samoa Cookhouse
78 Cookhouse Lane, Samoa, CA 95564
707.442.1659 / www.samoacookhouse.net
▲ If you've eaten lobster at Newick's in Dover, New Hampshire, or cracked a few crabs at the Boiling Pot in Rockport, Texas, you'll love this old-fashioned seafood restaurant next to the beach.

Art of Wine
308 Second Street, Eureka, CA 95501
707.268.0626 / www.humboldtartofwine.com
▲ Exhibitions of local art seem perfectly matched with the excellent Northern California vintages selected by owners Byron and Hilary Alexander.

———

A s both executive director of Humboldt Arts Council and curator of the Morris Graves Museum of Art, Jemima Harr is one of the most accessible arts organization leaders in the state. The museum's very popular family programs and vastly expanded special event offerings are participatory manifestations of Harr's energetic style of arts administration.

"During my four years here at the museum we've gone through quite a few changes, especially in terms of family programming and programming targeted at making the children of Humboldt County feel comfortably at home whenever they came into the museum. We've initiated a Second Saturday program for young people, using local artists and musicians and performers to create a fun learning environment. The rest of our programming has vastly expanded, through art instruction, adult education, and summer programs for youth.

"Our attendance is now close to 30,000 a year, with as many as 2,400 visitors coming through during our Arts Alive! openings. And having an expanded range of programs has also increased our numbers of volunteers, who now want to be part of all the activity taking place here. Our exhibition program has evolved from being primarily concerned with what's taking place in the Humboldt area to including exhibitions from across the country in our own calendar. Having an opportunity to see national exhibitions that are new and exciting has energized our local audience and made visiting the museum more of a pattern in the community's life."

———

A graduate of Humboldt State University, artist Thao Le Khac draws upon the vibrant landscape of Northern California in her work. She also employs recollections of childhood years in Vietnam in creating her colorful images of rural splendor.

"For me having the Open Studios Tour as a way to familiarize people with my work has been a great experience. It's a two-weekend *show and the people who came into my studio on those weekends were a really great mix of artists, community elders, and art students. My goal was to just have a great time in feeling connected to the community, and sell some art on the side. I'm happy with the results of being on the Open Studios Tour.*

"I teach art in local elementary schools as a way to support my art. Getting the work out into places where people will actually see it is one of the challenges of being an artist in this area. I combine gallery shows with restaurant shows and exhibitions in other venues . . . it's the life of an artist in Humboldt County, where everyone seems to have an artistic side to them. Life is very slow here, and in 15 minutes you can be in the redwoods or hiking on a sand dune. There's pristine, epic rivers just thirty minutes east of here, and for artists this whole part of the state is alive with inspiration."

Fallbrook

he communities bordering a 125,000 acre military base might seem to be unlikely places for an arts conscience to flourish, yet that's exactly what's taken form in the far northern end of San Diego County. In this picturesque countryside setting of avocado groves, horse farms, eucalyptus forests, and commercial flower fields, the sights and sounds of whatever it takes to fulfill the mission of the 100,000 individuals attached to Camp Pendleton are woven into the fabric of everyday life. In this region of small towns it's the presence of military professionals that's provided an enduring stability since the base's 1942 founding.

Navigate away from the base, however, and Southern California's beauty envelops the area, from beaches of Oceanside's flawless stretch of Pacific Ocean coastline to the rugged canyons of Fallbrook's east borders to Camp Pendleton's wide reach. Fallbrook is the visual art focal point of a spread-out regional art scene whose key components include the Oceanside Museum of Art in downtown Oceanside, the Avo Playhouse in the town of Vista, Fallbrook Art Center on the town's Main Street, the Old Town Community Theatre in Temecula, and the New Village Arts Theatre in Carlsbad. Considered as a whole these building blocks of an art infrastructure form a "creativity crescent" running from southwest to northeast, following the military base's boundaries.

As is the case with many of the leading Art Towns of California, the region's Westernized roots can be traced back to the founding of a Mission church by the Franciscan Order of Padre Junipero Serra. The 1798 establishment of Mission San Luis Rey in what came to be called Rancho Santa Margarita y Las Flores led eventually to the lucrative

Fallbrook's Art Campus provides this north San Diego County community with a setting for the study of art as well as its fabrication.

cattle ranching business run by Irish-born Richard O'Neill (not to be confused with the soccer-playing namesake of downtown Fallbrook's popular JJ Purdy Landers Irish Pub, the best bet for a Guinness between San Diego and Pasadena). The original Mission church, whose impressive architecture signifies this as the largest of the Franciscans' 21 California Mission churches, serves today as the anchor to an historic Oceanside neighborhood. Its counterpart, the Mission San Antonio de Pala, was established in 1816, 20 miles east on the outskirts of present-day Fallbrook for the purpose of Christianizing the region's Indigenous population. Referred to as the Luiseño Indians by the Mission's Spanish priests, the present-day descendants of those Indigenous people have resurrected their Pala Tribal identity through initiatives such as the economic powerhouse of Pala Casino Resort & Spa. Though Mission San Antonio de Pala stands as a restored historical monument, the Francis-cans eventually turned the keys over to today's administrators, the Barnabite Fathers.

Downtown Fallbrook's cluster of art galleries, along with its centrally-located public sculpture garden, an art center with year-round changing exhibitions, a promising film festival as well as community theatre, and its expansive complex of working artists' studios attached to an art instruction center, lends this community of 30,000 residents a sense of momentum and purpose. Other elements supporting the community's art scene, such as a slate of outdoor summer art festivals and an open studios tour, have added to the diversity of Fallbrook's arts programming while developing a distinct arts culture independent of what's taken place 25 miles south in the Art Town of Escondido.

Housed in what once was the community's 1950s-era pharmacy, the Fallbrook Art Center serves a central role as far north San Diego County's leading venue for a broad range of visual art and fine crafts shows. Its exhibitions, which change every four to six weeks, run the gamut from wildlife art to surveys of the region's most promising student artists, to fine art glass sculpture, national juried exhibitions of themed art, and juried invitational exhibitions covering contemporary as well as traditional creative techniques. In addition to its innovative shows the art center also functions as a daylong gathering spot for local creative types through its charming Cafe des Artistes, whose infusions of espresso, local wines, soup, and salads have proven to be as important to sustaining artistic imaginations and motivations as they are attractive to the community's ever-increasing numbers of cultural tourists. Local art, as well as work from the

Year-round classes keep the Art Campus at Fallbrook busy most days and nights.

art center's larger exhibitions, is displayed on the cafe's walls, while live entertainment from local singers and jazz musicians entertains the cafe's dinner crowd on weekends.

The art center's central location in downtown Fallbrook places it just steps away from the art galleries, community theatre, artist studios complex, and art education center. Brandon Gallery, an artist-run cooperative space, represents the work of nearly three dozen artists drawn from Fallbrook and the region. While many of the gallery's artists are also members of the Fallbrook Art Association, the gallery extends its reach past San Diego County for events such as its annual Small Works All Media Competition, while balancing its monthly exhibitions by member artists. The association's two annual exhibitions, a fall Open Juried Show and spring's Membership Show, are part of its regular slate of events that includes painting workshops led by art pros from across Southern California, and monthly exhibitions of members' art at Fallbrook Public Library. Blue Heron Gallery, another of the town's Main Street art venues, exhibits a wide range of fine arts, jewelry, and fine crafts by living and deceased artists. Works by the likes of Maynard Dixon, Gene Kloss, Joseph Henry Sharp, Margaret Tafoya, Francisco Zuniga, and Childe Hassan can be found here. Fallbrook Fine Art, one of North San Diego County's largest commercial art spaces, exhibits a wide range of painting and sculpture in its Main Street storefront arts venue. In addition to a group of Russian impressionist painters the gallery balances a selection of established regional talents such as Carol Lindemulder, Carly Castillon, and Joe Milazzo with the likes of Robert Rivera, Xiaogang Zhu, Wayne Justus, and Don Sieber.

One of the region's most popular arts events takes place on the shaded grounds of Welburn Gourd Farm, whose expanses of acreage are home to one of the nation's top producers of gourds in all shapes, sizes, and species. Thousands of gourd artists, collectors, wholesalers, and retailers crowd their way along the farm's narrow strip of blacktop road each June during the farm's Annual International Gourd Art Festival.

A brief stroll from Main Street's concentration of art exhibiting venues leads to the complex of the Art Campus at Fallbrook. On its south end the campus is home to a rambling main structure as well as several outbuildings that all serve as the creation points for art. This facility serves as the working environment for several sculptors, ceramists, and tile mural specialists. The north side of Fallbrook's Art Campus is a combined series of art education classrooms as well as facilities for the creation of hot glass objects and several kilns for firing ceramics. While the Art Campus offers its own slate of year-round classes in disciplines such as photography, printmaking, painting, and ceramic, this facility is also used by out-of-area groups for short-term rentals that range from single artist projects to weekend-long intensives in oil painting. Among the organizations making use of the three classrooms is the Scottsdale Artists School, an Arizona-based powerhouse that since its 1983 founding has brought together many of the nation's top painters and sculptors with thousands of art students from all ages and skill levels. Scottsdale Artists School organizes six summer session classes through the facilities of the Art Campus at Fallbrook, making full use of the region's extraordinary landscape in its plein air painting workshops.

Two performance venues serve the needs of Fallbrook's musicians, actors, and dancers. Downtown's Mission Theatre, built in 1946 and seating 306, is a renovated space whose interior mainly serves as the home stage for the community theatre presentations of C.A.S.T. Productions, whose offerings have a family-friendly focus. The Bob Burton Center for the Performing Arts, a 532-seat theatre on the campus of Fallbrook High School, serves as the venue for the Fallbrook Music Society's year-round presentations of symphony orchestras, virtuoso recitals, and chamber music performances. The society has forged close links with the Redlands Symphony Orchestra, whose musicians are mainly drawn from the teaching faculty and advanced level music students at the University of Redlands. The orchestra's music director, Jon Robertson, is a former concert pianist whose 25-year tenure at the helm of Redlands Symphony Orchestra has established the organization as among the stalwarts of Southern California's classical music scene. Fallbrook Film Festival, a newly formed organization, uses the Mission Theatre as the home base for its three-day staging in late April. Cafe des Artistes and the environs of JJ Purdy Landers Irish Pub round out the festival's screening venues, which are complemented by an exhibition of Hollywood memorabilia in the Fallbrook Art Center and film industry workshops in the classrooms of the Art Campus at Fallbrook. With an emphasis on showcasing the work of emerging filmmakers the festival's initial season saw the screening of nearly 100 shorts, documentaries, and features.

Venues

Fallbrook Art Center
103 South Main Street, Fallbrook, CA 92028
760.728.1414 / www.fallbrookart.org
▲ As the leading exhibition venue in far North San Diego County, this downtown Fallbrook facility organizes exhibitions covering a wide range of media, motifs, and talents.

Brandon Gallery
105 North Main Street, Fallbrook, CA 92028
760.723.1330 / www.brandonartfallbrook.com
▲ With more than 30 member artists and more than 30 years of history behind it, this artists cooperative gallery has established itself as an important venue for local creative talents.

Art Campus at Fallbrook
310 East Alvarado, Fallbrook, CA 92028

760.728.6383 / www.artstudiosoffallbrook.com
▲ Serving both as a studio resource for working artists and as an art education facility for emerging to experienced artists, this multidimensional facility is Fallbrook's center of creativity.

Fallbrook Fine Art
128 North Main Street, Fallbrook, CA 92028
760.728.0700 / www.fallbrookfineart.com
▲ This commercial gallery represents the work of Russian impressionists, Western Realists, and motifs in between those points.

Blue Heron Gallery
113 North Main Street, Fallbrook, CA 92028
760.731.9355 / www.blueherongallery.net
▲ One of the leading Southern California art resources for masterworks in painting, furniture, and fine crafts.

Events

Fallbrook Film Festival
949.306.3465 / www.fallbrookfilmfestival.com
▲ A three-day, late April screening of new and recent work by emerging film talents at venues throughout downtown Fallbrook.

The Art of the Flower Festival
760.728.1414 / www.fallbrookart.org
▲ This early April, outdoor art fair on Main Street focuses on expressions of floral beauty in painting, sculpture, and fine crafts.

Sustenance

Aqua Terra Restaurant
2001 South Highway 395, Fallbrook, CA 92028
760.728.5881 / www.palamesa.com
▲ Fallbrook's only full-service restaurant and sushi bar with an outdoor deck overlooking the tees on a long, uphill par 4, Aqua Terra is also a popular gathering spot for locals and out-of-towners who want to kick back with a glass of wine and catch a Chargers game on the plasma screen.

Cafe des Artistes
103 South Main Street, Fallbrook, CA 92028
760.728.3350
▲ Chef Michael Calvanese brings a Mediterranean touch to his

menu of soups, sandwiches, salads, and dinner specials. Locally produced wines and an old-fashioned soda fountain.

JJ Purdy Landers Irish Pub
125 South Main Street, Fallbrook, CA 92028
760.731.0839
▲ There's not a better place around for fish and chips, a pint of Guinness, and sports action on the tube.

Brothers Bistro
835 South Main Street, Fallbrook, CA 92028
760.731.9761 / www.brothersbistro.net
▲ A superb wine list, romantic patio, and attentive service make Ron and Dee Nusser's Italian cuisine outpost a locals' favorite.

Garden Center Cafe
1625 South Mission Road, Fallbrook, CA 92028
760.728.4147 /
▲ This popular and lively cafe has a charming setting that brings the outdoors in, where it discovers a range of salads, sandwiches, and light entrees.

Slumber

Pala Mesa Golf Resort
2001 South Highway 395, Fallbrook, CA 92028
760.728.5881 / www.palamesa.com
▲ One of the best golf courses in San Diego County is the 18-hole, par-72 Championship Course adjoining the landscaped grounds of this 205-acre resort on Fallbrook's eastern fringe. Huge guest rooms with terraces and balconies, fitness pavilion, outdoor pool, sushi bar, cocktail lounge, and the excellent Aquaterra restaurant.

Blue Heron Farm Bed & Breakfast
5910 Camino Baja Cerro, Fallbrook, CA 92028
760.643.0092 / www.blueheronfarmbandb.com
▲ This comfortable inn is part of an organic farm whose main product, baby lettuce, grows year-round in the region's temperate, coastal climate.

Rodeway Franciscan Inn
1635 South Mission Road, Fallbrook, CA 92028
760.728.6174 / www.choicehotels.com
▲ With free wi-fi, a pool, and affordable rates, this 50-room motel is convenient to Fallbrook's art galleries.

As the Fallbrook Art Center's executive director, Mary Perhacs runs a facility whose year-round exhibitions and events are at the very center of social life in this north San Diego County unincorporated village.

"Our town's slogan is aptly 'Find Fallbrook.' While we are actually quite accessible, the town is a discovery you come upon after driving through groves and nature preserves that surround it, a rarity in Southern California. The town is personal and friendly, and its residents diverse, qualities attractive to artists and art lovers alike. The historic downtown is the hub of the art scene with galleries, the Art Center, and the School of the Arts an easy walk from one to the other.

"Fallbrook is a place where artists can have their privacy while enjoying the camaraderie of an established artist community. The lifestyle of an artist living in Fallbrook can be whatever they want it to be. Of course, being in Southern California, money is a challenge, but sadly that is often the case in the life of an artist. We promote our national level shows drawing local, regional, and out of state cultural visitors. Due to the diversity of the Fallbrook Art Center's show schedule, we appeal to a wide audience.

"Over the last year, we've made great strides in pulling together the arts in Fallbrook with a focus on collaboration. Our measuring stick of success is the formation of an Art Alliance joining the town's visual and performing arts groups, approaches from nearby art communities to partner with the Fallbrook Art Center on exhibitions, and the joint venture of Fallbrook School of the Arts with the Scottsdale Artists School."

Gallery owner, photographer, guitar player, antiquities expert, and Studebaker owner Robert Sommers says that he's happy he chose Fallbrook as the home base for his art and antiquities business. "If I told you about all the amazing stuff that comes through here . . . just walks in the door tucked in a shopping bag, you wouldn't believe me," he says.

"I painted and drew starting early in life and had the good fortune to be raised in a family that truly appreciated the art and spirit of Native American cultures. I started selling some of my collection of Native American art in the early '90s and found art dealing to be a *great way to counterbalance what came across to me as a sterileness in the prevailing art world. I've found Fallbrook to be an ideal environment in which to set up a business that would be right at home on Canyon Road in Santa Fe. With Internet communications and travel so easy these days I feel that Fallbrook lacks for nothing as a place to set up a focused, specialized type of art gallery. In terms of having access to walk-in buyers this community has exceeded my expectations. I'm especially appreciative of the educated and genuinely curious individuals who are in the Marines and step into my gallery open to learning about the art, the furniture, the jewelry, and everything else that's displayed in here.*

"I'd like to see more galleries opening in Fallbrook, maybe even turning our nice little downtown into a very well-known destination for people who like art and who enjoy visiting the environments where art's made and sold. And of course we really need to get serious about doing whatever we can to bring more art instruction into our local schools. The incredible strides forward that were made in art education just up until recently are worth protecting."

Healdsburg

For more than a century, Sonoma County's combination of climate, geography, and culture have attracted the types of individuals who are masterful at both conceptualizing and creating. The region's talent base is plugged into industries that depend upon innovation, and from one end of the county to the other there's tangible proof that the arts play a significant and appreciated role in enhancing the region's communities and the quality of life enjoyed by its residents. Among those communities is Healdsburg, whose location close to the county's north boundary with Mendocino County places its 11,500 residents within a 65-mile radius of San Francisco's Ghirardelli Square. Framed on its northeast by the 3,457-foot heights of Geyser Peak and on its west by 1,948 foot Queens Peak, Healdsburg's surrounding farmlands along both Dry Creek Valley and Alexander Valley are bisected by the Russian River, whose waters have spelled success for the area's multitude of vineyards, wineries, and family farms.

The community's downtown is comprised of a profusion of attractive storefronts whose businesses are in part oriented toward the needs and impulses of Healdsburg's year-round stream of tourists. Many are drawn toward this place in the hopes of finding a Northern California wine country community whose tourism business hasn't overwhelmed the historic look and feel of the town, and once they stroll onto the manicured grounds of Healdsburg Plaza Park, they know their search is over. With its broad walkways, gazebo bandstand, Florentine-style fountain, expansive flower beds, and tall trees, this homage to California's historic connection to Mexico's gracious take on living is more than the centrally located meeting ground for both local residents and tourists, it's also Healdsburg's front porch. The plaza's four sides

Home to the Raven Players, this 1949 movie palace has been turned into Healdsburg's Performing Arts Theatre.

border on a series of bookstores, art galleries, boutiques, gourmet shops, and sidewalk cafes. Even nearby streets hold surprises worth investigating, such as the Healdsburg Avenue site of the Hand Fan Museum and its international collection of a once-essential accessory no woman could do without. This being the heart of some of the world's most renowned wine country it's no surprise that wine tastings are intertwined with Healdsburg's appeal, and storefronts representing the likes of Todd Hollow Vineyards, Gallo of Sonoma, Souverain Vineyards, and Pezzi King Vineyards contribute to the downtown shopping experience.

The area's arts community is represented throughout Healdsburg in many ways, including commercial galleries, nonprofit exhibition spaces, artist-run galleries, alternative exhibition sites in cafes and restaurants, and during the summer months through a series of outdoor exhibitions and events on the Plaza. On Tuesdays from early June through August the late afternoon and early evening hours are occupied by Tuesdays in the Plaza, an event featuring local musicians performing zydeco, blues, jazz, and world beat from the plaza's gazebo/bandstand, and local farmers selling fresh produce from nearby tables. Healdsburg's farmers get a second weekly shot at reaching the community's foodies at the larger Farmers Market on Saturday mornings from May through November behind the Vine Street parking lot.

Healdsburg's venues for visual as well as performing arts fan out from Plaza Park to its adjoining streets. One of the best places to get a sense for the direction of Sonoma County's contemporary artists is the Hammerfriar art space on Healdsburg Avenue. Its selection of represented artists emphasizes regional painters, photographers, and sculptors such as ceramic sculptor Penny Michel, Petaluma photographer Randall Ingalls, and Native American painter Frank LaPena, whose Wintun ancestors once occupied the site where Healdsburg sits. Artist Marc Cabell Harris exhibits his richly-hued paintings and drawings in a museum-like setting overlooking the plaza. Huntington Wine Cellars on Front Street uses its former railroad station facility as both a tasting room and gallery, emphasizing regional artists such as landscape photographer Lance Kuehne, sculptor Keith Hoefer, and painter Else Gonella. Janet Howell Fine Art on Plaza Street uses its former bank building for exhibitions of contemporary work by California artists such as Carmel landscape painter Melissa Lofton, and Big Sur painter Reed Farrington. Erickson Fine Art Gallery has a national scope in its roster of contemporary artists, while the Palette Art Café on Healdsburg Avenue serves as a venue for exhibitions by established, experimental, and emerging art talents from throughout the region. Live music on weekends and a Thursday Night Jazz Series collaboration with the Healdsburg Jazz Festival attract an arts-appreciative clientele, and the cafe's range of exhibitions has broadened the community's reputation among art circles. Healdsburg's 4-mile long Foss Creek Pathway serves as the site for five works of public art installed along the bike trail's north-south route on the west side of town through a collaborative effort between city government and the Voigt Family Sculpture Foundation. Independent bookseller Levin and Company's Center Street location is also home to the Upstairs Art Gallery artists cooperative, whose more than 30 member artists exhibit their work on the bookstore's mezzanine. Plaza Arts Center, a nonprofit education and exhibition venue, has an alternative approach to the art business. It uses its Plaza Street location for two types of visual art shows. Those held in the East Gallery usually have

---

Healdsburg's community theatre activity was lifted out of its doldrums when the Healdsburg Plays & Players organization allied with several new faces in relaunching the Raven Players as an in-house stage company of the Raven Performing Arts Theatre. Operating in tight quarters with a playhouse under renovation hasn't derailed the acting company from pursuing its goal of becoming the North Sonoma County's top professional theatre.

a theme and are juried, while its Showcase exhibitions feature artists in a juried, four-week show contained inside 8 linear feet of wall space, with the center taking a small commission on sales. The center also runs a Resident Artist program for 18 artists who commit to a year of exhibiting art in the center's West Gallery and 15 monthly hours of volunteer gallery staffing, with the artists paying monthly studio rent and the center taking a small commission on sales. The resident artists are each allocated 8 linear feet of wall space, plus a display window rotation.

Jazz music isn't limited to the weekend performances at the Palette Art Cafe. Friday and Saturday evenings see the lobby of Hotel Healdsburg turn into another venue courtesy of the Healdsburg Jazz Festival, whose 10-day staging in late May and early June showcases dozens of leading music talents in a range of Healdsburg and Sonoma County venues. While many of the

Art galleries, bookstores, wine tasting rooms, and superb restaurants draw year-round visitors to Healdsburg.

festival events are ticketed, free concerts in Plaza Park draw large audiences when Tuesday in the Park's focus shifts toward the jazz side, as do several free performances at the Palette Art Café and Hotel Healdsburg. With nearly 20 years of concerts under its belt, Russian River Chamber Music has established itself as North Sonoma County's premier presenter of classical and new music, using Healdsburg Community Church as the primary performance venue for its October to May season. The local music and theatre programming has the potential to expand exponentially once the Raven Performing Arts Theatre completes the total renovation to its facility on North Street. It's presently being used for a variety of purposes such as the Raven Players and Imaginists stage productions, Healdsburg Ballet's concerts, and first-run movies on weekends. The Raven Players are active year-round, presenting a season of five plays.

Celebrate your inner geisha, or flaunt your Scarlet side, at this one-of-a-kind jewel.

An interesting side trip away from Healdsburg's weekend crowd of tourists involves driving north along the Old Redwood Highway (CA 128) until it merges with Highway 101 in the community of Cloverdale. Though located just 15 miles from Plaza Park, the distinctly local flavor and agricultural business focus of Cloverdale's quiet downtown brings to mind what Healdsburg must have resembled before its cultural and culinary tourism sectors took off. The sole destination for an art aficionado's journey to Cloverdale is a visit to the First Street Gallery and its array of quality artists selling their work at very reasonable prices. This 12-member, artist-owned space typically has some great ceramic pieces as well as abstract paintings on display, and from June to October it collaborates with the Cloverdale Arts Alliance in staging a 14-artist exhibition of contemporary sculpture on the Cloverdale plaza. Those who drop by on summer Friday evenings can groove to the free Friday Night Live concerts on the plaza. Another arts-fulfilling jaunt takes a shorter, southerly route out of Healdsburg to the community of Windsor, the place where the Russian River Valley broadens its shoulders to accommodate hundreds of acres of prime vineyard landscape. From June through August the Thursday evening Summer Nights on the Green series of free concerts and classic films draws a family-friendly audience, while the Windsor Art Council, which exhibits local artists' work on the walls of Windsor Town Hall, avails itself of the Town Green for its annual Windsor Fine Arts Show on a weekend in mid-May.

Venues

Raven Players / Raven Performing Arts Theatre
115 North Street, Healdsburg, CA 95448
707.433.6335 / www.ravenplayers.org
▲ Healdsburg's community theatre company has high hopes and lots of patience.

Palette Art Café
235 Healdsburg Avenue, Healdsburg, CA 95448
707.433.2788 / www.palette-art.com
▲ Exhibiting regional artists, showcasing regional jazz talents, and serving up Healdsburg's favorite cup of joe.

Voigt Family Sculpture Foundation
Foss Creek Pathway, Healdsburg, CA 95448
707.857.1733 / www.voigtfoundation.com
▲ Geyserville-based, regionally focused, and loaded with innovation, they've turned a bike path into one of the state's largest public sculpture venues.

Upstairs Art Gallery
306 Center Street, Healdsburg, CA 95448
707.431.4214 / www.upstairsartgallerysite.com
▲ Get the best of both worlds when browsing the shelves of Levin and Company bookstore by dropping by this artist-run gallery space on the bookstore's mezzanine.

Howell Fine Art
101A Plaza Street, Healdsburg, CA 95448
707.431.2684 / www.jhowellfineart.com
▲ After she positioned the Carmel Art Association's gallery near the top of that Art Town's visual arts pyramid, gallerist Janet A. Howell set her sights on Plaza Park as a perfect site for exhibiting the best of Monterey Peninsula's art talent, plus several exciting newcomers.

Hammerfriar
139 Healdsburg Avenue, Healdsburg, CA 95448
707.473.9600 / www.hammerfriar.com
▲ The leading regional venue for Sonoma County's top contemporary artists.

Events

Healdsburg Jazz Festival
707.433.4644 / www.healdsburgjazzfestival.org
▲ Summer in Healdsburg gets off to a great start when this 10-day celebration of American music mastery fills various venues with large, enthusiastic crowds.

Summer Nights on the Green
Windsor Town Green, Windsor, CA 95492
707.838.1260 / www.townofwindsor.com
▲ Twelve Thursday nights of free concerts and movies.

Cloverdale Sculpture Exhibit
Cloverdale Plaza, Cloverdale, CA 95425
707.894.4410 / www.cloverdaleartalliance.org
▲ Sixteen week exhibition of three-dimensional work from 14 local artists.

Slumber

Honor Mansion
14891 Grove Street, Healdsburg, CA 95448
707.433.4277 / www.honormansion.com
▲ This Victorian retreat on a peaceful street offers a pool, 24-hour espresso machine, gym access, sunset sherry hour, and 13 elegant rooms.

Les Mars Hotel
27 North Street, Healdsburg, CA 95448
877.431.1700 / www.lesmarshotel.com
▲ Boutique hotel near Plaza Park with 16 rooms, European elegance, and a pool.

Hotel Healdsburg
25 Matheson Street, Healdsburg, CA 95448
707.431.2800 / www.hotelhealdsburg.com
▲ Midsize hotel in downtown Healdsburg with a spa, Dry Creek Kitchen restaurant, pool, lobby bar scene, fitness room, and gardens.

Sustenance

Cyrus
29 North Street, Healdsburg, CA 95448
707.433.3311 / www.cyrusrestaurant.com

▲ Located inside Les Mars Hotel and featuring photographer Andy Katz's work on its walls, chef Douglas Keane's forum delivers cuisine worth every point of its four-star status.

Zin Restaurant & Wine Bar
344 Center Street, Healdsburg, CA 95448
707.473.0946 / www.zinrestaurant.com
▲ A bistro-style menu and comprehensive wine selections are a winning formula for co-owners Scott Silva and Jeff Mall.

Bear Republic Brewing Company
345 Healdsburg Avenue, Healdsburg, CA 95448
707.433.2337 / www.bearrepublic.com
▲ The best burgers in town, plus the award-winning Red Rocket Ale.

When he stepped into the leadership post at Healdsburg's Raven Performing Arts Theater, Executive Director Tom Brand became the unofficial steward of the facility's classic, postwar marquee featuring an agitated blackbird wearing a red bow tie.

"We recently changed the colors on our building after receiving comments from dozens of our supporters that the old color scheme was looking tired. So we now have red as the background color instead of turquoise. At night with the neon lit up the marquee looks great. On the building's interior we've slowly been renovating this old, 600-seat move theatre . . . it's been challenging to figure out how to maximize the potential for the stage while not letting go of the numbers of seats. There are similar projects taking place across the country at older theatres with lots of personality.

"The Raven operates like a hybrid falling somewhere between traditional community theatre and a swingin' roadhouse. For our audience it's important to keep things fun and keep things diverse, and having a flexible administrative structure helps us stay that way. By our being open to all sorts of community voices, Healdsburg has been able to warm up to us.

"The Raven Players are our resident theatre company. We work with them to help their productions make full use of the building's capacity. Initially we were a theatre serving the 11,000 residents of the community but as our reputation for compelling theatre has spread, our numbers of visitors and returning local residents has jumped."

As board president of the Plaza Arts Center, sculptor and photographer Robert Weiss guides the center's affairs. While 18 resident artists exhibit their work in the center's West Gallery, the center also organizes juried exhibitions and numerous events serving local residents and artists.

"A brilliant guy named Bob Schneider, who is also an artist, got the concept for Plaza Arts Center going and he found it grew quickly. We're now organized as a 501(c)3 and use the proceeds of three large fund-raising events each year to put together around 25 educational art classes that are taught by local artists to the community at a very low cost, and to meet the gallery's expenses. There are no paid staff at the arts center, but instead we rely on the volunteer expertise of 50 individuals who give of their time to help the arts center function.

"Resident artists are required to staff the gallery for a certain number of hours each month, and when they sell their work they're splitting the proceeds of the sale with the arts center. We raise money for the center through events like the annual "Opera in the Garden," which is a phenomenal event for 135 people with opera singers outdoors in a beautiful garden, along with food and wine from a top restaurant and vineyard. Our other big events are art auctions, and we make those occasions as specific as we can for various arts needs around the community. We do all we can to try and fill the art education gaps that exist in our public schools.

"Healdsburg is filled with galleries that exhibit all kinds of art, but only some of which comes from local artists. And that's why the opportunity to exhibit at the Plaza Arts Center is so important to the artists who are from here and might not otherwise get a chance to show their work in town."

Idyllwild

On days when Los Angeles's air quality seems only a slight improvement over the tailpipe emissions of a 30-year old pickup tooling down the I-15 corridor, the towering outline of the San Jacinto Mountains disappears. But centuries ago, in the days before Henry Ford started tinkering in his garage, the Cahuilla Indians who fished and hunted in the area now occupied by Riverside County rarely wandered far from the San Jacinto Peak's 10,800-foot foothills. Neither did the desert-dwelling Agua Caliente Indians lose sight of that same peak's eastern boundaries. These indigenous cultures knew that when times got tough in the lowlands they could always rely upon the high altitude refuge of the San Jacinto's alpine streams, towering pines, and relief from summer's heat.

Because those highlands remained difficult to reach they were largely spared the impacts of Southern California's sprawl. For decades communities in this alpine forest grew at a snail's pace when compared to those at lower elevations. In one corner of the San Jacintos a place named Strawberry Valley became a summer retreat for tuberculosis patients. Eventually that area evolved into the town of Idyllwild, and by the early 1900s its promoters conjured up an unofficial title of Idyllwild Among the Pines, which was a far more attractive identity than that of a town full of wheezing geezers. The combined attributes of Idyllwild's 5,300-foot elevation along with its two-hour driving distance from either LA or San Diego have preserved this community's unhurried and uncrowded quality of life, which today is enjoyed by 3,500 local residents.

For artists whose idea of paradise is a pristine setting in the San Bernadino National Forest's alpine heights, within an easy drive of

Most of Idyllwild's art spaces are clustered under the pines at the center of town.

everything from an international airport to desert badlands, Idyllwild offers the best of all worlds. Drive out of town heading southeast on Highway 74 and within an hour you're in Palm Desert, soaking up the rays and checking out sculpture along El Paseo. Head the opposite way on Highway 74 and in less than two hours the steep walls of Laguna Canyon open to spectacular ocean vistas. This confluence of topography is exactly what attracts Idyllwild's artists and visitors to the community's nearly 20 art galleries, coffeebars, and fine crafts stores.

But it's not only the appeal of a walkable art district set underneath a canopy of giant pines that lures cultural tourists into Idyllwild. Being within easy reach of Art Towns such as Palm Desert to the east and Laguna Beach to the west makes Idyllwild's Art Town success even more noteworthy given the realities of its competitive, regional arts markets. Realizing this, the Idyllwild arts community long ago determined that a series of near-monthly special events emphasizing their Art Town's unique qualities would be a revisitable strategy for attracting regional interest, which in turn would translate into heightened media focus on the local gallery scene.

That effort and planning started paying off when the community's popular First Saturday series of monthly gallery exhibition openings teamed up with a program titled "Saturday Morning Art Cafe," which offers art instruction workshops in casual settings. Idyllwild's arts sector also took the step of framing the community's Saturday gallery walks and art cafes as specially themed events, rolling out a steady stream of not-to-be missed soirees such as the Annual Art Walk & Wine Tasting in October; the Art Treasure Hunt in August, the 3-D Art Festival in June, and the trio of Art Alliance of Idyllwild member exhibitions slated throughout each year. With few exceptions, Idyllwild's art galleries are located within walking distance of each other in the town's commercial center. More than a dozen galleries participate in the local tradition of coordinated, opening receptions for new exhibitions, including Willow Creek Gallery, Artisans Gallery, Two Babes in the Woods Fine Art & Antiques, Baker Galleries, Courtyard Gallery, Mountain Metals, Mason Fine Art Gallery, Everitt's Minerals & Gallery, Idyllwild Gallery of Fine Art, the Four Corners Gallery, and Flying Pigments Studio.

While the ponderosa pine hillsides surrounding Idyllwild offer visitors one of Southern California's most accessible access points to the national forest's 275 miles of mountain biking, hiking, and horseback riding trails, another of the community's most notable assets is the year-round visual and performing arts programming on the campus of Idyllwild Arts Academy. Dedicated to fostering a distinctly arts-focused approach to the education of students in the 9th to 12th grades (as well as a few postgraduates), the academy site is also home to the Idyllwild Arts, a multidisciplinary session attracting more than 1,300 learners of all ages to the academy's campus from mid-June continue through mid-August. The program's early classes focus on the visual arts (painting, sculpture, ceramics), poetry, and Native American creative traditions. In late July the program's focus shifts to performing arts, and though theatre is represented here, the emphasis is placed on chamber music, orchestra, and master class training in violin, piano, cello, and wind instruments. The academy's mid-August Music Festival week attracts large audiences into Idyllwild for its nightly concerts on campus, while the popular programs and exhibitions staged during mid-July's Native American Week take place after with the annual presentation of a group exhibition in the Parks Exhibition Center. During its September to May academic year the academy presents a more limited slate of public programs, with events such as lectures by visiting artists and writers, student exhibitions in the Parks Exhibition Center, and stage productions in the 350-seat Foundation Theatre.

Idyllwild Arts Academy's 205-acre campus bordering Strawberry Creek is the September through May home to nearly 250 full-time students. On most afternoons a steady stream of students can be found in downtown Idyllwild's Candy Cupboard, an old-fashioned sweet shop and candy store.

Even the short break separating the summer-long Idyllwild Arts from the start of Idyllwild Arts Academy's academic year is full of action, as the annual staging of Jazz in the Pines brings dozens of

Summer's intensive art programs attract top professionals to the mountainside setting of Idyllwild Art's campus.

world-class music professionals and thousands of jazz-loving listeners to town for a weekend-long presentation of concerts, recitals, and social events. It's not at all unusual for Jazz in the Pines to present a dozen or more acts on each of its two-day runs, with performances starting just before noon and concluding around dusk.

In the best Art Towns there's always one business or art center or even a bar that functions as a central gathering point for the local creative community. Cafe Aroma's continuing impact on Idyllwild's artists, poets, musicians, and authors is pervasive. Its presence helps renew and sustain an already vibrant art scene while encouraging continued growth of the community's arts horizons. Owned by a retired mathematics professor from the University of California at San Diego, Cafe Aroma opens early every day and closes conveniently late (and even later on weekends) to accommodate not only the communing instincts of the region's artists and outdoor recreation enthusiasts but to also provide an ideal setting for the presentation of live music in the form of jazz, blues, and soloists. Some of the best nights on Cafe Aroma's stage are the ones when local resident and cowboy music legend Herb Jeffries "The Bronze Buckaroo" decides to saunter up to the microphone and lend his polished presence to the goings on. If you're in Idyllwild on one of these rare nights, consider yourself forturnate. Of course the local arts community regards Cafe Aroma's wall space as a prime spot for hanging paintings, and owner Hubert Halkin is more than obliging through the cafe's rotating schedule of exhibitions. Being that Halkin is, after all, a retired professor emeritus from UCSD in the lovely Art Town of La Jolla, it's only slightly less startling to find out that in addition to running along all of its caffeinated tracks (coffeebar, restaurant, live music venue, art gallery, social club) there's yet another facet to this gemstone. In one cozy corner of the cafe's candlelit interior is an unofficial though extraordinarily well-stocked library whose book borrowing policy of "return at your leisure" always seems to result in more books filling these shelves than Cafe Aroma has room for . . . an indication that local residents have interests extending beyond the edges of their television screens. There's a distinctly Italian touch running through the cafe's lunch and dinner menus, a direction well suited to chef Frank Ferro's creative talents. This explains why local folks know that on those evenings when they want to take in the pleasures of a bowl of linguine and clams, accompanied by a very reasonably priced bottle of pinot grigio, and then linger over their tiramisu while Jamie Olsen & the Hillbillies gets the crowd fired up on the dance floor . . . that it's only common sense to phone in your reservation earlier in the day.

Venues

Parks Exhibition Center
52500 Temecula Road, Idyllwild, CA 92549
951.659.2171 / www.idyllwildarts.org
Closed Monday
▲ Exhibits student work during the academic year, and visiting artists' work during the summer. Also hosts a year-round slate of poetry readings, artist lectures, and artist demonstrations.

Artisans Gallery
54-425 North Circle Drive, Idyllwild, CA 92549
951.659.9091 / www.idyllwildartisans.com
Open Daily
▲ This welcome addition to Idyllwild's art scene represents many of the area's most accomplished painters, photographers, and sculptors.

The Courtyard Gallery
26120 Ridgeview Drive, Idyllwild, CA 92549

951.659.2774 / www.courtyardgalleryidyllwild.com
Open weekends and by appointment
▲ Seven artists, each creating a range of interesting, contemporary work.

Idyllwild Gallery of Fine Art
54245 North Circle Drive, Idyllwild, CA 92549
951.659.1948 / www.idyllwildgallery.com
▲ More than 100 talented fine craftsmen from across the nation are represented in Idyllwild's oldest gallery.

Four Corners Fine Art
54967 Pine Crest Drive, Idyllwild, CA 92549
951.533.7564 / www.elenakern.com
▲ Artist-owned space with rotating shows by visiting artists.

Two Babes in the Woods
55750 South Circle Drive, Idyllwild, CA 92549
951.659.9595 /
▲ Antiques, original art, jewelry, and collectibles.

Events

Jazz in the Pines
52500 Temecula Road, Idyllwild, CA 92549
760.320.5272 / www.idyllwildjazz.com
▲ This late August event presents dozens of leading jazz musicians on the Idyllwild Arts Academy campus.

Idyllwild Music Festival
52500 Temecula Road, Idyllwild, CA 92549
951.659.2171 / www.idyllwildarts.org
▲ This weeklong culmination of the annual Idyllwild Arts summer program spotlights achievement in traditional chamber and orchestra performance.

Isis Theatre Company
www.isistheatrecompany.com
▲ Local theatre company presenting its performances in the Idyllwild Town Hall.

Slumber

Silver Pines Lodge and Creekside Cabins
25955 Cedar Street, Idyllwild, CA 92549
951.659.4335 / www.silverpineslodge.com

▲ This sprawling, 1923 hunting lodge once housed Idyllwild's movie house.

Quiet Creek Inn
26345 Delano Drive, Idyllwild, CA 92549
800.450.6110 / www.quietcreekinn.com
▲ This secluded refuge alongside Strawberry Creek offers fireplaces, Adirondack chairs, a hot tub, and 6+ acres of solitude.

Strawberry Creek Inn
26370 Highway 243, Idyllwild, CA 92549
951.659.3202 / www.strawberrycreekinn.com
▲ This 10-room B&B has lots of country charm in a contemporary mountain-style setting.

Sustenance

Cafe Aroma
54750 North Circle, Idyllwild, CA 92549
951.659.5212 / www.cafearoma.org
▲ Idyllwild's liveliest spot for the caffeine crowd also attracts artists of all varieties. If you spot Herb Jeffries holding court at his usual table, be sure to stop by and pay your respects to this music legend who used to perform with the Duke Ellington Orchestra as "The Bronze Buckaroo."

Oma's European Restaurant & Bakery
54241 Ridgeview Drive, Idyllwild, CA 92549
951.659.2979 /
▲ This Dutch-style bakery specializes in European pastries and hearth-baked breads.

Gastrognome
54381 Ridgeview Drive, Idyllwild, CA 92549
951.659.5055 / www.gastrognome.com
▲ High-style dining in a romantic setting featuring a family or two of garden gnomes.

Idyllwild Cafe
26600 Highway 243, Idyllwild, CA 92549
951.659.2210 / www.idyllwildcafe.com
▲ If your breakfast fantasies feature fluffy pancakes surrounded by sausage links, see Kelly at this local favorite.

L andscape painter Elena Camargo Kern lives in neighboring Hemet, California, and is the owner of Four Corners Fine Art Gallery in Idyllwild.

"Idyllwild is an artists' dream town. It would be impossible not to find inspiration simply by looking out a window or walking down the street. The fresh, clean air, the beauty of the pine trees, the majesty of Lily Rock and Strawberry Creek, and the hiking trails make Idyllwild a plein air painters' paradise. There is wildlife in abundance, wildflowers in spring, concerts in summer, and a crystalline blanket of snow in the winter. Idyllwild attracts artists and collectors from all parts of southern California. We're a weekend destination just two hours from the noise and gridlock of Los Angeles. Our town has accommodations ranging from B&B's to lodges and inns, all of which are reasonably priced. Most of the restaurants have live music on weekends, and pet owners enjoy the town's dog-friendly atmosphere.

"The Art Alliance of Idyllwild has a season that begins in March with an art auction and culminates in October with our Art and Wine Walk, which grows larger each year. Wineries come from as far away as San Luis Obispo County. There's a winery and live music at each gallery, so visitors can sample new wines and buy art in a festive atmosphere. Local artists design commemorative wine glasses that serve as a ticket to each gallery, and at the evening's end we have a drawing for a gift basket filled with wine bottles and gift certificates. In September there's the plein air painting festival showcasing artists from California and beyond. Saturday we all paint at locations throughout the town, then on Sunday morning after a champagne brunch the awards are given out and the art gets sold."

A rt gallery owner Chris Maxson has for nearly 10 years advocated Idyllwild's beauty and artistic flavor to audiences across Southern California.

"The art focus of the town of Idyllwild is diverse and cohesive. Idyllwild's primary reason for being is the arts. The Idyllwild Arts Academy, a boarding high school for visual and performing arts during the school year and a favorite summer place for over 2,000 students from ages 5–95 in the summer, hosts almost nightly performances and exhibits that are free and high caliber. The weekend Jazz Festival in August is the largest event on the school's campus. Other *popular festivals include the chamber music and band festivals in the summer, the Painters' Edge lecture series, the Poetry weeks, and the Native American exhibitions. The First Saturday Events of the Art Alliance of Idyllwild include local artist shows as well as Gallery Tours, a 3D Festival, Art Treasure Hunt and a plein air festival, culminating in the Art Walk and Wine Tasting the first Saturday in October.*

"The audience for these events includes local residents who enjoy living in Idyllwild and choose Idyllwild as a second home or retirement option because of the art and cultural events. More and more we see these newcomers joining organizations and participating in the development of Idyllwild's art scene. Regional visitors will come back for Art Alliance events and the Arts Academy does a great job of promoting its Jazz Festival. Each organization has a following and promotes events to their "off the hill" advocates as well as local residents. My estimate is that some events may have a 75 percent on the hill audience, like the ICRC Speaker's Series. The plein air festival seems to be a more local event because part-time and full-time residents want to meet the artists and buy a painting for their cabin on the hill."

Laguna Beach

The crescent shaped swoop of white sand separating downtown Laguna Beach from the Pacific Ocean's waves has lured artists, sun worshipers, and fun seekers to this Orange County arts haven for more than a century. Framed on its north and south entryways by rugged cliffs and shielded from nearby development's sprawl by the San Joaquin Hills to the east, Laguna Beach has managed to hang onto its particular charm even though it's just an hour's drive south of downtown Los Angeles.

Artists have played a fundamental role in defining the Laguna Beach experience ever since its early days, when painter Norman St. Claire closed his San Francisco studio in 1903 and decamped for the warmth, sunshine, and relaxed lifestyle of Southern California. St. Claire settled down in Laguna Beach and started painting its coastal splendor. As those plein air landscapes began catching the attentions of art collectors, it didn't take long before other painters began dropping by Laguna Beach on their own painting excursions. And once they realized that St. Claire hadn't been conjuring the sensual perfection of his Laguna Beach representations, an art colony was born. Within the span of a decade Laguna Beach developed a national reputation as an art colony whose little black book of local talents was on an equal footing with the Connecticut arts colony of Old Lyme, where Miss Florence Griswold's summer boarding house was patronized by many of American painting's leading figures.

Being well-informed of the latest trends rippling through the art world meant that denizens of Laguna Beach's art colony were quick to catch wind of the latest craze in French painting circles. Impressionism, which flaunted its intense colors and painterly inexactitude in cap-

Laguna Beach's heritage as one of the nation's foremost centers of impressionism is cele-brated in year-round exhibitions at the Laguna Art Museum.

turing the joie de vivre of a perfect afternoon underneath the Provençal sun was something this art colony's creative types could relate to. It turned out that the requisites for executing a compelling Impressionist variant on the local plein air painting style provided a perfect fit for both the artists and the setting of Laguna Beach.

By July of 1918 the community had developed its art reputation to regional acclaim, allowing what's now the Laguna Art Museum to open its doors with an exhibition covering nearly 100 works of art cre-ated by a group of 25 leading local talents. The successful outcome of that effort is considered the validation of Laguna Beach as one of America's most important art communities. In many ways that burst of early 20th century creativity has never slowed down, and present-day Laguna Beach has become home to a wide range of art galleries, performing arts events, and renowned arts festivals. And it also explains why so many Laguna Beach artists continue their pursuit of impres-sionism with a conviction evident throughout this Art Town's galleries and festivals.

Visitors to Laguna Beach are faced with the need to decide which of the community's three zones of art galleries they'll tackle first. The town's 50 or so commercial galleries are more or less equally divided between those along the Pacific Coast Highway in the North Coast Highway cluster (North Gallery Row), Central Downtown, and South Coast Highway. In practical terms the North Gallery Row venues begin at the Laguna Art Museum's dramatic precipice and continue along a very walkable stretch of landscaped streets. The Central Downtown cluster in Laguna Beach's most visited area covers the oldest and most gallery-dense part of town. Further on down are the South Coast Highway galleries, which are interspersed along a stretch of mixed development. A monthly First Thursdays Art Walk connects all three gallery zones with free shuttle buses and is an ideal way to absorb the local visual art scene's big picture.

While the coastal Pacific views from walkways surrounding Laguna Art Museum's hilltop location are mesmerizing, the works of art displayed in its two levels of exhibition space also provide creative inspiration. Known as an institution whose interests embrace both national and regional Southern California art movements, the museum offers an illuminating mix of contemporary and traditional art exhibitions whose observations often address the values, aspirations, and perspectives of the Laguna Beach art community. Many museum visitors head straight to those spaces displaying paintings by California impressionists such as Colin Campbell Cooper and William Wendt, preferring the museum's traditional area of emphasis. Other visitors exercise the option to bypass those subdued exhibition spaces in favor of the museum's latest installations of bold, memorable works installed through its contemporary art program. The museum's Plein Air Invitational has turned out to be an early October celebration of all things Impressionist and beyond.

What sets Laguna Beach apart from other Art Towns and what provides this community with a year-round advantage over other destinations is its capacity to sustain three of the nation's most prominent visual art festival events, each drawing tens of thousands of weekly visitors into town during their late June through August runs. The oldest of these is the Festival of the Arts, whose roots trace back to a 1932 event timed to lure visitors attending the Olympic Games in nearby Los Angeles. Staged as a multiperformance, multimedia extravaganza of creative expression, it was conceived as part art fair, part theatre festival, part studio tour, and part vaudeville comedy . . . and audiences loved it from the start. The festival's headline hit was Lolita Perine's Living Pictures, a series of staged, live tableaux using actors, props, and special lighting to re-create scenes depicted in famous paintings. These events remain vital components of Laguna Beach's art scene, with Ms. Perine's show renamed as Pageant of the Masters and the Festival of the Arts now grown into a summer-long, 140-artist art fair. The Festival of the Arts also programs a full schedule of community-focused art workshops from September through May and offers young audiences a summer workshop program. Both festivals take place on a 6-acre park along a winding road leading into downtown Laguna Beach.

Just a Frisbee toss away on Laguna Canyon Road's south side sits the 3-acre site of the Sawdust Art Festival. Its founding in 1967 was in part an effort to allow a diverse, nonjuried collection of painters, craftspeople, jewelers, and sculptors access to the arts audiences patronizing their peers across the canyon since the days of the Great Depression. The Sawdust Art Festival has broadened its impact on Laguna Beach's art scene through ventures such as the annual Art Studio Tour of Laguna Beach, its Winter Fantasy holiday season market, and weekend art classes from September through April.

With year-round productions that typically cover world premiers, musicals, and recent Broadway hits—all in the course of a single season—it's not surprising the Laguna Playhouse consistently draws over 110,000 theatre-goers each year to its Moulton Theatre home on Laguna Canyon Road. This Actors Equity organization has been the originating theatre for numerous productions that have toured nationally and internationally, frequently working with top Los Angeles playwrights, actors, and artistic directors. Laguna Playhouse also offers the community an intriguing series of youth-focused stage training workshops and full-scale productions through its Theatre for a New Generation series and its Youth Theatre program.

A perfect setting for everything from volleyball to beachside painting, Laguna Beach captures Southern California's beauty at its best.

From its humble beginnings in the parlor of a local arts patron the Laguna Playhouse has evolved through many phases of growth and several theatre buildings. With its need for expanded production and administrative space reaching a new interpretation of critical mass, the organization has again set its sights on facilities expansion.

Though it's within easy reach of the nation's entertainment center, Laguna Beach has developed a series of popular, locally-focused, arts events. Several organizations serve the community, booking stage pros and musicians from the nearby metropolis. The Laguna Beach Cultural Arts Department's July through early September series of concerts in Bluebird Park offers free Sunday evening presentations of jazz, salsa, rock, and Afro-pop. Music in the Park is the formal title of this 5 PM to 7 PM gathering of Laguna Beach locals. An equally popular series of concerts but with a twist running through classical, jazz, chamber music, and world music is staged from October through May as part of the Laguna Beach Live! series at several local venues, including Laguna Art Museum, Laguna College of Art & Design, and Laguna Playhouse.

Venues

Laguna Art Museum
307 Cliff Drive, Laguna Beach, CA 92651
949.494.8971 / www.lagunaartmuseum.org
$10 admission / Open daily
▲ Spectacular location overlooking the community's gorgeous beach and quaint business district. Presents innovative contemporary shows and the best of California impressionism.

The Laguna Playhouse
606 Laguna Canyon Road, Laguna Beach, CA 92651
949.497.2787 / www.lagunaplayhouse.com
Ticket prices vary / Open year-round
▲ One of the region's oldest theatre organizations, the Laguna Playhouse doesn't shy away from producing new and controversial plays.

The Redfern Gallery
1540 South Coast Highway, Laguna Beach, CA 92651
949.497.3356 / www.redferngallery.com
Open daily
▲ One of the very best places for early to recent California impressionism, as well as traditional landscape and wildlife work.

Sherwood Gallery
460 South Coast Highway, Laguna Beach, CA 92651
949.497.2668 / www.sherwoodgallery.com
Open daily
▲ Downtown art space representing contemporary fine crafts and painting since 1976.

Peter Blake Gallery
326 North Coast Highway, Laguna Beach, CA 92651
949.376.9994 / www.peterblakegallery.com
Open daily
▲ Compact, elegant gallery representing leading talents from Southern California and the nation.

Sue Greenwood Fine Art
330 North Coast Highway, Laguna Beach, CA 92651
949.494.0669 / www.gcgallery.com
Closed Monday
▲ Laguna Beach's prominent contemporary art space represents the likes of Gloria Gaddis, Gary Nisbet, Sally Chiu, Patrick LoCicero, and David Kroll.

Events

Festival of the Arts / Pageant of the Masters
650 Laguna Canyon Road, Laguna Beach, CA 92651
949.494.1145 / www.foapom.com
Ticket prices vary / July and August
▲ Established artists exhibiting underneath 6 acres of eucalyptus trees, and a nightly spectacular that's unlike any other.

Sawdust Art Festival
935 Laguna Canyon Road, Laguna Beach, CA 92651
949.494.3030 / www.sawdustartfestival.org
$7 Admission / Late June through August
▲ Wonderfully funky with lots of talent, this summer festival is ideal for families and art lovers of all persuasions.

First Thursdays Art Walk
949.683.6871 / www.firstthursdaysartwalk.com
Free / Year-round
▲ More than 40 Laguna Beach galleries keep their doors open late on the first Thursday of each month. Free shuttle bus service from 6 PM to 9 PM.

Slumber

Laguna Riviera
825 South Coast Highway, Laguna Beach, CA 92651
949.494.1196 / www.lagunariviera.com
▲ Great views of the Pacific and within walking distance of downtown.

Best Western Laguna Brisas Spa Hotel
1600 South Coast Highway, Laguna Beach, CA 92651
949.497.7272 / www.lagunabrisas.com
▲ Ocean view rooms and a resort-style pool.

Casa Laguna Inn & Spa
2510 South Coast Highway, Laguna Beach, CA 92651
949.494.2996 / www.casalaguna.com
▲ European style and service make this retreat one of the region's finest.

By the Sea Inn
475 North Coast Highway, Laguna Beach, CA 92651
949.497.6645 / www.bytheseainn.com
▲ This 36-room, Mediterranean themed hotel is close to the art museum and galleries, offers in-room wi-fi, has a pool, and will even loan out its beach umbrellas.

The Carriage House
1322 Catalina Street, Laguna Beach, CA 92651
949.494.8945 / www.carriagehouse.com
▲ Traditional Laguna Beach style and comfort reigns at this six-room B&B, within easy walking distance of the galleries.

Sustenance

Mozambique
1740 South Coast Highway, Laguna Beach, CA 92651
949.715.7100 / www.mozambiqueoc.com
Open daily
▲ Unique atmosphere with live entertainment, seating environments, and grilled specialties with a surprising twist.

The Beach House
619 Sleepy Hollow Lane, Laguna Beach, CA 92651
949.494.9707 / www.thebeachhouse.com
Open daily
▲ Forty years as Laguna Beach's favorite spot for seafood.

230 Forest Avenue Restaurant & Bar

230 Forest Avenue, Laguna Beach, CA 92651

949.494.2545 / www.230forestavenue.com

Open daily

▲ Great wine list and lively atmosphere combine to make chef Marc Cohen's presentations shine.

242 Cafe Fusion

242 North Coast Highway, Laguna Beach, CA 92651

949.494.2444

▲ Sushi chef Miki Izumisawa's talents win the Laguna Beach sushi debate year in and year out.

———————————

N*ow the public relations representative for the Sawdust Art Festival, Cynthia Fung has been involved with the event since her childhood years. Born and raised in a family of Laguna Beach artists, she's spent most summers employed by the festival, working in every imaginable job, from flipping burgers to punching admission tickets.*

"My childhood friends were kids whose parents were festival artists, so you could say this place is my comfort zone. I've performed here as a musician and have worked in the music business outside of my time here at the festival. Laguna Beach is the kind of community that inspires people to feel a sense of joy in this small, artistic, California beach town environment. It's always exciting to see the artists coming back here year after year, seeing the people who buy their art every summer. One of our requirements for artists is that they have to be residents of Laguna Beach, all 200 of them.

"There is a population of emerging young artists interested in exhibiting at the Sawdust Art Festival, and each year around 20–30 new artists put in a request to become a Sawdust exhibitor. The addition of new artists is based on a lottery system, and by pure luck of the draw young artists are able to move off our waiting list to join the 200 other Laguna Beach exhibitors for the annual summer show.

"The Sawdust Art Festival began in 1965 when a group of the original founding members came together in response to changes occurring at the famous Festival of Arts and Pageant of the Masters. A small group of artist-exhibitors within the Festival of Arts, called the Art Guild, decided the show needed to become a fully juried show, a political move that upset many artist-exhibitors, including some of the founding

members of the Festival of Arts. The first fully organized Sawdust Art Festival started in 1967, and many of the 65 artists who exhibited that first year are still coming back each summer."

Artist Dale Terbush, whose Illuminist-style paintings are sold at galleries in North America, Asia, and Europe, has been closely associated with the Laguna Beach art scene for more than three decades, both as an exhibiting artist and as an occasional resident.

"A large part of my professional career is the result of the friends I made and the skills I learned while I was living in Laguna Beach. I first got there in 1979 and it still had that sense of being Southern California's haven for painters. In those days there were only three winding roads in and out of town, but then with the development of multimillion dollar homes up toward Newport Beach a lot of that feeling of isolation was lost as the roads got widened and the coast's rolling grasslands disappeared."

"There was a lot of pressure in the 1980s that came along with the real estate boom. I remember the way that the Pottery Shack used to just leave hundreds of pieces of dinnerware, coffee cups, vases, and bowls stacked on the sidewalks in front of the store and walk away in the evening knowing their things wouldn't be disturbed or stolen . . . a true 'honor system.' It was remarkable, a Laguna Beach fixture that had been doing business that way since 1936. I realized change was on its way when one day I drove past the store and all of the once unsecured plates and things were now under plexiglass. There were still all the great coffee shops, the quiet restaurants, and the galleries, but a Malibu sort of influx began buying up homes in the neighborhoods. For ten years I participated in the Festival of the Arts, which was part of the Pageant of the Masters and was a great place for me to meet the people who would become collectors of my work."

"It's still an incredibly beautiful place, the kind of community that makes you feel certain excitement just driving into town. There are many great artists still living there and without question I'd recommend it to any landscape artist who needs inspiration and natural beauty."

La Jolla

rom its location atop a rocky cliffside in La Jolla, the Museum of Contemporary Art San Diego commands one of the most spectacular Pacific Ocean vistas of any site along California's legendary coastline. It's close enough to the relentless crashing of waves that sprays of salty seawater occasionally reach MCASD's panoramic windows, a reminder that like many of the state's coastal communities, La Jolla's roots extend deep into an oceanside culture.

The seaside resorts and fishing boats that supported many decades of La Jolla's working class are long gone. Neighborhood grocery stores and beach cottages have given way to vacation condos and high-end boutiques. Todays visitors to La Jolla are more likely than not in pursuit of a different bounty, the fashionable handbags, baubles, cocktail dresses, and stiletto heels coveted by the decidedly international stream of shoppers drawn to this breathtakingly beautiful Art Town throughout the year.

Located less than a half-hour's jaunt from the heart of bustling, downtown San Diego, this community of nearly 45,000 residents was one of the first Southern California towns to experience the dramatic surge in real estate values that characterized the region's development from the mid-1980s onward, when median La Jolla home values reached near 7-figure heights. And despite the impact of more recent adjustments in property values, it's safe to state that the prospects are slim to none that La Jolla's chic nightclubs and restaurants will be transformed into the outlet stores and fast food joints found just a hop, skip, and jump down Interstate 5. There is plentiful evidence of the anecdotal variety that life has become more challenging for retailers, realtors, and restaurant owners accustomed to smoothly surfing the

Museum of Contemporary Art San Diego delivers internationally significant exhibitions to La Jolla's culture vultures, while its cafe is one of the best places to observe artists at leisure.

economic tides that brought Gucci, Prada, and Gautier to the storefronts along Girard Avenue.

La Jolla was originally home to a thriving culture of American Indians, people whose basic survival skills included fashioning clothing, baskets, and vessels from whatever materials were available. The community's modern arts history began taking shape in the late 1800s, when Anna Held underwrote the dozen cottages comprising the Green Dragon Colony, a creative-minded refuge for many of California's foremost literary, music, and visual arts luminaries. Mexican ceramics craftsman Cornelio Rodriguez, who arrived here in 1928 along with his brothers Abraham and Ubaldo, was among the next generation of artists whose efforts broadened La Jolla's reputation as an arts colony. The Rodriguez brothers evolved their La Jolla Canyon Clay Products Company into one of the Southwest's leading producers of the roof tiles, floor tiles, and adobe bricks used in developing the distinct, Mission-style architectural motif of structures found from San Diego to Los Angeles.

The community's performing arts traditions can be traced back to the years following WWII, when vacationing Hollywood actors such as Gregory Peck would collaborate with members of San Diego's stage and music professionals in productions at the Summer Playhouse, precursor of what today is nationally renowned as the La Jolla Playhouse.

Regarded as among the very best American theatre companies for not only the quality of its productions but also the unflagging support it's given to playwrights ranging from household names to off-the-radar emerging talents, La Jolla Playhouse has served as the proving ground for dozens of productions that have gone onto both Broadway and Hollywood. It's launched productions such as Jersey Boys, Billy Crystal's 700 Sundays, the Who's Tommy, Dracula the Musical, Big River, and When Grace Comes In. In 1993 La Jolla Playhouse received a Tony Award naming it America's Outstanding Regional Theatre. Located on the bucolic grounds of the University of California at San Diego, just a few minutes drive north of the community's business district, La Jolla Playhouse presents its creative gems on the stages of a three-theatre complex. Its most recent addition is a flexible, black box style facility capable of seating 400 patrons, while its main stage theatre seats nearly 500.

That same commitment to supporting new directions in creative expression is but one of the key elements of the success underlying the national and international reputation of the Museum of Contemporary Art San Diego. While the institution's primary, 15,000 square feet of exhibition facilities are in La Jolla, MCASD also offers an equally dynamic exhibition experience in several structures on the site of downtown San Diego's historic Santa Fe Depot, a Spanish Mission Revival masterpiece adjoining the city's waterfront. In La Jolla, MCASD's vibe reflects a decidedly urban approach to the exhibition and program values expressed inside its Robert Venturi designed facility. Add to this MCASD's long-standing commitment of serving as an accessible exhibition facility for the region's emerging and midcareer artists, along with its outreach toward the contemporary arts community in neighboring Tijuana, Mexico, and the result is a contemporary art museum both shaping and reflecting the character and aspirations of its region. Through its audience-focused balancing of constituencies, MCASD resolves concerns about elitism that fray community connections at some art museums.

Due to an organized effort by neighborhood preservationists, MCASD's most recent, 1996 renovation of its La Jolla site, a $9.75 million project designed by architects Robert Venturi and Denise Scott Brown, was only able to add the 4,500 square foot Axline Court to the museum's 10,500 square feet of exhibition space, necessitating MCASD's welcomed expansion in downtown San Diego.

MCASD traces its roots back to the 1941 founding of the La Jolla Art Center on the site of what once had been the home of Ellen Browning

Art + Design

7661

766

La Jolla's contemporary art galleries are enthusiastic proponents of the region's established and emerging creative talents.

Scripps. Several name changes and architectural renovations later, MCASD solidified its art world reputation by becoming an early collector of works by the likes of Donald Judd, Andy Warhol, Frank Stella, and Claes Oldenburg. The museum also pursued innovative programs such as an artist residency initiative that invited the visual art world's top talents to La Jolla to lead artist workshops as well as create works destined to become part of the museum's permanent collection. The residency program remains an important connection to the international contemporary art world, though the program's artists are now housed in MCASD's downtown Jacobs Building, a 10,675 square foot treasure once used as a baggage facility for the city's main railroad station. With MCASD firmly planted in La Jolla, the community is able to access a contemporary art viewing experience equaling that found in many urban centers. To live in La Jolla is to know that misty mornings can become transformational experiences to be spent among art by the likes of Bruce Nauman, Vik Muniz, Ellsworth Kelly, Frida Kahlo, Christo, Andy Goldsworthy, and Vanessa Beecroft, at least until the fog burns off.

As is the case in communities whose early reputations as art colonies eventually come full circle and turn into a real estate free-for-all, sustaining an art business in La Jolla requires not only deep pockets but a decided sense of brinksmanship. Many of the nearly three dozen venues identifying themselves as art galleries have found it necessary to diversify away from traditional painting, photography, and sculpture. In a surprising number of art spaces it's not uncommon to see functional art, rugs, handblown wine glasses, and even gift cards vying for impulse buyers' attention.

Despite these distractions, several art galleries present their exhibitions with consistent attention to the quality. Joseph Bellows Gallery on Girard Avenue stands out as one of the nation's foremost photography galleries, while the roster of talents represented in Quint Contemporary Art's one-artist and group exhibitions strives toward an international standard of achievement. Stalwarts such as K. Nathan Gallery on Fay Avenue and Alcala Gallery are known for their changing inventories of works by early California impressionists. Tasende Gallery, located within a few steps of MCASD on Prospect Street, has long served as the anchor of La Jolla's contemporary art gallery scene. With a star-studded roster featuring the likes of Wayne Thiebaud, Louise Nevelson, Roberto Matta, Mark di Suvero, and Lynn Chadwick, no La Jolla art excursion is complete until one's passed through Tasende's glass doors.

Venues

The Village Gallery
La Jolla Art Association
7734 Herschel Avenue, Suite G, La Jolla, CA 92037
858.459.1196 / www.lajollaart.org
▲ La Jolla's resident artists work hard at rolling out the welcome mat to this Art Town's visitors. One of their most noteworthy efforts is The Village Gallery, which stays open daily from 11 AM to 5 PM, exhibiting the creations of the La Jolla Art Association's more than 100 accomplished members. Located just a pleasant, two-block stroll from the crush of tourists on Prospect Street, in a neighborhood filled with cafes and locally-owned shops.

Museum of Contemporary Art San Diego (MCASD)
700 Prospect Street, La Jolla, CA 92037
858.454.6985 /www.mcasd.org
$10 admission / Closed Wednesday
▲ Stunning location with important exhibitions by leading international and regional artists, as well as shows addressing San Diego's contemporary arts talents. Fantastic terrace views of the Pacific.

La Jolla Playhouse
2910 La Jolla Village Drive, La Jolla, CA 92037
858.5550.1010 /www.lajollaplayhouse.org

Ticket prices vary / Open year-round
▲ Famed for presenting sophisticated productions and edgy works by new and established playwrights. Located on a secluded corner of the UCSD campus. Saturday matinees are pay-as-you-can performances.

Tasende Gallery
820 Prospect Street, La Jolla, CA 92037
858.454.3691 / www.tasendegallery.com
Closed Sunday and Monday
▲ Blue chip contemporary art within sight of MCASD's front doors.

Joseph Bellows Gallery
7661 Girard Avenue, La Jolla, CA 92037
858.456.5620 / www.josephbellows.com
Closed Sunday
▲ From Paul Caponigro and Walker Evans to Minor White and Wynn Bullock, this gallery represents top contemporary and historic talents in photography.

Quint Contemporary Art
7739 Fay Avenue, La Jolla, CA 92037
858.454.3409 / www.quintgallery.com
Closed Sunday and Monday
▲ Representing a noteworthy and accomplished roster of mid-career and emerging contemporary artists from San Diego, and beyond.

Events

La Jolla Festival of the Arts
858.456.1268 / www.lajollaartfestival.org
▲ This late June, two-day event showcases nearly 200 artists in various disciplines on the East Campus of the University of California San Diego.

La Jolla Music Society's Summerfest
858.459.3728 / www.ljms.org
▲ An extremely active, year-round presenter of classical and pop music as well as dance, the society's extraordinarily popular Revelle Series and its Summerfest draw audiences from across Southern California.

La Jolla Gallery & Wine Walk
858.454.5718 / www.lajollabythesea.com
▲ This late September ticketed event pairs La Jolla's art galleries with many of its leading restaurants in an evening of gourmet entertainment.

Slumber

The Grande Colonial La Jolla
910 Prospect Street, La Jolla, CA 92037
888.530.5766 / www.thegrandecolonial.com
▲ Ocean views and European luxury in this romantic getaway. Don't miss the rooftop sundeck's breathtaking sunset vista.

Best Western Inn by the Sea
7830 Fay Avenue, La Jolla, CA 92037
858.459.4461 / www.bestwestern.com
▲ Ocean views and a swimming pool, in a downtown location.

The Bed & Breakfast Inn at La Jolla
7753 Draper Avenue, La Jolla, CA 92037
888.988.8481 / www.innlajolla.com
▲ Historic residence with 13 private rooms, one block to the beach and close to MCASD.

La Valencia Hotel
1132 Prospect Street, La Jolla, CA 92037
800.451.0772 / www.lavalencia.com
▲ This historic hotel has been a La Jolla landmark since its 1926 opening, now with 116 rooms, fitness center, three dining spots, and a tropical pool.

La Jolla Inn
1110 Prospect Street, La Jolla, CA 92037
888.855.7829 / www.lajollainn.com
▲ Great views, afternoon tea service, convenient to downtown, and balconies are among this 23-room establishment's assets.

Redwood Hollow Cottages
256 Prospect Street, La Jolla, CA 92037
858.459-8747 / www.redwoodhollow-lajolla.com
▲ Beautifully maintained, these seven cottages are holdovers from the way LaJolla charmed visitors nearly a century ago.

Sustenance

Cafe Lavande
7644 Girard Avenue, La Jolla, CA 92037
858.459.9940 / www.cafelavande.com
Closed Sunday
▲ European style in an intimate setting with an affordable menu and wine list.

La Jolla Brewhouse
7536 Fay Avenue, La Jolla, CA 92037
858.456.6279 / www.lajollabrewhouse.com
Open Daily
▲ Best place in town to grab a burger, watch the Padres game, and sip a La Jolla Red Ale.

Nine-Ten
910 Prospect Street, La Jolla, CA 92037
858.964.5400 / www.nine-ten.com
Open Daily
▲ From its gorgeous setting adjacent to downtown's top hotel, this highly regarded restaurant has consistently been rated as one of the region's best.

As a member artist and president of the La Jolla Art Association, painter Pierce Harrah oversees the affairs of one of Southern California's most influential groups of artists.

"I paint with acrylics on canvas in an expressionistic manner, painting the landscape, people, animals, and anything else in an experimental way with lots of color. I've ended up in art and in La Jolla because of the tremendous feelings of community and camraderie that exist here. Local artists tend to be very aware of the community's very strong flow of tourists and they're challenged in many ways to find effective ways to exhibit their art in places where visitors will find it. La Jolla has many fine art galleries but there's not the same sense of interest in local artists as you find in places that have similar reputations. The LaJolla Art Association has its own gallery but because the cost of renting a commercial space is so high our front windows cannot be easily seen from the street, so visitors have trouble finding us. Our situation isn't that uncommon, but if a place like La Jolla truly wants to retain the presence of a 90-year-old group like ours then

we'll all have to do some creative thinking about what it takes to sustain people as artists. Many of the most influential California artists were in some way connected to the La Jolla Art Association, from the plein air painters of the early 20th century to the Modernists and contemporary artists of today. What we really need is for someone, whether its the city or a corporation or a private individual, to meet us halfway."

———————————

Artist and art gallery owner Dottie Stanley is one of La Jolla's best known proponents of the need to develop innovative ways for sustaining the presence of locally created art in the community's most prominent regular and alternative exhibition venues. She is the founding president/director of Allied Artists Association of San Diego.

"We do quite a number of things, but one of the things we like doing most is working with nonprofit charitable organizations to help them raise money by using art in the context of auctions or straight sales. We've found this to be a nice way of getting exposure for the artists and simultaneously helping those groups that are working on behalf of our neediest citizens. It's a win-win way to help artists and nonprofits. We've been effective in partnering with groups, like the Patrons of the Prado, which raise money for events and places inside Balboa Park, and at the same time get money into the hands of the artists who created the work. We're also very active in several of downtown San Diego's most prominent office buildings, where we exhibit for-sale work in shows that rotate every month. These shows have turned out to be very effective ways for selling our art and for getting exposure to the kinds of people who would like to buy art but who just can't find the time to spend visiting galleries.

Allied Artists is only three years old, so there's still a degree of maneuvering taking place as we decide what exactly it is that we're going to aim for. One opportunity that's taking shape involves becoming part of the move to turn a former military facility into a center for arts organizations and artists studios."

Mendocino

T he further one drives toward Mendocino along California's Pacific Coast Highway, the easier it is to understand why Santa Cruz is referred to as Southern California's northern border. Cross the Golden Gate Bridge and the coastal landscape changes in dramatic fashion as sandy beaches give way to rugged cliffsides and dense pine forests replace clusters of oak trees clinging to grass covered hills. In some ways this tectonic landscape shift provides a visual rationale for the ill-fated Bear Flag Rebellion of 1846. Its leaders, who wanted to break away from California's Monterey-based Mexican administration and become a U.S. Territory, understood that the realities of their daily lives had practically no connection to the lives of their frontiersmen living hundreds of miles south. Of course in today's 20-20 hindsight, with the California State flag bearing a more than passing resemblance to the rebels' Bear Flag, at least some of the justifications for Major John Fremont's uprising against Mexico's authority have likely been vindicated, if not exactly adopted.

The Gualala Point Regional Park marks Mendocino County's southern reach, while its northern limit lies just south of the Cape Mendocino Lighthouse, a historic relic that's now been meticulously restored and relocated to Mel Combs Park in Shelter Cove. The 126 miles separating this county's coastal extremes are filled with the scenic places and tranquil communities that attract both artists and art lovers. Clusters of galleries highlight the entire route, making places such as Gualala, Point Arena, Elk, Albion, Westport, Ukiah, and Willits well worth the time and effort of a visit. But it's the adjacent communities of Fort Bragg and Mendocino on north Mendocino County coast where the concentration of visual and performing arts venues, festivals, and talents has reached a critical mass. If not exactly on a par with the likes of Carmel, Laguna Beach, and La Jolla, Mendocino nonetheless functions with the diversity of expressions and standards of across-the-board quality that keep arts-savvy visitors coming back for repeated stays.

Getting here is no easy task and requires advanced driving skills. One chooses to either whipsaw north from San Francisco along Highway 1's punishing series of hairpin turns, blind curves, and small town speed traps, or slalom through the redwood groves and vineyards lining Highway CA-128's westward wiggle from Highway 101. Impatient types who thrive on rewards after completing

Sitting atop Mendocino Headlands, the historic residence now serving as the community's visitor information center is a perfect first stop on any Mendocino's itinerary.

complex tasks will be ecstatic at the end of their journey into Mendocino when the astonishing beauty of this community of less than 1,000 residents and its adjacent Mendocino Headlands State Park jump into view. Arriving here on a sunny day when the number of tourists is not overwhelming is to instantly understand why Hollywood directors hauled their crews up here to use Mendocino as a setting for films such as *East of Eden, Cujo, The Summer of '42, Racing with the Moon, Forever Young,* and *The Majestic.* It's that spectacular a place.

As is the case in many of California's Art Towns, Mendocino's creative expressions range across the performing and visual arts. For visitors in an exploring mood there are more than two dozen art galleries scattered along the community's broad streets, providing an ideal excuse to log in a walking tour through residential areas filled with Victorian homes. In recent years art afficionados have benefitted from the art-focused developments a short drive north of here. The lofty cost of living and doing business inside Mendocino's town limits has been a boon to Fort Bragg, justifying the once-daunting ten-mile drive separating these communities and thereby creating a larger and more diverse regional fine arts scene. Still in firm possession of its historic roots as a blue collar counterpart to its button-down neigh-

Several charming courtyards beckon Main Street's tourists to stop and smell the roses.

bor, the downtown streets of Fort Bragg look as if they were transplanted from a mid-1960s San Francisco neighborhood, except that instead of Italian bakeries and pharmacies, its storefronts are filled with art galleries and a collection of locally owned restaurants, coffeebars, and boutiques.

What distinguishes Mendocino's art scene are the long-standing presence of the Mendocino Art Center (MAC), and the impressive range of talents at work among the community's large population of artists. While the art center's path to its present-day stability has not always been smooth, its role in coalescing Mendocino's spirit as a hotbed of creativity has been evident ever since its 1959 founding by artist Bill Zacha, whose bronze bust rests at the entrance to the Zacha Sculpture Garden Commemorative Walkway. The MAC is well-known among creative types for its Artists in Residence Program, which offers talents working across a range of media the opportunity to live on-site for anywhere from one to nine months. It's structured in much the same way that the Fine Arts Work Center in Provincetown, Massachusetts, provides its artists with residencies on Cape Cod. Mendocino Art Center's year-round offerings of fine art workshops, not only give attendees and local residents an opportunity to learn firsthand from many of the region's most distinguished talents, they also provide art mentoring and exhibition programs for elementary, middle, and high school students. Several gallery spaces are part of the art center's complex, and on the second Saturday of each month they become filled with new waves of art and artists during the center's exhibition openings. The art center's curatorial balance ensures that local and regional talents from across Northern California as well as the center's Artists in Residence are showcased as frequently on its gallery walls as are artists from elsewhere in the nation. Also located on the grounds of Mendocino Art Center is the rustic, 81-seat jewelbox Helen Schoeni Theatre, which is home to Mendocino Theatre Company. The organization takes a contemporary look at American stagecraft, offering nothing but recent works in its mainstage season of six productions, all presented on a year-round schedule along with the plays of its Jump Start Productions theatre for young audiences.

Music performance is an integral part of Mendocino's art scene. The two July weeks of concerts offered by the Mendocino Music Festival serve as showcases for chamber music, virtuoso recitals, big band orchestras, jazz combos, world beat groups, and folk musicians. While many of the festival's 22 concerts are staged inside an 800-seat tent set up on the grounds of Mendocino Headlands State Park, the organization also makes use of cozier confines throughout Mendocino and Fort Bragg such as the Evergreen Methodist Church, Mendocino Presbyterian Church, Preston Hall, and the Mendocino Hotel. Mendocino Opera Fresca presents its August to April series of classic concerts locally in Preston Hall and also at the Heritage House in nearby Little River and in Fort Bragg's Cotton Auditorium. In a community like Mendocino, which has served as the setting of numerous Hollywood films, the cinematic arts are not an unknown entity, which is why the annual Mendocino Film Festival has become a success in its few years of existence. Presented in late May and early June, the festival makes use of several local venues in screening a wide range of films, taking a specific interest in films concerning the arts.

With nearly 20 years of achievement behind it, the four-day Mendocino Coast Writers Workshop has helped hundreds of writers hone their skills, thereby kicking careers into gear through its intense schedule of agent/editor workshops, author readings, and evening social gatherings. Outside the conference's early August session, local writers gather for the intriguing series of readings and performances presented by Mendocino Stories in the Garden Room of the Mendocino Hotel.

Mendocino's creative spirit has attracted artists of all disciplines to its picturesque setting north of San Francisco.

California's artists seem to have a knack for organizing themselves into entrepreneurial ventures that take the form of art associations and cooperative galleries, and the direct marketing platforms of street fairs and online galleries. Mendocino's artists have established their mastery of those vehicles ever since the late 1950s when Bill Zacha turned his attention toward establishing a permanent art center on the ashes of a burned down residence. One of the town's most popular gallery destinations is on the upstairs level of a Main Street building housing the Artists' Cooperative of Mendocino, whose windows overlook the Pacific Ocean horizon. Nearly 20 local artists, most of them accomplished in their field, fill out the gallery's roster. Mendocino's commercial art spaces emphasize local and regional artists in their exhibitions, with fine crafts having an especially prominent profile in places such as the Highlight Gallery on Main Street. Panache Gallery fills its two Mendocino locations with a balance of two-dimensional art, sculpture, and jewelry.

Venues

William Zimmer Gallery

45101 Ukiah Street, Mendocino, CA 95460
707.937.5121 / www.williamzimmergallery.com
▲ Regarded as one of the top West Coast contemporary galleries, representing national and international talents.

Mendocino Art Center

45200 Little Lake Street, Mendocino, CA 95460
707.937.5818 / www.mendocinoartcenter.org
▲ Secluded but hardly sedate, Mendocino Art Center rotates exhibitions through its galleries with the same sense of purpose applied to the manner in which it rotates artists through its residency program.

Coastside Gallery & Graphics

45055 Albion Street, Mendocino, CA 95460
707.937.4960 / www.coastsidegallery.com
▲ The home base of master landscape painter Kevin Milligan.

Opera Fresca

707.937.3646 / www.operafresca.com
▲ What started as a lark in 1996 has turned into an emerging regional powerhouse with an ever-expanding performance schedule reaching far beyond Mendocino's city limits.

Artists' Cooperative of Mendocino
45270 Main Street, Mendocino, CA 95460
707.937.2217 / www.artgallerymendocino.com
▲ Run by accomplished artists in an amazing location.

Mendocino Coast Writers Conference
707.962.2600 / www.mcwc.org
▲ Four August days of connecting, learning, and writing.

Panache Gallery
45110 Main Street & 10400 Kasten Street, Mendocino, CA 95460
707.937.0947 / www.thepanachegallery.com
▲ This prominently located gallery represents a roster of regional and national artists in a range of media.

Mendocino Theatre Company
45200 Little Lake Street, Mendocino, CA 95460
707.937.4477 / www.1mtc.org
▲ Performing in a theatre on the grounds of Mendocino Art Center and focused on presenting contemporary plays.

Events

Mendocino Music Festival
Mendocino Headlands State Park, Mendocino, CA 95460
707.937.2044 / www.mendocinomusic.com
▲ Nearly two dozen concerts spread across two July weeks at venues in Mendocino and Fort Bragg.

Annual Summer Arts & Crafts Fair
Mendocino Art Center, Mendocino, CA 95460
707.937.5818 / www.mendocinoartcenter.org
▲ More than 60 artist booths fill the art center's grounds on a mid-July weekend.

Mendocino Second Saturday
707.937.5818 / www.mendocinoartcenter.org
▲ Coordinated exhibition openings with galleries open until 7:30 PM.

Slumber

Mendocino Hotel & Garden Suites
45080 Main Street, Mendocino, CA 95460
707.937.0511 / www.mendocinohotel.com

▲ Watch migrating gray whales frolic off the Headlands from the grounds of this centrally located, historic 1878 hotel with an outstanding restaurant, the popular Garden Room cafe, and the Lobby Bar's selection of regionally-crafted draft beers. With 51 rooms spread over its 2 acres of landscaped gardens, there's something here for every price range.

John Dougherty House
571 Ukiah Street, Mendocino, CA 95460
707.937.5366 / www.jdhouse.com
▲ Set in a quiet neighborhood yet close to the galleries, restaurants, and art center, with seven smartly furnished rooms and a cabin. A Mendocino classic.

Little River Inn
7901 North Highway 1, Little River, CA 95456
707.937.5942 / www.littleriverinn.com
▲ Located on a bluff overlooking the Pacific coastline just a few miles south of Mendocino, this spa resort has a spectacular view from its friendly bar, plus jaw-dropping vistas from many of its rooms.

Sustenance

Moody's Organic Coffee Bar & Gallery
10450 Lansing Street, Mendocino, CA 95460
707.937.4843 / www.moodyscoffeebar.com
▲ Computer stations, free wi-fi, organic smoothies, gravity-brewed espresso, and monthly exhibitions of local art make Moody's a must-visit.

Grey Whale Bar & Cafe
45020 Albion Street, Mendocino, CA 95460
707.937.0289 / www.maccallumhouse.com
▲ With rotating exhibitions of local painting and photography, this cozy hideaway inside the MacCallum House Inn is an ideal spot for enjoying chef Alan Kantor's highly regarded take on culinary arts, as the bar is part of his larger MacCallum House Restaurant.

Mendocino Market
95051 Ukiah Street, Mendocino, CA 95460
707.937.3474

▲ No visit to the Headlands is as complete as when a picnic lunch from Mendocino Market provides the pasta salad, sandwiches, and cabernet sauvignon.

Hill House Inn / Cabot Cove Bar & Grill
10701 Palette Drive, Mendocino, CA 95460
707.937.0554 / www.hillhouseinn.com
▲ Live music and a friendly social scene combine with spectacular vistas and local wines to make this popular nightspot a must-visit.

As vice president of the Artists Cooperative of Mendocino, painter Jessica Jade Norris is a six-year veteran of the challenging task of surviving Mendocino's high cost of living and competitive exhibition opportunities.

"I've been with the co-op for 4 years and it's been great to be part of this community of artists. Our gallery space was secured about 20 years ago in a space that has a spectacular view of the coast. So even though people have to walk up a flight of stairs to get to us they really don't mind because the view and the art never disappoint them.

"There's been a very strong focus on the arts in Mendocino Village, with events like the Second Saturday receptions being important ways this art community continues providing people with reasons to come here throughout the year. I do about three independent shows a year at venues like restaurants and hotels, and occasionally I'll have work at the Mendocino Art Center. By far the best place to exhibit and sell my work has been the cooperative gallery, because everyone who comes to Mendocino has to walk right past us as they explore the community.

"This is the kind of place where it seems that most of the people living here are creating art of one type or another. We have a large group of artists making a full-time living from their work, and on weekends there's a surprising number of artists who stay in their studios painting."

As executive director of the Mendocino Art Center, Peggy Templer oversees a multitiered organization whose operations include one of the nation's top artist residency programs in addition to year-round art education classes, rotating exhibits in several gallery spaces, and even outdoor art festivals and special events.

"Organizations like ours that offer such a wide range of programs relating to the arts are in a constant state of adjustment as we work through fluctuations in the economy and trends in the art world. That's just the reality of being in this line of work . . . you've got to listen carefully to what artists are telling you, just like you need to listen to what the general public tells you. It's very challenging to sustain the magnitude of activity that a community like Mendocino expects from its art center. We've discussed the possibility of limiting some of our programs but every time we dig into the process of deciding where and how to cut back the community jumps to its feet and changes our mind.

"Our artist residency program is a highly competitive program attracting far more applications than we have places to fill. And in the past few sessions I've noticed that the artists coming here are highly skilled already, even the ones at early points in their careers. Most come for nine months, and we charge low rents as a way to encourage them to stay, work on their art, and also hold down part-time jobs in the community.

"Our exhibitions are not only important ways for the art center's members to show their work but also present the local art community with art that's from outside the area, and provides us with a way to acknowledge the achievements and contributions made by Mendocino artists to the community."

Monterey

From the funkiness of Santa Cruz on its north boundary to the flashiness of its south shores, Monterey Bay's communities and even those inland from its Pacific Ocean waters have inspired prodigious amounts of creativity. Not many years ago the presence of artists and art galleries on the bay's south end was defined by whatever might catch the eye of tourists to Cannery Row, the waterfront entertainment and shopping development that today encompasses hotels, restaurants, and nearly 100 retail storefronts. But with artists being the flexible types that they are, things took a turn for the better when the growth of neighboring Pacific Grove's art scene started a creative migration toward Monterey's downtown. The combined impacts of Monterey's and Pacific Grove's arts development have started evolving into a potentially significant Monterey Peninsula art scene that's entirely separate from the goings on in nearby Carmel. Nearly a dozen exhibition venues have sprung up in the past few years, paralleling an ever-expanding range of programming in venues such as the Pacific Grove Art Center, whose galleries and performance space are located in a historic structure formerly housing the community's Masonic Hall. The spirit of entrepreneurial creativity that lifted Pacific Grove's creative community into view has had a similarly enterprising impact on the vitality of Monterey's art scene. There's also been a number of creative developments in the community of Seaside, which lies to Monterey's east and includes the 4,000-student campus of California State University–Monterey Bay.

The region's most prominent art exhibiting institution is the Monterey Museum of Art, which maintains its primary exhibition facility on Pacific Street in the community's historic district, while also

Just as the Gold Rush attracted thousands of hardworking fortune seekers to the mid-1800s Sierra Nevada foothills, so did an early 1900s fishing boom attract the strong of back to Monterey's canneries, fishing fleet, and shipping terminals. Author John Steinbeck, who was raised in nearby Salinas, chronicled their lives. (Photo © Kerrick James)

presenting visual art shows in the four gallery spaces attached to La Mirada, a historic adobe home on Via Mirada near the Monterey Peninsula College campus. The college's MPC Art Gallery serves as another of the region's key exhibiting venues, mounting shows whose reach extends past the campus community to include influential contemporary art and photography talents from across the state. Cal State University at Monterey Bay (CSUMB) has developed its facilities on one section of the former Fort Ord's decommissioned 45,000 acres. Creativity in all of its permutations is nurtured by the institution's teaching faculty, and the exhibitions offered by both the students and faculty of CSUMB's Visual and Public Art Department have developed a reputation for their boldness. Inside the space of a few years CSUMB has turned itself into one of the region's creativity hotbeds.

Monterey, which once was the center of Spanish Colonial life on the West Coast, was annexed into the United States as part of the 1848 Treaty of Guadalupe Hildago. Prior to 1848 the official U.S. government presence in Monterey was a consular office. Many of the community's historic structures surviving from that era are located in what's now designated as the Old Monterey district. The Monterey Art Museum

(MAM) is one of that historic neighborhood's most recognizable presences. With the flexibility of having two exhibition facilities MAM presents a wide variety of exhibitions surveying contemporary art, California impressionism, contemporary fine crafts, and photography. The museum's MontereyNOW exhibition series provides a focused look at the emerging contemporary art talent of the region, presenting quarterly shows in the museum's Coburn Gallery. A popular Third Thursday Open House offers free admission to local residents for an evening of social networking, while a similar though less frequent effort targeted toward young collectors is called Arts Lounge@La Mirada. Another of the museum's popular events, is its Food for Thought Lunchtime Series of lectures on art history and present-day art issues. The Monterey History & Art Association operates several important cultural facilities including the Maritime Museum of Monterey, the Casa Serrano on Pacific Street, the Perry-Downer House on Van Buren Street, the Mayo Hayes O'Donnell Library on Van Buren Street, and the Fremont Adobe on Hartnell Street. The museum's Doud House on Van Buren Street is also the home of Studio One, the work environment of painter Erin Lee Gafill and photographer Tom Birmingham.

Since the time John Steinbeck's 1945 novel *Cannery Row* hit bookshelves, Monterey's identity has been closely tied to the rough and tumble life that celebrated author detailed in his work. Though the days when the community was best known for its sardine industry are long gone, Steinbeck's legacy lives on in not only the tourist destination of Cannery Row but also on the grounds of the National Steinbeck Center in nearby Salinas. Part of a broad-scale effort to revitalize the historic core of what historically has been an agriculture-based community, the center offers year-round visual art exhibitions in both its Art and Cultural Gallery and in the Gabilan Gallery, in addition to a comprehensive schedule of films and lectures. The center's annual Steinbeck Festival in early August attracts a wide range of authorities and literature lovers to the Valley of the World, which was Steinbeck's way of describing his hometown of Salinas.

One of the surviving remnants of Steinbeck's *Cannery Row* is the memorial on Wave Street marking the place where pioneering ecologist Ed Rickets, the marine biologist who inspired Steinbeck's Doc character, crossed paths with a southbound express train in May 1948. Two art galleries have staked their claim to Cannery Row in recent years, battling perceptions about there being a limited local market for paintings not containing a seagull or two. Gallery at 417 is making its presence felt through the talents of its dozen members, all of whom are accomplished local artists. Those efforts are paralleled by the activities

Interior of the Monterey Museum of Art

and exhibitions taking place inside Monterey Peninsula Art Foundation Gallery, whose Cannery Row digs represent nearly 30 local artists. Also worth a downtown Monterey art visit is the alleyway adjoining the popular Portola Plaza Hotel. It serves as the home of Venture Gallery, yet another of Monterey's artist-owned spaces and displaying the creations of more than two dozen area painters and jewelers.

Pacific Grove's heritage as a summer retreat was inspired by the Chautauqua movement in the late 1800s, and though its final Chautauqua took place in 1926 the community retained its appeal as a supportive setting for alternative thinkers. One of the foremost intellectuals to leave their mark on Pacific Grove was architect Julia Morgan, who is best known for her long-term tenure as the technical genius behind William Randolph Hearst's massive castle, which is located 90 miles south of here. Over the course of several years she oversaw the design and construction of Asilomar, a complex of Arts & Crafts structures that today is used as a conference center run by the state's park system.

Famed as the wintering grounds for hundreds of thousands of monarch butterflies, the eucalyptus trees in George Washington Park are part of the community's Monarch Grove Sanctuary and attract visitors from mid- November through March. This steady stream of mariposa fans also delivers art buyers into local galleries in a quest for monarch memorabilia. The Pacific Grove Art Center's trio of galleries provide local and regional artists with numerous opportunities to participate in showcase exhibitions, with one of its galleries dedicated to photography. The center reshuffles its exhibition deck monthly and offers year-round art education programs for all ages and skill levels.

The area's densest concentration of commercial art galleries is located along Grand Avenue and Forest Avenue, which turn into ground zero during Pacific Grove's monthly Art Walk on second Fridays. Another Forest Avenue space, the Loft Gallery/Studio, showcases locally crafted glass alongside the work of regional painters, while Lysakov Art Company, painter Victor Lysakov's exhibition site and studio, grows by leaps and bounds each year. Possibilities Art Studio & Gallery is artist S. L. Greek's atelier, while Trotter Galleries is reliably strong with California impressionists. Hauk Fine Arts on Fountain Avenue has a varied roster of California artists both traditional and contemporary, while Anton Gallery on Hawthorne Street cuts a distinctly different swath by representing a national group of decidedly contemporary artists. Lisa Coscino Gallery on Grand Avenue has a California slant to its roster of nearly 50 emerging and midcareer contemporary artists, demonstrating that in several important ways the art buyers coming in for a look at the galleries tend toward more contemporary tastes than what's exhibited in the galleries of nearby Carmel.

Paperwing Theatre Company, Monterey's live theatre counterpart to Carmel's Pacific Repertory Theatre, reaches its audience in the Monterey Peninsula's competitive marketplace by offering theatre with a zany and manic twist. Some of its recent offerings include "Nuncrackers!," "One Flew Over the Cuckoo's Nest," "Killer Joe," and "Reefer Madness."

Venues

Monterey Museum of Art
559 Pacific Street, Monterey, CA 93940
831.372.5477 / www.montereyart.org
▲ With exhibitions at two local venues and full slates of programs, MMA set the pace for Monterey's art scene.

Pacific Grove Art Center
568 Lighthouse Avenue, Pacific Grove, CA 93950
831.375.2208 / www.pgartcenter.org
▲ Exhibitions, instruction, performance, and music with a local talent emphasis.

Gallery at 417
417 Cannery Row, Monterey, CA 93940
831.645.9923 / www.galleryat417.com
▲ This smartly run, twelve-artist cooperative gallery on Cannery Row showcases the work of leading local talents.

National Steinbeck Center
Central Avenue, Salinas, CA 93901
831.775.4728 / www.steinbeck.org
▲ More than 10,000 square feet of exhibition space dedicated to the legacy of a great American writer.

Paperwing Theatre Company
320 Hoffman Avenue, Monterey, CA 93940
831.675.0521 / www.paperwingtheatreco.com
▲ Monterey's downtown stage company maintains a humorous outlook.

Asilomar Conference Grounds
800 Asilomar Avenue, Pacific Grove, CA 93950
866.654.878 / www.visitasilomar.com
▲ Early 20th Century masterpiece of Arts and Crafts design.

Hauk Fine Arts
206 Fountain Avenue, Pacific Grove, CA 93950
831.373.6007 / www.haukfinearts.com
▲ Representing contemporary and traditional California artists.

Lisa Coscino Gallery
216 Grand Avenue, Pacific Grove, CA 93950
831.646.1939 / www.lisacoscinogallery.com
▲ One of the region's best places for discovering the contemporary art scene's next big names.

Lysakov Art Company
305 Forest Avenue, Pacific Grove, CA 93950
831.375.7100 / www.lysakovartcompany.com
▲ Artist Victor Lysakov's expressionistic paintings and prints.

Anton Gallery
701 Hawthorne Street, Monterey, CA 93940
831.373.4429 / www.antongallery.com
▲ Hawthorne Mansion space representing a distinguished group of established figures in the contemporary art world.

Monterey Live
414 Alvarado Street, Monterey, CA 93940
831.375.5483 / www.montereylive.org
▲ 100-seat venue for music, spoken word, jazz, and theatre.

Events

Pacific Grove Art Walk
Pacific Grove Chamber of Commerce, Pacific Grove, CA 93950
831.373.3304 / www.pacificgrove.org
▲ More than a dozen art venues stay open late on the second Friday of each month.

Art on the Plaza
Old Monterey Business Association, Monterey, CA 93940
831.655.8070 / www.oldmonterey.org
▲ Custom House Plaza hosts more than 60 artist exhibitors during this March show.

Monterey Jazz Festival
9699 Blue Larkspur Lane, Monterey, CA 93940
831.373.3366 / www.montereyjazzfestival.org
▲ This mid-September event delivers three days of top international music talent to venues across Monterey.

Slumber

Lighthouse Lodge and Suites
1150 Lighthouse Avenue, Pacific Grove, CA 93950
831.655.2111 / www.lhls.com
▲ Sixty-four-room hotel and a 31-unit complex of suites with lots of traditional charm.

Hotel Pacific
300 Pacific Street, Monterey, CA 93940
831.373.5700 / www.hotelpacific.com
▲ One hundred five-room, Spanish Colonial-style hotel in downtown Monterey.

Old Monterey Inn
500 Martin Street, Monterey, CA 93940
831.375.8284 / www.oldmontereyinn.com
▲ Nine rooms and a quaint cottage in this Tudor-style inn.

Sustenance

The Planet Ultra Lounge
2110 N. Fremont Street, Monterey, CA 93940
831.373.1449 / www.theplanetmonterey.com
▲ Comedy club, restaurant, and live music venue make the Planet Ultra a local favorite.

Old Fisherman's Grotto
39 fisherman's Wharf, Monterey, CA 93940
831.375.4604 / www.oldfishermansgrotto.com
▲ The longest restaurant presence on Fisherman's Wharf serves great seafood with consistency.

Cibo Restaurant
301 Alvarado Street, Monterey, CA 93940
831.649.8151 / www.cibo.com
▲ Lively bar and an art-filled interior plus great food make Cibo a winner.

---

*A*rtist Barbara Svetlik is a member of the Monterey Bay Plein Air Painters Association and a founding officer of Gallery at 417, Monterey's leading artist-run gallery, located in a historic structure on Cannery Row. Her work is widely exhibited throughout the region.

"Artists living on the north side of Monterey Peninsula don't have the benefit of having a year-round influx of cultural tourists like you'll find in Carmel. So without that kind of reputation it's something of a surprise when visitors walk down Cannery Row and find us here because we presume that they assume all the galleries are in Carmel.

"We have very reasonable rent and a really great location for showing the work of our 12 member artists. Having Gallery at 417 allows us to show our art in the one place where people are most likely to see it, and it gives us a place to interact with each other as well as with the people buying our art. My original intention wasn't to get into the gallery business, but once the location became available I saw it as that diamond in the rough and set out to pull the original group together.

"We're heading into our fifth year, and we've found that selling art on Cannery Row hasn't been as difficult as we first thought it would be. Lots of our buyers are the people who come to Monterey for conferences and end up staying in one of the Cannery Row hotels. People seem to like the paintings that capture an attraction in Monterey that they've already visited."

---

*S*ince arriving in the bucolic setting of Monterey, Executive Director E. Michael Whittington has brought to the Monterey

Museum of Art a decided sense of forward thinking change, as witnessed through his rapid expansion of the institution's exhibitions and programs.

"The legacy that we're dealing with at the museum is one in which from the late 1800s positioned this community at the focal point of central and northern California's art history. Its wonderful tradition of plein air landscape painting was joined in the 1950s and 60s by the masterful photography of Adams and Weston along with many other leading photographers of the time. At the museum we've taken great strides to honor that Monterey Peninsula legacy by positioning ourselves in ways that foster the development of the region's 21st-century arts community.

"We've become very strong advocates of contemporary art, some of which originates in our area and its diverse group of artists, but much of which also represents the entirety of what's taking place artistically throughout northern and southern California, with the Monterey Peninsula serving as an axis point for what's happening statewide. We feel we're in a unique position to disseminate California contemporary art to other parts of the country.

"We're challenged by the need to present exhibitions at two different facilities in downtown Monterey and feel that in the next few years we'll be under some pressure to further expand our programs and facilities to meet the community's needs."

Mount Shasta

rom Taos, New Mexico, to Banff, Alberta, high-country Art
Towns are scattered along the Rocky Mountains. But the West's
tall peaks don't end with the Rockies. In central California the
Sierra Nevada range is punctuated by the likes of 14,246-foot White
Mountain, while northern California's inland is dominated by Cascade
Range's 14,162-foot Mount Shasta. On that peak's southwest foothills
is the town of Mount Shasta (elevation 3606), where 3,700 residents
enjoy an alpine climate and yearly snowfall averages of 104 inches on
local streets. Along with nearby small towns such as Dunsmuir,
McCloud, and Weed, the southern end of Siskiyou County supports a
year-round art scene reflecting the significance of the region's creative
community.

The mid-1850s California Gold Rush brought hordes of prospectors into Siskiyou County searching for the veins of gold like these discovered at Yreka, which today is famous for once being the home of
Yreka Bakery, the nation's only place where the cinnamon rolls came
wrapped inside a palindrome . . . go figure. While the 49ers didn't find
gold on Mount Shasta's slopes, local lumber mills prospered by chewing away at the forest, and by the time new railroad tracks brought passenger trains through the area in 1887 the pump was primed for rapid
growth. Today, with all but a few lumber mills existing only as memories, Mount Shasta's economy thrives on the year-round tourism that
keeps art gallery cash registers ringing. Fly fishing on the many rivers
and streams surrounding the mountain brings well-heeled anglers
into town, joining winter's skiers and snowboarders at the Mount
Shasta Board & Ski Park, along with summer's parade of mountain
climbers, rock climbers, and hikers.

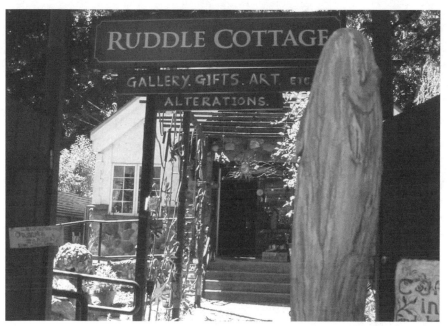

Nearby Dunsmuir has become a hotbed of creativity, providing the Mount Shasta area with a half dozen venues exhibiting locally created art.

Until recently the area's art exhibitions, performances, and live music mostly took place in Mount Shasta venues, but that dynamic is changing as the area's art scene has expanded into the neighboring communities of Dunsmuir and Weed. The well-kept buildings lining Dunsmuir Avenue and Sacramento Street are squeezed into a narrow valley bordered on its west by Interstate 5 and to the east by the Union Pacific's rail line and the Sacramento River. The north-south transportation business has historically been important to Dunsmuir, whose "railfan" switching yard is where crews were changed and trains were redirected. One of the town's most popular summer events is its early July Railroad Days, which features an art walk and community parade. Boxcar Gallery, the most likely place in town for discovering railroad memorabilia, is one of five Sacramento Avenue art spaces. The Brown Trout Gallery does double duty as a live music venue, coffee shop, and exhibition venue for local talents, while Window Box Bonsai Accents & Art Gallery manages to strike a balance between selling plants and exhibiting art. The Rostel Gallery emphasizes work from the region's large community of photographers. Ruddle Cottage features the work of mixed media artist Jayne Bruck-Fryer, who creates art across a range of formats that include mosaics, painting, sculpture, and jewelry. In mid-September these art venues are joined by the community's studio

Year-round supplies of glacial snowmelt have attracted seekers and healers to the slopes of Mount Shasta for centuries.

galleries for the Saturday staging of Dunsmuir Art Walk, a daylong event coordinating exhibitions in nearly a dozen venues. The Blue Sky Room on Dunsmuir Avenue, part of Sengthong's Thai Restaurant, is probably the only place between Oakland and Portland where customers can both catch a performance by an established recording artist and enjoy an order of summer rolls from the bar menu. The list of talents who have played the Blue Sky Room continues to grow, making this live music venue one of Northern California's premier nightclubs.

As is the case in Art Towns such as Sedona and Asheville, there is a large and influential spiritual community living in the Mount Shasta area. Many local artists have become full-time residents of Mount Shasta through their connection to the numerous healing centers, spirit guides, and holistic health care practitioners who have contributed to the region's reputation for tolerance. From high country explorations into energy vortexes on Mount Shasta's slopes to retreats featuring massage, mineral springs, and sweat lodges, when it comes to the realm of new age spirituality Mount Shasta has it all. Several downtown art galleries exhibit the work of Mount Shasta artists. The Gallery in Mount Shasta and Gallery 319 are a two-location art business representing painters, sculptors, photographers, and fine craftspeople from mainly the

Siskiyou County area, including Pamela Sexton, Terry Lawhon, Alice Nathan, Lisa Schneider, David Joaquin, and Eric Marshall. Photographer Kevin Lahey's namesake gallery on Mount Shasta Boulevard features his color-saturated, large format images of mountains, wild places, trains, and individuals. The best place to find fine crafts by local talents is downtown Mount Shasta's Velvet Elephant Fair Trade, which carries creations from across the oceans in addition to its local art. From April to September a good place to come across local artists' work is the Alpine Community Marketplace on Main Street, which offers art, crafts, and music on Saturdays from 10 AM to 3 PM in an open-air setting.

For a community with a small population Mount Shasta enjoys access to the sort of lively performing arts scene more common in destination towns. During the summer months the Mount Shasta Resort's free Summer Concert Series features musicians from across the region, while bluegrass music has its moment under the spotlight during Labor Day weekend's annual Blackberry Festival in Mount Shasta City Park. City Park is also the venue for the summer-long Cool Mountain Nights concert series as well as August's Mount Shasta Art & Wine Festival. One Shasta event that opens local minds to new considerations of life's creative possibilities is the weekend-long Shasta Yama, an international celebration of Japanese taiko drumming. Staged in late July in Shastice Park, Shasta Yama is the creation of musicians Russell Hisashi Baba, Jeanne Aiko Mercer, and Mark Miyoshi, Mount Shasta residents who are internationally respected educators and performers of this centuries-old music form. The three October days of the Mount Shasta International Film Festival have had a significant impact on the community since the festival started screening films in 2004. Started by local resident Jeffrey Winters the festival screens nearly four dozen features, shorts, and documentaries at venues such as the Mount Shasta Cinema and the Ford Theater on the College of the Siskiyous campus in the town of Weed, which is located 10 miles to the north. The

Without having the benefit of a community art center serving as a central location for visual art exhibitions, educational workshops, chamber music concerts, and theatre performances, the Mount Shasta creative community has developed an innovative way to work around the problem. One of the most prominent of these is the early August event "Art in the Garden," staged inside Native Grounds Nursery and featuring visual artists as well as performing artists in an evening celebration of the region's wealth of talent.

literary-minded side of Mount Shasta's creative community has spawned the Mount Shasta Writers Series, whose open mic poetry readings at the Mount Shasta Library are precisely the kind of social gatherings the solitary-minded writing community needs. The series also coordinates visits and workshops featuring established authors and poets, as well as the publication of the Moving Mountain literary journal. Downtown Mount Shasta is home to the Stage Door Coffeehouse & Cabaret, a multifaceted center of creativity whose environment provides local artists, writers, music lovers, and java heads with everything from free wi-fi to a comprehensive selection of regionally crafted draft brews. Located in the center of Mount Shasta Boulevard's funky mix of art galleries, bookstores, boutiques, and cafes, the Stage Door presents local, regional, and national entertainers from Celtic rockers to introspective folkies on its very busy stage.

The campus of College of the Siskiyous in Weed offers a wealth of fine arts programming through its arts, music, and theatre departments. The institution's Performing Arts Series, staged in the Kenneth W. Ford Theatre, delivers a wide range of professional talent to Mount Shasta area audiences, presenting the likes of Chinese acrobats, touring ballet companies, and Broadway-style theatre as its season, which is in addition to the college's own production schedule of eight concerts and plays. Another of the region's hotbeds of creativity is the college's COS Art Gallery, which exhibits work by its art students and art faculty, as well as regular shows featuring established artists from Northern California.

Venues

Stage Door Coffeehouse & Cabaret
414 N. Mount Shasta Boulevard, Mount Shasta, CA 96067
530.926.1050 / www.stagedoorcabaret.com
▲ One of Northern California's premier live music venues, this downtown Mount Shasta coffeehouse and cafe also serves up burgers, salads, and free wi-fi.

The Gallery in Mount Shasta
201 N. Mount Shasta Boulevard, Mount Shasta, CA 96067
530.926.2334 / www.thegalleryinmtshasta.com
▲ This downtown art space represents many of the region's top talents. It's 319 Gallery, located at 319 N. Mount Shasta Boulevard, specializes in exhibiting the work of regional photographers.

Kevin Lahey Photography
304 N. Mount Shasta Boulevard, Mount Shasta, CA 96067
530.926.3906 / www.kevinlahey.com
▲ This downtown Mount Shasta venue exhibits the full range of images captured by one of the region's best known photographers.

Ruddle Cottage
5815 Sacramento Avenue, Dunsmuir, CA 96025
530.235.2022 / www.ruddlecottage.com
▲ This comfortable and attractive art space on historic Sacramento Avenue exhibits the multimedia expressions of Jayne Bruck-Fryer, an artist committed to using recycled materials in her creations.

Rostel Gallery
5743 Sacramento Avenue, Dunsmuir, CA 96025
www.nrcpa.org
▲ Photographers John Rickard and Rika Noda established this Dunsmuir exhibition and education space in an old hardware store as a forum for Northern California's photography community.

Events

Mount Shasta International Film Festival
530.926.4537 / www.shastafilmfest.com
▲ An early October screening of dozens of short films, feature films, and documentaries at venues in Mount Shasta and on the College of the Siskiyous campus.

Dunsmuir Art Walk
530.235.0963 / www.dunsmuir.com
▲ Historic Dunsmuir's South River Arts District springs into full gear for this daylong event featuring music, art, and performances on a sunny, mid-September afternoon.

Art in the Garden
Native Grounds Nursery, Mount Shasta, CA 96067
530.926.0667 / www.siskiyouartscouncil.org
▲ This early August gathering of the region's artists and art supporters in the bucolic setting of a plant nursery provides an ideal reason to schedule a Mount Shasta visit.

Slumber

Mount Shasta Ranch Bed & Breakfast

1008 W.A. Barr Road, Mount Shasta, CA 96067

530.926.3870 / www.stayinshasta.com

▲ A comfortable ranch house built in 1923 with four guest rooms, a carriage house, and a cottage with mountain views and rural quiet.

The Mount Shasta Resort

1000 Siskiyou Lake Boulevard, Mount Shasta, CA 96067

530.926.3030 / www.mountshastaresort.com

▲ Offering 15 hotel rooms, 15 studio units, and 50 private chalets, this year-round resort features a golf course, restaurant, tennis courts spa, massage therapists, and incredible views of Mount Shasta.

Evergreen Lodge

1312 South Mount Shasta Boulevard, Mount Shasta, CA 96067

530.926.2143 / www.stayinshasta.com

▲ This 20-room motel features a swimming pool, hot tub, and affordable rates.

Sustenance

Black Bear Diner

401 West Lake Street, Mount Shasta, CA 96067

530.926.4669 / www.blackbeardiner.com

▲ Bob and Laurie Manley exhibit chain saw carving master Ray Schultz's bear sculptures at their popular eatery, which since its founding in 1995 has grown into a 38-location franchise success story. Don't miss a chance to try Bob's BBQ pork ribs.

Trinity Cafe

622 North Mount Shasta Boulevard, Mount Shasta, CA 96067

530.926.6200 / www.trinitycafe.net

▲ Chef Jennifer Stout's seasonal menu featuring local produce and wild game has put this high country bistro's reputation on firm footing. Tiny bar, smart wine list, and friendly staff.

Seven Suns Coffee & Cafe

1104 South Mount Shasta Boulevard, Mount Shasta, CA 96067

530.926.9701

▲ The community's favorite morning buzz is the friendly vibe served at this caffeine station.

Tucked into a somewhat secluded niche along the short but eminently enjoyable gallery row on Dunsmuir's Sacramento Street, the verdant surroundings of artist Jayne Bruck-Fryer's Ruddle Cottage lend this unique art space the charm of an English teahouse while providing a delightful backdrop for displaying the artist's lines of original and recycled art.

"Here in Dunsmuir we have inexpensive rent, affordable home prices, and lovely views of rivers and mountains. We are a community that appreciates our quality of living. We have an ideal environment for artists, and we all enjoy each others' company. Dunsmuir has fresh air and our faucets flow with glacial waters from the slopes of Mount Shasta, water that flows from Mount Shasta's lava tubes straight to the Sacramento River. And if you ever need a rest from our panoramic mountain views there's incredible trout fishing just across the street in the Sacramento River.

"We welcome new artists to the community and help them whenever they ask for advice. It's always a pleasure to converse with new people and exchange ideas. As a small community with lots of artists Dunsmuir's always looking for ways to elevate its profile as the exact sort of place cultural tourists enjoy visiting. I'm pleasantly surprised at the number of people who seek me out at Ruddle Cottage, asking for advice and some true directions."

As executive director of the Siskiyou Arts Council, artist Lauri Sturdivant brought to the high country her experience as a founding member of the West Marin Open Studio Group. In her spare time she's an instructor in the county's "Special Arts for Special Children" program.

"One of the biggest attractions for artists thinking of making a move here from the Bay Area or even in some cases Southern California are the much more affordable studio rents and home prices. But then you walk into one of our grocery stores and realize that you'll be paying higher prices for your food, so it kind of evens out. And when it snows things around here can totally shut down. Some artists stick around for seven months a year then get out of here in the winter, but most just struggle through the conditions.

"When you think about the way the county works it's Mount Shasta that serves as the hub for a large area that extends as far north as Yreka, where there's the wonderful contemporary gallery called Liberty Arts, and as far south as Dunsmuir, which has attracted several new art galleries. In between those points is Weed, which has several art galleries as well as the College of the Siskiyous art department and art gallery, and Mount Shasta itself."

Nevada City

In the mid-1800s the first of many California land booms swept through the Sierra Nevada region, bringing with it hordes of prospectors, prostitutes, and politicians whose minds were set on getting their share of the Gold Rush. In many instances the legacy of those years survived in the form of closed mine shafts and forlorn ghost towns. But in other places the Gold Rush's spectacular wealth left behind enduring communities whose civic parks, streetlights, and fire departments were the direct result of mining's rippling economic impacts. Nevada City, home to 3,000 or so full-time residents and widely considered to be the most complete and authentic surviving Gold Rush community, is one of those towns. In many ways it's a living history museum whose collection of brick commercial buildings, narrow sidewalks, and wrought iron balconies could serve as a Disney movie set, completed by the sounds of Deer Creek's rushing waters and the mountain winds whistling through nearby pine forests.

Though bearded prospectors attired in flannel shirts and riveted dungaree pants manufactured by a San Francisco tailor named Strauss are long gone from Nevada County, their legacy has never faded far from public view. It lives on in different ways, such as in the historic photographs and awesome locomotives exhibited at the Nevada County Historical Society's impressive Narrow Gauge Railroad Museum. Its exhibits include treasures such as the 1901 steam-powered automobile used by the owner of Gold Blossom mine on his daily rounds, and several mammoth, meticulously restored steam engines that from time to time chug down the museum's 300-feet of narrow gauge rail. Memories of a storied past also live on in the form of numerous cabins that once served as residences for the city's working

Reminders of the Gold Rush glory years are memorialized throughout the Sierra Nevada foothills.

class, now assets inside a National Historic District that includes 93 Nevada City structures listed on the National Register of Historic Places. The district's limits also preserve what once was known as the town's Chinese Quarter, which in the 1880s extended along Commercial Street and contained retail and service businesses serving the county's then thousands of Chinese residents. Their contributions to the region's prosperity extended across the mining, forestry, and agricultural sectors and included the building of the Transcontinental Railroad. Today the legacy of California's first influx of Chinese laborers is kept alive through the productions staged by Community Asian Theatre of the Sierra (CATS), a multicultural performance group whose reach extends beyond the walls of its Commercial Street quarters. Using the historic, 1863 Nevada Theatre for its main stage presentations, CATS produces and performs material dealing with the contemporary issues impacting both the Asian American demographic of California and the state's recently arrived Asian immigrant community.

For a community whose population exceeds the 3,000 mark Nevada City is overflowing with performing arts talent. In addition to the aforementioned CATS, there's the Off Broadstreet company's season of a half dozen comedies and musicals staged in its Commercial Street performance space. Year-round productions are the specialty of the Foothill Theatre Company, whose more than 30 years of performances on the Nevada Theatre's historic stage have evolved into its present format of seven annual productions, including an annual turn at a Shakespeare classic in nearby Grass Valley. The company also organizes an impressive community outreach and education program that includes Studio FTC's Summer Shakespeare Camp, an apprentice program for teens, and a series of subsidized matinee performances for students.

The area's leading presenter of classical music is Grass Valley–based Music in the Mountains, whose slate of more than 30 annual concerts is organized around seasonal festival formats. Paul Perry, the organization's artistic director/conductor, has in his 25 years at the helm developed an exemplary and dynamic range of community outreach and education programs that have broadened his audience's numbers, lowered its average age, and simultaneously expanded the region's cultural horizons. On the education front Music in the Mountains organizes a range of programs that even metropolitan orchestras are hard-pressed to match. These initiatives include the Young Composers Program, the Donner Mine Music Camp, a Young Musicians Competition, the annual KinderKonzert, and in-classroom programs throughout Nevada County schools. For older listeners there's another ambitious level of events such as the annual Northern Sierra Food, Wine & Music Celebration in March, the Swing Along Golf Tournament in September, an October Home Tour, and the July 4th Picnic & Pops concert.

The fun and farce never seem to let up at Music in the Mountains. As Artistic Director and Maestro Paul Perry prepared for his final curtain call after 25 years as the organization's guiding light, he tweaked his audiences by inserting his own "dancing maestro" logo into various spots of Music in the Mountains season program. Sharp-eyed music savants who caught on early to Perry's ploy won everything from dinner with the orchestra's pianist to a champagne-fueled limo ride to the festival's opening night bash.

Innovation in music presentation is also the calling card of Nevada City's Music City Music Events, which uses local venues such as the Odd Fellows Hall on Spring Street and the Miners Foundry Cultural Center to showcase everything from Led Zeppelin tribute bands to Afro-beat dance legends. The one-time blacksmith shop that today has grown into the Miners Foundry Cultural Center traces its Nevada City roots back to 1855, when the demand for precision-built mining equipment attracted machinists and ironworkers to the Sierra Nevada foothills. Fast-forward to modern times and the foundry's

Carefully maintained and meticulously restored, downtown Nevada City would still look like home to any prospector.

blacksmithing anvils have been replaced by two performing arts venues capable of seating 250 and 300 music lovers, along with all the add-ons required for a state-of-the-art conference center. Concert promoters bring a steady stream of established recording artists in a wide spectrum of music genres to the foundry's Great Hall stage, while community organizations such as gardening clubs use the foundry's Stone Hall for their botanicals shows.

During the summer months Nevada City turns into a hub for various festivals. Pioneer Park's expanses on Nimrod Street host everything from the Nevada County Concert Band's free Sunday performances to the muscle car mania of June's Pioneer Classic Car Show. Downtown's sloping jumble of streets attracts its share of visitors for events such as Friday's Downtown Nevada City Market on York Street; the three July weekend stagings of Summer Nights, which closes off the streets for a festival combining art, cars, and music; and the annual Nevada City Bicycle Classic. One of the top North American bicycle racing events, the Classic's June staging attracts top professional riders for its series of competitive races around downtown Nevada City's jigsaw of asphalt.

Thousands of spectators crowd onto the city's sidewalks during these races, causing consternation in the minds of some downtown business owners but bringing broad grins to the faces of barkeeps and baristas.

The commercial gallery scene in Nevada City is alive and well, bolstered by several venues pitching in as alternatives to the cluster of galleries along Broad Street. Taylor-Drake, an exhibition venue for handcrafted home furnishings from Ohio, is located in the historic confines of the National Hotel, a 42-room Victorian landmark radiating Gold Rush-era charm. Tanglewood Forest Gallery represents the work of Marci Wolfe, whose intricately crafted masks and dolls have a worldwide following. Nevada City Picture Framing showcases the work of local artists in its rotating shows. Mowen Solinsky Gallery exhibits the region's top talents in jewelry, fine crafts, and photography, in addition to paintings and sculpture. Photographer Steve Solinsky and sculptor John Mowen have included some of the state's leading contemporary artists in their gallery's roster, staging monthly exhibitions by the likes of painters Carol Aust and Susan Dorf, wood turner Jerry Kermode and photographer Phil Borges. Julie Baker Fine Art uses its Commercial Street location for a decidedly contemporary approach to the art business, representing artists such as painters Alexandra Eldridge, Eric Blum, and Willie Long. The gallery's focus indicates an evolving sense of artistic depth taking root in these Sierra foothills.

Venues

Julie Baker Fine Art
246 Commercial Street, Nevada City, CA 95959
530.265.9278 / www.juliebakerfineart.com
▲ Ambitious art space with a focus on the national contemporary art scene and beyond.

Mowen Solinsky Gallery
225 Broad Street, Nevada City, CA 95959
530.265.4682 / www.mowensolinskygallery.com
▲ Owned by two of the region's top creative talents, this gallery stays in front of the regional art scene.

Foothill Theatre Company
530.265.8587 / www.foothilltheatre.org
▲ Performing from the historic Nevada Theatre's stage this firmly established, professional theatre organization presents a year-round slate of productions and community outreach programs.

Miners Foundry Cultural Center
325 Spring Street, Nevada City, CA 95959
530.265.5040 / www.minersfoundry.org
▲ One of Northern California's top venues for live music from established and emerging recording artists.

Music in the Mountains
530.265.6173 / www.musicinthemountains.org
▲ At a point in history when many classical music organizations barely stay afloat, Maestro Paul Perry did the impossible by building what once had been a pip-squeak of an event into a classical music giant presenting more than 30 concerts in the new Amaral Family Festival Center.

Events

Nevada City Bicycle Classic
530.263.3388 / www.ncclassic.com
▲ For nearly 50 years the stars of professional bicycle racing have battled along Nevada City's downtown streets.

Nevada City Film Festival
916.548.7716 / www.nevadacityfilmfestival.com
▲ This four-day screening of features, shorts, and documentaries takes place at several local venues and includes the work of local and emerging filmmakers as well as established professionals.

Slumber

Red Castle Inn
109 Prospect Street, Nevada City, CA 95959
805.265.5135 / www.redcastleinn.com
▲ Live like you found the Treasure of Sierra Madre in this seven-room Gothic Revival mansion in the middle of town. Great views, spectacular gardens, afternoon tea, and restful quiet.

Outside Inn
575 E. Broad Street, Nevada City, CA 95959
530.265.2233 / www.outsideinn.com
▲ This renovated, 1930s-ear motor court features themed rooms and a subdued aura of hipness. From the Rock Climbing Suite to the Celestial Room, this affordable hideaway fits the traveler's needs.

The National Hotel
211 Broad Street, Nevada City, CA 95959
530.265.4551 / www.thenationalhotel.com
▲ This historic survivor of downtown Nevada City's Gold Rush days is a 42-room reminder that there's still gold in those steep Sierra hills.

Northern Queen Inn
400 Railroad Avenue, Nevada City, CA 95959
530.265.5824 / www.northernqueeninn.com
▲ This complex of motel rooms, cabins, and chalets even has its own on-site narrow gauge railroad (pulled by Engine #5), plus a pool and spa. You can't go wrong starting the day with a Popeye Omelette in the Trolley Junction restaurant.

Nevada City Inn
760 Zion Street, Nevada City, CA 95959
530.265.2253 / www.nevadacityinn.net
▲ This conveniently located motel offers 27 guest rooms and seven cottages, free wi-fi, and a pets-friendly policy.

Harmony Ridge Lodge
18883 E. Highway 20, Nevada City, CA 95959
530.478.0651 / www.harmonyridgelodge.com
▲ Nestled up against the towering pines of Tahoe National Forest, this 10-room inn is loaded with local art and high Sierra charm.

Sustenance

Citronee Bistro & Wine Bar
320 Broad Street, Nevada City, CA 95959
530.265.5697 / www.citroneebistro.com
▲ Downtown's most enjoyable setting for a selection of craftsman's cheeses and superb California wines.

Stonehouse Restaurant
107 Sacramento Street, Nevada City, CA 95959
530.265.5050 / www.stonehouse1857.com
▲ Romantic and rustic, this outstanding restaurant inside a historic structure features live music on weekends and Celtic Jams on the first and third Wednesdays of each month.

New Moon Cafe
203 York Street, Nevada City, CA 95959
530.265.6399 / www.thenewmooncafe.com

▲ Taking advantage of the region's bounty, New Moon Cafe changes its menus seasonally and offers wines to complement the moon's changing cycles.

PJ's of Nevada City
106 Argall Way, Nevada City, CA 95959
530.265.9091 / www.pjsnavadacity.com
▲ Great place to pick up a few sandwiches and a bottle of Arizona Ice Tea before heading to the bike races, car show, etc. Try the Gold Club on sourdough.

Cafe Mekka
237 Commercial Street, Nevada City, CA 95959
530.478.1517
▲ Local art, open mike readings on Wednesdays, and hyper-caffeinated coffee.

---

*A*s executive director of the Foothill Theatre Company, Karen Marinovich oversees the direction of a respected stage organization whose reputation for presenting new material as well as classics regularly fills its performing venues in both Nevada City and Grass Valley.

"Our home venue, the Nevada Theater, was built in 1863 and is a beautiful place to perform in, but a place that's not set up for modern theatre. There's no real backstage to speak of, no wings to the stage, and it's a venue that's also used for a weekend film series so all of our sets have to be dismantled on the evenings when the films are screened, then reassembled the next day. We have a very talented production staff that is ingenious in the ways they work around these limitations. Our maximum capacity is 242 great seats on the Nevada Theater's main floor. There is a balcony in the theatre but we don't use it because the sight lines are restricted.

"Our artistic director, Carolyn Howarth, is the person responsible for developing our season and while she knows what people say they want to see on our stage she also knows how to introduce material that may not be familiar to our audience members but will fall within the boundaries of the material they enjoy seeing. We're in the process of rethinking our New Works Series, which will be presented in a 99-seat black box facility in Grass Valley at the Center for the Arts. We're also bringing back in 2009 our summer Shakespeare series at the North Star Museum in Grass Valley."

As co-founder of the downtown Nevada City art space known as the Mowen Solinsky Gallery, sculptor John Mowen provides leading artists of the Sierra Nevada foothills with a sophisticated setting for display of paintings, sculpture, fine crafts, and jewelry. Now in its sixth year, this collaborative venture between Mowen and photographer Steve Solinsky has evolved into one of Central California's destination art galleries.

"Back in the 1980s when I moved here there were a number of very good artists in the area who were living out in the woods and doing their own thing. Today the artists in this part of the state have developed a strong sense of community through events like the annual studio tour, which is a huge event on the Nevada City arts calendar, and the dozens of restaurants and coffee bars that are showing local art on their walls and rotating it monthly. You now have artist studios the keep regular hours so visitors can drop by to spend time talking to the artist. There's been a widespread evolution of the way local artists interact with not only each other but with the people coming here to enjoy the art.

"We're also experiencing an influx of younger artists who are not only attracted to the area for its stunning natural beauty but who also are coming here to participate in the arts, either through the work they create in their own studios or by learning in the studios of the experienced artists working in the Sierra Nevada. I think we'll be able to sustain the creative vitality of Nevada City through the presence of this up and coming generation of artists. This isn't going to be the kind of place where artists need to fit into a 'starving artist' mold to survive. I think Nevada City's going to move beyond that and become something far more significant."

Ojai

Sestled into a narrow valley and less than 30 miles from the Pacific Coast, the community of Ojai exudes a timeless and historic beauty that's purely Californian. Its alluring combination of Spanish Mission Revival architecture and modern vernaculars are celebrated along the pedestrian friendly, tree-shaded streets of a downtown drawing visitors throughout the year.

While Ojai's historic roots can be traced to an 1837 Spanish land grant to Fernando Tico, the contemporary history of Ojai began taking shape in the years leading up to 1922. That's when Ojai was first visited by educator, philosopher, and spiritual visionary Jiddu Krishnamurti. His enduring legacy includes decades of serving as a spiritual guide for the likes of Greta Garbo, Charlie Chaplin, Jackson Pollock, Aldous Huxley, and Ann Morrow Lindbergh. Krishnamurti's influential presence among Hollywood's leading figures brought a steady trickle of Dusenbergs up the winding road from Ventura. As that road improved it started to also bring visitors who saw great potential in Ojai's attractive combination of seclusion and unspoiled natural beauty. Hollywood Director Frank Capra was among those who fell under Ojai's spell when he used the community as a stand-in for Shangri-La in his 1937 film "Lost Horizon."

Through its six decades of presentations the Ojai Music Festival has showcased the artistry of composers such as John Adams and Lukas Foss, the talents of conductors Kent Nagano, Michael Tilson-Thomas, and Esa-Pekka Salonen, and the leadership of music directors such as Pierre Boulez, Aaron Copland, Robert Spano, and Pierre-Laurent Almard.

Built in 1918, the elegant, Spanish Mission Revival structure that once was the Saint Thomas Aquinas Catholic Church has now become home to the Ojai Valley Museum.

Capra's reinvention of Ojai as a long-lost paradise tucked into a Nepalese mountain valley wasn't the first time local residents adjusted their cultural bearings. In the early 1900s the community went by the title of Nordhoff, an exceedingly unromantic moniker whose replacement name of Ojai (derived from the area's indigenous Chumash tribe's word for "nest") was championed by industrialist Edward D. Libbey. Sensing that a name change wasn't the only thing the town needed, Libbey also underwrote the redevelopment of downtown's business district, overlaying East Ojai Avenue with a series of design and architectural flourishes that included construction of a bell tower and an Arcade structure whose tall archways still provide shoppers and tourists with relief from Ojai's intense, midday sun.

Though today's Ojai has accommodated a certain amount of commercial development on lands where vaqueros once raised livestock, its overall sensibility is of a community that, if not bypassed by the march of time, at least has hung onto most of its traditional charm. Those qualities have proven extremely effective frameworks for promoting Ojai's accessibility from Los Angeles, just a two-hour drive south. One of Ojai's more popular visitor lures (especially for those on their second or third Ojai experience) revolve around the community's fascination with books. Two very engaging booksellers, Local Hero Books, which dabbles in regionally produced wines as well as a full

Home to philosophers, artists, gurus, and musicians, the Ojai Valley also was a central force in the life of ceramist Beatrice Wood, who passed away in 1998, just one week after celebrating her 105th birthday.

range of new titles, is located along the downtown Arcade. Ojai's other destination for literature lovers is Bart's Books of Ojai, whose selection of used and new titles exceeds 10,000 volumes stored both indoors and outdoors on bookshelves surrounding the shop. Readers who arrive after sunset (the end of Bart's regular business hours) pay for their selections from Bart's 24/7, outdoor bookshelves by sliding their bills through a slot on the shop's front door.

For visual artists this Art Town of 8,000 residents offers easy access to an enviable range of natural resources to refresh one's views on life and provide new subject matter for painting or sculpting. Ojai's cost of living somewhat shelters artists with relief from the worst of Southern California's high prices, with homes in Ojai Valley averaging just short of $500,000. With its healthy flow of year-round visitors Ojai has been able to sustain a cluster of commercial art galleries along its historic downtown's streets, most representing the work of local artists. Mid-October's Ojai Studio Artists Tour opens the doors of more than 50 valley-area studios for a self-guided exploration of some of Ojai's creative nooks and crannies. Since far more artists live and work in Ojai than there are local galleries with available wall space, studio tours are an effective, though once a year, way to discover the art community's depth. Outside of the studio tour weekend a good place to find local artists' work is the Ojai Cafe Emporium, a popular bakery and lunch spot featuring changing exhibitions. Artist Leslie Clark's space, Nomad Gallery, reflects the source of inspiration for her work in the tribal cultures of Saharan Africa, while the emphasis at Studio 84 West is on a national group of two dozen painters and sculptors. Primavera Gallery represents fine crafts artists, while Human Arts Gallery has both paintings and fine crafts in addition to jewelry. Janis' Art Workshop has a handle on the garden art scene, while Firehouse Pottery & Gallery, located in a former firehouse on South Montgomery Street, is home to Frank Massarella's elegantly crafted studio work as well as a Clay School for aspiring potters and a gallery representing a selection of clay artisans from across the West. Also located on South Montgomery Street is the Ojai Center for the Arts, a multidisciplinary education and presentation facility that includes an art gallery and theatre. The center's Art Branch offers year-round art classes in addition to its slate of one-artist, invitational, and survey exhibitions. One of the most respected figures in American contemporary ceramics, Beatrice Wood, made her home in Ojai's Happy Valley until her 1998 passing at the age of 105. Ms. Wood's home

An honor system, fresh air, strong espresso, and a breathtaking inventory are hallmarks of Bart's Books, Ojai's beloved literary outpost.

has become the Beatrice Wood Center for the Arts and is affiliated with the Besant Hill School. A series of changing exhibitions now fill the center's galleries and sculpture garden, located on a spectacular piece of property in the mountains overlooking Ojai's town center.

Theatre 150, which recently moved into an improved performance space on Matilija Street, operates as the community's professional stage company and presents a diverse slate of productions for adults and children. Established in the mid-1990s, the organization presents both theatre and music, relieving Ojai locals from the need to drive into Ventura or Santa Barbara to catch some live entertainment. Ojai Center for the Arts is home to the eight-production season series offered by its Art Center Theater, with material ranging from *Its a Wonderful Life* to a popular showcase series featuring works by local playwrights.

Ojai's Libbey Bowl, a 1500-seat amphitheatre in Libbey Park, is the preferred venue for a diverse range of musical and theatrical presentations by local and outside promoters. The most prominent of these, Ojai Music Festival, is a multiday event in early June and featuring a wealth of top international talents in classical music, chamber music, and orchestra. Over the 60-plus years of its success the festival has added on a full schedule of workshop, social, educational, and culinary programs, setting the tone for what is widely considered the high point of Ojai's summer arts season.

Venues

Ojai Center for the Arts
113 S. Montgomery Street, Ojai, CA 93023
805.646.0117 / www.ojaiartcenter.org
▲ Multidisciplinary facility with gallery, theatre, dance, and music.

Bart's Books of Ojai
302 W. Matilija Street, Ojai, CA 93023
805.646.3755 / www.bartsbooksojai.com
Open daily 9:30 to Sunset
▲ Eclectic and famous bookstore with picnic tables and sunshine.

Beatrice Wood Center for the Arts
8560 Ojai-Santa Paula Road, Ojai, CA 93024
805.646.3381 / www.beatricewood.com
▲ Gorgeous home in Happy Valley exhibiting changing shows of contemporary art, with an emphasis on ceramics.

Firehouse Pottery & Gallery
109 S. Montgomery Street, Ojai, CA 93023
805.646.9453 / www.firehouse-pottery.com
▲ Gallery of contemporary ceramics with a clay art school.

Nomad Gallery
307 E. Ojai Avenue, Ojai, CA 93023
805.646.1706 / www.nomadgal.com
▲ Artist Leslie Clark is inspired by the tribal peoples of Saharan Africa.

Primavera Gallery
214 E. Ojai Avenue, Ojai, CA 93023
805.646.7133 / www.primaveraart.com
▲ Fine crafts gallery with national and regional talent.

Studio 84 West
602 E. Ojai Avenue, Ojai, CA 93023
805.646.3812 / www.studio84west.com
▲ Represents national and local painters and sculptors.

Theater 150
316 E. Matilija Street, Ojai, CA 93023
805.46.4300 / www.theater150.org
▲ Innovative stage crafts and music performances.

Events

Ojai Music Festival
2101 S. Signal Street, Ojai, CA 93023
805.646.2094 / www.ojaifestival.org
▲ Prestigious and vibrant celebration of international music excellence, with extensive community outreach programs throughout the year.

Ojai Studio Artists Annual Studio Tour
www.ojaistudioartists.com
▲ More than 50 local talents participate in this October weekend event.

Village of Tales—Ojai Storytelling Festival
201 Park Road, Ojai, CA 93023
805.646.8907 / www.villageoftales.org
▲ Annual celebration of a traditional art form in Libbey Bowl on a May weekend.

Slumber

Su Nido Inn
301 N. Montgomery Street, Ojai, CA 93023
805.646.7080 / www.sunidoinn.com
▲ This luxurious, fully equipped boutique hotel in a Spanish Mission Revival home on a secluded side street is within easy strolling distance of downtown's art scene. Its nine guest rooms and suites are arranged around a cobblestone courtyard whose fountain and picnic tables make Su Nido a perfect setting for enjoying a bottle of local wine.

The Lavender Inn
210 E. Matilija Street, Ojai, CA 93023
805.646.6635 / www.lavenderinn.com
▲ This fully renovated 1874 schoolhouse offers an immersion into Ojai's lifestyle. Located within view of the heart of Ojai, this boutique hotel with eight guest rooms is surrounded by lush gardens and is also the home of the Ojai Culinary School. Offering demonstrations as well as classes led by visiting chefs and Ojai culinary authorities, the school's course offerings range from pastries to healthful living to ethnic cuisine.

Ojai Valley Inn & Spa
905 Country Club Road, Ojai, CA 93023
805.646.5511 / www.ojairesort.com
▲ One of the world's top-rated resorts on 220 acres with 308 rooms, 18 holes of championship golf, 31,000 square feet of spa, several restaurants, and historic works of art.

The Ojai Retreat–A Hilltop Inn
160 Besant Road, Ojai, CA 93023
805.646.2536 / www.ojairetreat.org
▲ Located several miles from the center of town, this inn's lush, landscaped grounds provide an ideal setting for meditative getaways in its dozen, beautifully appointed rooms. Five secluded acres, spectacular views, and an art-filled environment.

Ojai Cottage
1484 East Ojai Avenue, Ojai, CA 93023
805.646.9779 / www.ojaicottage.com
▲ A private, 800-square-foot, two-level house with stone walls, fireplace, and quiet gardens. Up to five guests can be accommodated in this centrally located getaway.

The Capri

1180 East Ojai Avenue, Ojai, CA 93023

805.646.4305 / www.hotelojai.com

▲ This stylish, retro modern motel at the edge of downtown Ojai is close enough to be within walking distance of galleries and restaurants, but safely removed from the crowds. Spectacular pool and gardens, smartly appointed rooms, wireless Internet, bicycles, patios, and 42-inch plasma sets in each of its guest rooms.

Ojai Rancho Inn

615 West Ojai Avenue, Ojai, CA 93023

805.646.1434 / www.ojairanchoinn.com

▲ This 118-room inn, located next to the Ojai Valley Inn & Spa, is convenient to Ojai's galleries and restaurants. Affordable rates, an expansive swimming pool, gardens, and an on-site sauna.

Inn Harmony

308 North Signal Street, Ojai, CA 93023

805.640.6524 / www.innharmonyojai.com

▲ This lovely house in downtown Ojai is convenient to restaurants and galleries, with five guest rooms, free wi-fi, and a harmonious environment.

Sustenance

Ojai Cafe Emporium

108 S. Montgomery Street, Ojai, CA 93023

805.646.2723 / www.ojaicafe.com

▲ Downtown Ojai's breakfast favorite sidelines as a gallery for local artists.

Azu

457 E. Ojai Avenue, Ojai, CA 93023

805.640.7987 / www.azuojai.com

▲ Chef/owner Laurel Moore's Spanish tapas restaurant has earned a reputation for innovation.

Ojai Coffee Roasting Company

337 E. Ojai Avenue, Ojai, CA 93023

805.646.4478 /

▲ Downtown's jumpin' java jitter joint.

As executive director of Ojai Music Festival, Jeffrey P. Haydon oversees the affairs of one of the nation's most individualistic and treasured celebrations of classical and contemporary musical genius.

"Ojai's historically welcomed artists and in turn artists have welcomed Ojai's suspension of reality from the rest of the world. The mountains surrounding Ojai lend this beautiful valley a feeling of isolation and many artists need that type of setting to explore their creativity. From the music festival's standpoint that sense of freedom to explore was witnessed when composer Aaron Copeland selected the festival as the place where he tried his hand at conducting, and when composer Stravinsky elected to stage the premier of one of his works here at the festival. So Ojai has a way of convincing talented people to come here and try doing something that's untested, that's experimental, that's new.

"We're one of the more improbable music festivals you find anywhere. Our performing facility, Libbey Bowl, is just a bandshell with benches in the middle of a city park. But what we do have is a history of receptivity to the risks some artists need to take to figure out the next stages of their careers, and in Ojai they get to do that inside of a space of four days. We're truly an adventure on the leading edge of classical music."

———————

From his Ojai studio and gallery, located in a historic structure that once served as the community's firehouse, artist Frank Massarella carries on in the outstanding tradition of Ojai's master potters. His gallery represents the work of more than a dozen artists working in clay as well as fine art glass.

"I had been living in the San Fernando Valley, just scratching out a living as a full-time artist whose best sales came at weekend art festivals. Then, in 1982, I stopped by Ojai and found an affordable studio space in an alley, and that's where I finally started selling more of my work . . . to people from LA. Then, in 1999, the city's old fire station came on the market and I bought the building.

"Artists step into this space and their jaws drop when they see the concrete floors, tall ceilings, and the sunlight coming in through those old firehouse doors. And everyone appreciates the irony of locating an art studio that uses kilns in its process being located in an old brick building once dedicated to fighting fire.

"*Whenever I teach a workshop the list fills up with people from all corners of the state as well as Colorado, Arizona and Oregon. Artists love coming to a place like Ojai for a week or two to improve their skills and create art.*

"*One of the interesting things about living in Ojai is that you get decisions being made locally that impact the entire arts community, and I'm referring to the ways Ojai as a community is promoted as an Art Town. From what I've seen, there are a number of places that know how to do that the right way, and I wish Ojai would meet that higher level in promoting the arts already here.*"

Palm Desert

The Mojave Desert's forbidding climate places limits on those forms of life sustained under its glare. In parts of its vast emptiness an irrigated and air-conditioned form of civilization has defied nature's odds. One of those places is Coachella Valley, whose expanses of farms and clusters of master-planned communities follow the contours of the San Jacinto Mountains along the Mojave's westernmost fringe.

Drive into Coachella Valley from either direction on its main transportation artery of Interstate 10, and the concept of desert oasis springs to mind. Located less than a three hour drive from Santa Monica Pier, the valley's landscape could easily serve as a setting for anything from a Lawrence of Arabia fantasy to a Rat Pack romp, though one with Native American–owned casinos subbing for their counterparts in Sin City.

Along its irrigated sections the valley looks more like a suburban promised land than a sun-scorched wasteland. Ancestors of today's Agua Caliente Band of Cahuilla Indians chose the canyons and foothills below 10,800-foot San Jacinto Peak as their homeland. In contemporary times the Coachella Valley's largest communities have developed their own attributes and personalities. Considering them in a regional context it's easy to understand how this once forbidding landscape, with its present-day collection of assets such as Palm Springs' mid-century modernist architecture, La Quinta's gated compounds and Palm Desert's bustling art galleries and entertainment district, as well as a profusion of clothing-optional resorts geared toward sun worshipers of all persuasions, has experienced steady growth of both its tourism and residential population.

Generating the power to cool Coachella Valley's brutally hot summers is a full-time job for these wind turbines.

To live here is to accept the inevitability of six months of broiling sidewalks. Adapting to life here means resetting one's internal thermostat to the point where poolside brunching on a 106 degree morning feels comfortable. Kvetching about the heat is acceptable only on days when temperatures soar into the hundred-teens (meaning they've surged past 112 degrees). From mid-April through mid-October the relief offered by palms, shade structures, patio water misting systems, fountains, and powerful climate control systems take the edge off the valleys hottest months. As for the calendar's six other months, the climate offers reliably sunny and dry stretches whose temperatures fluctuate from the mid-60s to the upper 80s.

While some of California early 20th century painters considered the Mojave Desert's landscape to be an inspirational subject, it was creative minds from other art disciplines who jump-started the valleys creative climate. For entertainment industry professionals in need of a relaxing break from the hectic Hollywood scene, the region's tranquil emptiness had an immediate effect. As soon as the postwar economy brought improved highway connections from regional population centers, Palm Springs and its neighboring communities began turning into weekend havens for stage and screen personalities. And since it didn't escape anyone's attention that an absence of gossip columnists set the right tone

Changing exhibitions of public art have become a hallmark of El Paseo's vibrant art scene.

for some pre-papparazzi era debauchery, it's little wonder why the likes of early arrivals such as Bob Hope, Edgar Bergen, and Frank Sinatra were soon joined by Jackie Gleason, Kirk Douglas, and Dean Martin in claiming their shares of this desert paradise

In recent years the valley's growth trends have shifted towards Palm Desert resulting in an explosion of visual and performing arts events as well as amenities. Though Palm Springs remains the Coachella Valley's largest community and home to both an influential fine art museum and a popular community theatre, the focal point of the region's art scene has sunk its roots into Palm Desert's sands. The community's success as a destination for art lovers has been a driving force behind expansion of both its visual arts sector and its performing arts counterpart. Palm Desert's growing reputation as an Art Town has proven highly successful in developing the community's cultural tourism economy, attracting dedicated art collectors as well as socializing art afficcionados who consider gallery hopping in terms of a networking opportunity.

The concentration of dozens of art galleries along Palm Desert's famed El Paseo and its adjoining streets provides an ideal pedestrian-friendly context for visiting a multitude of exhibitions in just a few hours. Palm Desert's galleries exhibit a wide range of media and styles, ranging from Western art's historic scenes of cowboys, cattle, and endless skies, to the abstract expressions and every other iteration found in contemporary art. While most communities would hesitate to act on any urge to tweak what's proven in Palm Desert's case to be a formula for success (as the saying goes, if it's not broken then don't fix it), an act of civic daring has gilded this art town's lily, so to speak. An annual installation of public sculpture along the broad, landscaped median separating one side of El Paseo from the other has turned Palm Desert's showcase thoroughfare into one of the nation's best examples

He may indeed have been born to Italian immigrant parents in Louisiana, but Iron Eyes Cody milked his fictitious Native American ties for all they were worth, including this sidewalk star on Palm Canyon Drive.

of art's positive impact on the public commons. These extraordinarily visible works of three-dimensional art from prominent sculptors across the world have served as an enhancement to the art district's stature as a must-see arts destination.

El Paso's changing exhibitions, which typically favor contemporary expressions but also accommodate traditional sculpture forms, are sourced from both the permanent art collection administered through the city's Art in Public Places program, and from works loaned through what's officially known as the annual El Paseo Invitational Exhibition. From one year to the next as many as 20 works of art are installed along El Paseo's median. Palm

Palm Desert's ideal climate for outdoors activity is celebrated every weekend from October through May when more than 300 vendors of arts, crafts, and locally grown foods gather on the grounds of the College of the Desert for its Street Fair. Early April's annual Indian Wells Arts Festival on the grounds of the Indian Wells Tennis Garden is the Coachella Valley's top event for up-and-coming local art talent.

Desert's other thoroughfares, municipal parks, and civic buildings provide even more visibility for the community's Art in Public Places program by serving as temporary and permanent venues for art installations drawn from the city's 130-piece collection. Through its Art in Public Places initiative, which sets aside a percentage of city capital

Highly regarded for its collection of Native American artifacts, the Palm Springs Art Museum also presents beautifully designed exhibitions of contemporary art and Western realism.

improvement expenditures to fund art purchases, Palm Desert has enhanced the public environment by exhibiting art in accessible locations.

Several of Palm Desert's art venues boast dimensions rivaling those of medium-size art museums, especially Imago Galleries, Denise Robergé Art Gallery, Buschlen Mowatt Galleries, and CODA Gallery. Art afficinados in need of even broader visual stimulation need look no further than the Palm Springs Art Museum, located less than a two minute stroll from the busy sidewalks of North Palm Canyon Drive. Considered one of the most comprehensive contemporary art institutions in the region, this 125,000 square foot gem is home to a permanent collection covering everything from Agua Caliente basketry to the contemporary art's cutting edge. And while there's some emphasis placed on top-shelf names in the contemporary art world, the Palm Springs Art Museum also serves regional artists through its innovative, year-round slate of invitational and virtuoso exhibitions featuring talents drawn from established art careers as well as those just emerging into view in the fast-moving Southern California creative millieu.

The region's top venue for year-round performing arts is the McCallum Theatre, a 1127-seat showcase in Palm Desert featuring a range of professional presentations ranging from the Desert Symphony's concerts to touring Broadway plays, jazz masters concerts,

The presence of numerous galleries representing leading talents in contemporary art circles underscores Palm Desert's stature as an important meeting ground for artists, gallery owners, and collectors.

and locally-focused favorites such as the McCallum Theatre Institute's annual Choreography Festival and its Aesthetic Education Program. The valley's most prominent venue for community stage productions is the 230-seat Palm Canyon Theatre, located on a corner of Frances Stevens Park in a historic structure shared with the always entertaining gallery operated by the Desert Art Center. Housed in what once had been a school gymnasium, this Actors Equity theatre is known far and wide for its skillful collaborations with the Hollywood-tested expertise living throughout the Coachella Valley. If you love musicals, and one's onstage at the Palm Canyon Theatre, this stop on a local arts itinerary you won't want to miss. The venue also serves the community through a variety of ways such as its independent productions, Summer Theatre Camp, dance classes, and Third Sunday Improv comedy shows.

The Palm Springs International Film Festival, staged across two January weeks, is another of the area's most attention-grabbing annual arts events, and has become known for being first-out-of-the-gate among its many peer film festivals. Its screenings and forums take place in venues such as the Palm Canyon Theatre, the Annenberg Auditorium of the Palm Springs Art Museum, and local movie houses. The Palm Springs International Film Society also presents Palm Springs ShortFest, a weeklong program dedicated to the art of making short films, during the last half of August.

Venues

A Gallery Fine Art
73-956 El Paseo, Palm Desert, CA 92260
760.346.8885 / www.agalleryfineart.com
▲ Contemporary art space exhibiting painting, sculpture, art glass, fine crafts, and jewelry. Represents a national group of artists including Karen Naylor, Jeff Goodman, Joan Carson, Edith Bergstrom, and Patricia Qualls.

Palm Springs Art Museum
101 N. Museum Drive, Palm Springs, CA 92262
760.325.7186 / www.psmuseum.org
$12.50 admission / Closed Monday
▲ Downtown Palm Springs exhibition facility with a diverse range of special and permanent shows, as well as a must-see museum store filled with local creations.

McCallum Theatre
73000 Fred Waring Drive, Palm Desert, CA 92260
760.346.6505 / www.mccallumtheatre.com
Ticket prices vary / Open year-round
▲ Coachella Valley's best venue for national and international performing arts talent is just a short stroll from the visual arts action along El Paseo.

Palm Canyon Theatre
538 North Palm Canyon Drive, Palm Springs, CA 92262
760.323.5123 / www.palmcanyontheatre.org
Ticket prices vary / Open year-round
▲ Intimate and comfortable with great sight lines and a convenient location, Palm Canyon Theatre is the Valley's live stage favorite.

Imago Galleries
45-450 Highway 74, Palm Desert, CA 92260
760.776.9890 / www.imagogalleries.com
Closed Monday
▲ From Dale Chihuly to Jennifer Bartlett, William Wegman, Jun Kaneko, and Thurman Statom, Imago represents a wealth of blue-chip talents.

Denise Robergé Art Gallery
73-995 El Paseo, Palm Desert, CA 92260
760.340.5045 / www.plazaroberge.com

▲ Represents a strong roster of talents including Gloria Gaddis, Ron Pokrasso, Kirk Tatom, and Michael Kessler.

Adagio Galleries
193 South Palm Canyon Drive, Palm Springs, CA 92262
760.320.2230 / www.adagiogalleries.com
Closed Tuesday
▲ Palm Springs's most prominent visual arts venue celebrates art from the Southwest and Latin America.

Buschlen Mowatt Galleries
45-188 Portola Avenue, Palm Desert, CA 92260
760.837.9668 / www.buschlenmowatt.com
▲ Dramatic architecture is the ideal setting for the likes of Louise Nevelson, Robert Indiana, Bernar Venet, and Dirk DeBruycker.

CODA Gallery
73-151 El Paseo, Palm Desert, CA 92260
760.346.4661 / www.codagallery.com
▲ One of three CODA Gallery locations, this one defines the heart of El Paseo's art experience with talents such as Brad Aldridge, William DeBilzan, Carol Gold, and Chelsea James.

Events

Palm Springs International Film Festival
www.psfilmfest.org
▲ This early January presentation of feature films and forums is complemented by an August festival of short films.

El Paseo Art Walk
877.735.7273 / www.palm-desert.org
▲ Staged from October through May from 5 to 8 PM on the first Thursday of each month.

Indian Wells Arts Festival
760.346.0042 / www.indianwellsartsfestival.com
▲ Held in early April and featuring more than 200 artists and craftspeople.

Slumber

Quality Inn Palm Springs
1269 E. Palm Canyon Drive, Palm Springs, CA 92262
760.323.2775 / www.choicehotels.com

▲ Affordable and conveniently located midway between Palm Springs and Palm Desert.

Hilton Palm Springs
400 E. Tahquitz Canyon Way, Palm Springs, CA 92262
760.320.6868 / www.hilton.com
▲ Centrally located and elegantly designed, with a lively pool scene.

Villa Royale Inn
1620 Indian Trail, Palm Springs, CA 92262
800.245.2314 / www.villaroyale.com
▲ Historic and secluded, offering peace and quiet with mountain views and a lovely pool, in a garden setting.

Sustenance

Koffi
555 North Palm Canyon Drive, Palm Springs, CA 92262
760.416.2244 / www.kofficoffee.com
▲ Favorite of the creative class, this local landmark shares an enormous backyard with several antiques and home furnishings stores.

Sherman's Deli & Bakery
401 E. Tahquitz Canyon Way, Palm Springs, CA 92262
73-161 Country Club Drive, Palm Desert, CA 92260
760.325.1199 & 760.568.1350 / www.shermansdeli.com
▲ Postmodern in decor, this oasis of deli style serves the Coachella Valley's best pastrami on rye.

The Steakhouse
401 E. Amado Road, Palm Springs, CA 92262
888.999.1995 / www.sparesortcasino.com
▲ Located inside downtown Palm Springs's sophisticated casino setting, the Steakhouse is a chop lover's paradise.

***

Located in the heart of Palm Desert's bustling El Paseo arts district, A Gallery Fine Art represents an accomplished group of artists including sculptors Barrett DeBusk and Shirley Ruuska-Brown, painters Judith Marshall and Holly Cratty, and glass artists Kenny Pieper and Elizabeth Ryland Mears. Lisa Dempton is its gallery director.

"I think the desert itself lends the Palm Desert art scene a contemporary sensibility that's reflected in not only the kinds of painting and sculpture that gets sold in our galleries but also in the architecture prevalent in both residential ad commercial settings. That doesn't rule out the appeal that both Native American arts and the traditional Western art have for some buyers. If anything, having all kinds of art displayed in this modern environment lends the work a powerful sense of presence.

"The type of art market we have in Palm Desert is much more sophisticated than you'd normally expect for a community of this size. Collectors, whether they own a home in the area or are just in town for a few days, tend to be well traveled, well-informed, and aware of their preferences in art. There's a number of collectors in Palm Desert who play active roles in the leadership of art museums back in their home communities.

"Our growth curve for new galleries has leveled off a bit, but on the other hand those of us who have established our presences on El Paseo are seeing more people coming in during months that once were very quiet, as the community is attracting more year-round residents."

———

As public arts manager for the City of Palm Desert, Richard Twedt oversees not only the community's extensive permanent collection of paintings, sculpture, and pottery but also directs the highly successful El Paseo Invitational Exhibition of three-dimensional sculpture in the heart of Palm Desert's art district.

"Though ours was the first public art program in the area, there have been outdoor exhibitions of sculpture along El Paseo at least since the mid-90s. For example when I first got here there was an outdoors exhibition of twelve sculptures by Peter Voulkos (1924–2002), from his stacked series of bronzes. So one of my first efforts was developing a national advertising campaign for the El Paseo exhibition to allow us to maintain a high level of artistic achievement in terms of what got installed in each year's invitational show.

"The show has reached the point where we receive more than 200 entries from galleries and artists from across the country who want to be part of the El Paseo art scene. Our promotional efforts both online and in traditional arts newsletters and magazines has given Palm Desert the opportunity to extend its reach throughout the country, and

the artists are taking notice. They realize that a yearlong opportunity to exhibit their work in front of the types of individuals who have second or third homes in this area is well worth their effort.

"More than 30 art galleries are doing business in Palm Desert, and they do a good job of serving the art collectors who fly into town during the season. There are public works of art throughout the city, but it's the sculpture along El Paseo that visitors usually see first."

Redding

L ocated within easy reach of some of California's most spectacular natural assets, Redding sits far enough south to take advantage of long summer growing seasons yet is sufficiently north to be less than an hour's drive from the downhill runs at Mt. Shasta Ski Park. By most measures Redding is a hardworking town whose tourism economy has traditionally been centered around providing services for summer visitors to Lassen Volcano National Park (50 miles east) and to Shasta Lake, whose craggy shoreline encroaches on north Redding's urban boundary. In recent years local and state governments have made a concrete effort to give tourists and local residents a compelling reason or two to explore what's inside the city limits, and the results have included the development of Turtle Bay Exploration Park, an expansion of the Sacramento River Trail to nearly 10 miles of wide pathway paralleling the banks of one of the region's top fly fishing magnets, and a continuing effort to correct downtown Redding's urban planning miscues and regrettable development initiatives.

Before it grew to its present configuration as a city with 60 square miles and nearly 100,000 residents, Redding was a stop along the Siskiyou Trail connecting Portland and San Francisco. After the Shasta Dam was completed in 1945, the community's population swelled with an influx of retirees as well as young families, both groups having been motivated by Redding's affordable housing market. The nearly 8,000 full- and part-time students attending Shasta College occupy an attractive campus several miles removed from downtown's urban grid. In many art towns a leading educational institution will leverage its beneficial presence in fostering a downtown turnaround by infusing the

Restored to its original grandeur, downtown Redding's Cascade Theatre serves as the region's modern and busy performing arts center.

creativity and spending power of thousands of footloose college-age students into the economy. For now, downtown Redding has had its hands full in establishing its economic footing following the regions big box retail shopping mall development patterns of the past two decades.

As in many communities whose downtown streetscape is checkerboarded with vacancies, the ready availability of affordable downtown rentals has in Redding's case generated a level of interest from various components of its fine arts community. One of downtown's most visible success stories is the quite visible presence of the Cascade Theatre, a meticulously restored, 1935 movie palace whose 2004 renovation retained the Cascade's classic design and decor while outfitting the structure with the state-of-the-art technical features demanded by contemporary performing artists and presenters. This major venue's opening has not only resulted in the revitalization of Market Street buildings bordering Cascade Theatre, it's also turned around some perceptions about downtown's long-range prospects. On performance evenings when the facility's nearly 1,000 seats are filled for productions of the JPR/Cascade Theatre Performance series, or shows brought into Redding by outside promoters, downtown's potentials become more tangible. The Cascade Theatre serves as the Redding home of North State Symphony, an innovative classical music organization presenting itself as the community orchestra for three of the region's larger communities: Redding, Red Bluff, and Chico. Music Director Kyle Wiley Pickett's orchestra presents a season of five main stage concerts from September through April and supplements these efforts with an extensive slate of community outreach programs and youth education offerings. Redding City Musical

Theatre Company is another of the area art organizations using the Cascade Theatre for its productions of Broadway classics. Riverfront Playhouse, Redding's longest-standing community theatre organization, uses its own facility in downtown Redding for a slate of six productions presented year-round.

Redding's visual arts community makes its presence known through exhibitions organized in several noncommercial venues. One of these is the Sculpture Park at City Hall, a 2.5-acre space serving as an installation site for permanent works owned by the city and temporary installations selected through Redding's annual juried selection process. Redding City Hall and Redding Civic Center are also used as exhibition venues for changing shows organized by the city's Art in Public Places Committee. On the campus of Shasta College, the Shasta College Art Gallery presents a year-round exhibition program whose interests extend far beyond the talents of the institution's art students and teaching faculty, backing up its exhibitions with a series of artist lectures and art workshops led by the artists featured in its exhibitions.

Downtown Redding's 1907 City Hall is the home of Shasta County Arts Council, which uses the building's two levels for changing visual art exhibitions, education programs, video production studios, and a 150-seat performance venue. Through its exhibitions the gallery covers a range of constituencies and interests, providing a forum for youth groups, minority groups, artists from outside the community, disabled artists, and local artists' showcase exhibitions. From late September through October the gallery is home base for the annual Shasta County Open Studios Tour. On its performance side the art council's stage is used by a variety of local dance, stage, and music organizations including the Dance Project, Redding Children's Chorus, Northstar Opera Repertory, the North State Songwriters' Group, Redding Improv Players, the Traveling Bohemians, and the Oaksong Society for Preservation of Way Cool Music. Oaksong's annual Grey Pine Farm Summer Concert Series presents top names in music in a rural setting east of Redding, while its primary schedule of concerts and workshops takes place from September through April at Shasta Art Council's performance space and

While he's been widely praised for most of his efforts, including Redding's Sundial Bridge, Spanish architect Santiago Calatrava has also been subjected to criticism for some of his more controversial designs, such as an on-again, off-again project spanning the Grand Canal in Venice, Italy. Located underneath the Rialto Bridge, this fourth bridge over the Grand Canal has the sleek, gravity-defying appearance emblematic of Calatrava's work.

In a dramatic act of far-reaching brilliance, the combined vision and resources of an innovative public-private partnership resulted in the Sundial Bridge, one of the nation's architectural treasures, being built over the Sacramento River.

on the stage at Bernie's Guitars. The North Valley Art League, which organizes an annual Juried National Show combining local talents with artists from across the nation, operates the Carter House Gallery, which is primarily used for exhibiting work by the art league's more than 200 members. The Carter House also serves as the site for childrens' art classes, members' workshops, and the art league's Celebration Garden project.

Redding's Turtle Bay Exploration Park, which is located along the Sacramento River opposite the McConnell Arboretum & Gardens, is just a few city blocks removed from downtown's street life, but you would never know it from the nonstop activity taking place throughout its eye-popping range of science, history, and art events. Turtle Bay Museum uses its Koenig Art Gallery for exhibitions that change throughout the year. From late April through September the on-site Cafe at Turtle Bay hosts Twilight on the Terrace, a Friday and Saturday evening jazz music performance showcasing the region's leading music talents.

For contemporary art audiences, and especially for those who are interested in the exciting vernaculars being explored by the world's leading architectural geniuses, there's one darn good reason to pencil a Redding visit into one's itinerary. The Sacramento River behind Turtle Bay Exploration Park is the site of one of the most significant North American expressions of international architecture, the Sundial Bridge. This 700-foot-long masterpiece was designed by Santiago Calatrava, the Valencia, Spain designer of jaw-dropping structures such as Puente de Alamillo in Seville, Spain; the Milwaukee Art Museum; the Atlanta Symphony Center; and the Bilbao Airport Terminal in Spain. Now used by pedestrians traveling between the McConnell Arboretum and the Turtle Bay complex, Calatrava's 2004 bridge is a glass, steel, and cable reminder that Redding has the resources and vision to achieve artistic and cultural greatness.

One of the area's cluster of art galleries has taken root in Weaverville, located 30 miles west of Redding in a Trinity County logging community. Several art exhibiting venues concentrating on the creations of regional contemporary artists have turned Weaverville's Main Street into a counterpart to the San Jacinto Mountains creative community of Idyllwild. Several alternative art venues exhibit art in Weaverville, including the Meredith Vineyards Tasting Room, Garden Cafe, Christopher Robbins Pizzeria, and Mamma Lama Coffee House. Highland Art Center is Weaverville's largest exhibiting facility, as well as the location of a complex of six working artist studios. The first Saturday of each month features the Weaverville Art Cruise & Walk, a 5 PM to 9 PM gathering of local artists as well as artists from outside the area whose work is featured in one of the nearly two dozen Weaverville venues that celebrate this community's passion for creativity.

Venues

Sundial Bridge

Turtle Bay Exploration Park, Redding, CA 96003
530.243.8850 / www.turtlebay.org
▲ The majority of this architectural wonder's $23 million tab was covered by Redding's McConnell Foundation, which put Santiago Calatrava's 700-foot bridge to use as a pedestrian walkway across the Sacramento River connecting the Turtle Bay complex to the 20-acre McConnell Arboretum & Gardens.

Shasta County Arts Council

1313 Market Street, Redding, CA 96001
530.241.7320 / www.shastaartscouncil.com
▲ From its historic quarters in Redding's Old City Hall, this multi-faceted organization pounds a creative pulse into all corners of Redding community life.

Carter House Gallery

North Valley Art League, Redding, CA 96001
530.243.1023 / www.nval.org
▲ The art league's gallery, education, and presentation center is located in this historic home in a quiet neighborhood.

Highland Art Center

691 Main Street, Weaverville, CA 96093
530.623.5111

▲ This historic home in the center of Weaverville offers changing exhibitions of local and regional artists' work.

Events

ARTsMART Downtown
Downtown Redding Mall, Redding, CA 96001
530.241.7320 / www.shastaartscouncil.com
▲ This monthly event in downtown Redding showcases visual artists and local musicians on the first Saturday of each month.

Weaverville Art Walk
Downtown Weaverville
530.623.2760 / www.mainstreetgallery.org
▲ The first Saturday of each month coordinates visual art exhibitions in nearly two dozen Weaverville venues.

Slumber

Bridgehouse Bed & Breakfast
1455 Riverside Drive, Redding, CA 96001
530.247.7177 / www.reddingbridgehouse.com
▲ This quaint guesthouse in a quiet neighborhood is convenient to downtown as well as the Sundial Bridge in Turtle Bay. Four comfy rooms, each themed on a Sacramento River bridge.

Red Lion Hotel
1830 Hilltop Drive, Redding, CA 96001
530.221.8700 / www.redlion.com
▲ This 192-room, full service hotel has free wi-fi and a pool.

Hilton Garden Inn
5050 Bechelli Lane, Redding, CA 96001
530.226.5111 / www.hiltongardeninn.com
▲ Located in South Redding, with a pool, fitness room, and free wi-fi.

River Inn
1835 Park Marina Drive, Redding, CA 96001
530.241.9500 /
▲ Located in a quiet neighborhood in downtown Redding with Sacramento River views, and affordable rates.

Holiday Inn Convention Center
1900 Hilltop Drive, Redding, CA 96001

530.221.7500 / www.holidayinn.com
▲ Lots of rooms, an outdoor pool, on-site dining, and a 24-hour fitness center.

Sustenance

Tokyo Garden
1675 Hilltop Drive, Redding, CA 96001
530.221.6888
▲ Serving some of the best spicy tuna rolls in Northern California.

Jack's Grill
1743 California Street, Redding, CA 96001
530.241.9705 / www.jacksgrillredding.com
▲ Serving Redding's best filet mignon since 1940, this classic eatery has 17 bar stools and seats 46 in its booths. Don't even think of passing on the blue cheese salad dressing.

Nello's Place
3055 Bechelli Lane, Redding, CA 96001
530.223.1636 / www.nellosrestaurant.net
▲ Redding's classic Italian eatery has it all, from antipasto right down to the zabaglione.

A tireless advocate for Redding's artists and art community, Troy Hawkins tracks the comings and goings as well as the major and minor arts events taking place around Redding through his www.hawkmanstudios.com Web site.

"I was born and raised here and recently returned to Redding for its lower cost of living, relaxed lifestyle, and small town feeling. Growing up here as a young artist I felt there was little to do, but that's changed completely. Redding's now got several live music venues, a second Saturday Art Hop that uses different venues around town to exhibit art, summer music festivals, and a growing community of younger artists who moved here for the same reasons I did.

"We've also got these two organizations, the North Valley Art League and the Shasta County Arts Council, who are offering the community a diverse range of year-round art classes, exhibitions of paintings and sculpture from across the state, and expertise on things like grant writing for smaller organizations. When you consider it as a

whole you can easily see that things have really moved forward in the last few years.

"Most of the people around here are into outdoor recreation. We have easy access to water sports in the summer and to the ski areas in winter. There are state parks for hiking, bicycling . . . lots of ways to get out and clear your mind and enjoy life."

---

*A*s executive director of the Shasta County Arts Council, artist Gini Holmes has served the region's arts interests since 1997, overseeing the council's rapid growth in an era of rapid population expansion.

"Our building was once Redding's city hall and we have found that there's more than enough visual art space on our first floor, as well as an ideal performance space. The typical artist moving to Redding is coming here for a certain lifestyle . . . a quiet place where they can get work done but walk outside and be in the midst of out-standing natural beauty.

"The size of Redding's creative community would surprise lots of people. But professional artists aren't at all surprised . . . they just assume that there were going to be others who were in their age group. In Redding's downtown we are now seeing an effort made to remove a shopping mall's roof as a way of encouraging people to give the down-town a new look and maybe even find artists to occupy the apart-ments and condos already down here. There's a lot of new types of thinking taking place here . . . finally.

"The most powerful way that Redding's creative community could help guide its own future would be the initiation of a process whose goal is developing collaboration among art groups of all shapes and sizes. That would help in everything from promoting the events taking place every weekend to preventing the overlap of funding proposals. Our survival can only be assured if we collaborate with each other."

San Luis Obispo

F rom the sands of Avila Beach to the nearly 3,000-foot heights of the Santa Rita Mountains, there's an amazing diversity to San Luis Obispo's landscape. Its 45,000 residents enjoy uncrowded streets and uncomplicated access to some of the state's best beaches and parks, several of which are within easy pedaling distance of this bicycle-friendly community's downtown. It's also home to Cal Poly's (California Polytechnic State University) 6,000-acre campus and its 16,000 students. San Luis Obispo's character has been preserved through local government's vigilant bird-dogging of strict zoning regulations and intelligent growth policies concerning development proposals. As is the case in some California Art Towns, the desirable combination of a vibrant downtown, coastal location, and a college town lifestyle have ramped up real estate values to the point where $400,000 barely gets buyers into a San Luis Obispo home, though values typically drop by nearly 25 percent in some other areas of San Luis Obispo County.

Set in a landscape of rolling hills, San Luis Obispo's downtown is just 8 miles from the Pacific Ocean. The center of San Luis Obispo marks the spot where Padre Junipero Serra stood in 1772 when establishing what some historians consider to be the most architecturally significant of California's 21 Mission churches. Named in honor of a bishop, the Mission San Luis Obispo de Tolosa was the focal point of a regional economy that profited from the community's strategic location midway between Los Angeles and San Francisco. In modern times the Mission has retained its significant presence in the community's daily life. The facades of several downtown commercial buildings reflect the Spanish Mission Revival architectural elements

Once home to a large population of Chinese families, San Luis Obispo retains a few architectural reminders of its Chinatown past.

of whitewashed adobe walls and red tile roofs. For its part, the Mission refrained from building adobe walls to visually separate its gardens, walkways, and lawns from downtown's flow of humanity and commerce. One of the most striking aspects of downtown's vibrant commercial grid is its peaceful and accessible Mission Plaza, whose landscaped and tree-shaded grounds are integrated into the community's culture. Tucked into 2 acres bounded by San Luis Creek, the Mission's entryways, and the San Luis Obispo Art Center, Mission Plaza infuses downtown with a vivid reminder of the culturally rich legacy of Spain's colonial presence in California.

Right where San Luis Creek winds its way underneath Broad Street sits the San Luis Obispo Art Center, a key component of the San Luis Obispo County arts infrastructure. Its year-round education programs emphasize fine crafts and two-dimensional art instruction at all expertise levels. The center's exhibitions rotate on a gallery schedule that changes from four to eight weeks, primarily showcasing the work of artists from throughout San Luis Obispo County. Its expertise at successfully organizing individual, invitational, and group exhibitions indicates that the center has the potential to assume a more prominent role in the cultural fabric of San Luis Obispo. In the same way that the Lawrence Art Center in Kansas dramatically increased its regional impact after moving into a new facility built to meet its needs, so will the San Luis Obispo Art Center ultimately set out in a bold new direction. The center's most prominent annual event is the weeklong staging of the San Luis Obispo Plein Air Painting Festival, which draws more than 50 artists for its weeklong run in late September and early October. During the festival participating artists fan out across the county's dramatic terrain, guided by their creative compulsions as well as the shared desire to snag one of the festival's career-enhancing achievement awards.

Another of downtown San Luis Obispo's assets is its Public Art Program, which has used set-asides to fund the acquisition and installation of 30 significant works of art, including Paula Zima's popular Child & Bear Sculpture Fountain, one of nine art works installed in Mission Plaza. Nearly a dozen art galleries are part of the downtown San Luis Obispo art scene, while in nearby Morro Bay there's a cluster of several venues also exhibiting local artists. A monthly event keeping Morro Bay galleries open for later-than-normal hours is the Embarcadero Art Walk on the second Friday of each month. San Luis Obispo's version of that soiree is called Art After Dark and it takes place monthly from 6 to 9 PM on the first Friday of each month. All of the venues taking part in Art After Dark are great places to connect with

In addition to its year-round slate of exhibitions and workshops the San Luis Obispo Art Center organizes a highly regarded Annual Plein Air Painting Festival.

The verdant grounds of centrally-located Mission San Luis Obispo are bisected by the rushing waters of San Luis Creek.

local artists as well as its creative spirit. Arts Space Obispo's SLO Creamery on Higuera Street, a nonprofit venue run by the San Luis Obispo Arts Council, presents performance, as well as visual, art exhibitions and education programs, while the nearby Hands Gallery on Higuera Street has represented local as well as national contemporary fine crafts artists during its 14 years on San Luis Obispo's art scene. Peter J. Steynberg's namesake gallery is located in a quiet uptown neighborhood, though the compelling and contemporary work hung on its walls is anything but sedate. This decidedly unconventional gallery represents a number of the region's top established and emerging talents. On CalPoly's campus the University Art Gallery's innovative mix of national, international, and university talents is supported by the institution's arts-aware administration, presenting museum-quality exhibitions inside the Dexter Building. October's marathon version of a studio tour extends across three central coast weekends, with the first weekend's spotlight falling on artists living in the north part of San Luis Obispo County, while their south San Luis Obispo County brethren are placed front and center for the self-guided tour's second weekend. Apparently, all efforts at decorum are tossed off San Luis Point for the tour's third and final weekend, when all of its 250 participating talents (plus dozens of itinerant vendors selling whatnot at roadside stands throughout the county) compete against each other for cultural tourists' dollars snapping up paintings, sculpture, and jewelry.

Even though local foodies must leave their four-legged friends at home before they venture downtown for the wildly popular, six-block-long Farmers Market along Higuera Street from 6 to 9 PM, the market's crowds continue their weekly patronage of 120 farmers' and ranchers' stands, snapping up everything from the legendary barbecue beef ribs to fresh baked slices of pizza, flowers, and an amazing variety of locally grown fruits and veggies.

In the 1990s San Luis Obispo's municipal government partnered with CalPoly in developing the 1282-seat, $35 million Cohan Performing Arts Center, whose amenities also include a 170-seat recital hall and the 497-seat CalPoly Theatre, all of which came online in September 1996. Since then the facility has presented to both the on-campus and off-campus communities a range of performing art spectaculars. As is the case in many Art Towns with large universities the Cohan takes interest in everything from touring opera to Japanese taiko drumming, contemporary dance, world music, childrens' theatre, and even the inevitable appearance of CATS. San Luis Obispo Symphony, under the direction of Michael Nowak, presents a wide range of performance and education programs to regional audiences, from full-blown, black tie evenings in the Cohan (five of these each season, each with an intriguing theme), to treats such as an evening at Hearst Castle with the symphony performing the score of a Marion Davies film, and Labor Day Weekend's Pops by the Sea concert at the Avila Beach Golf

Home to CalPoly's nearly 16,000 students, San Luis Obispo's street art reflects the talents of its subversively smart residents.

Resort, a beer n' brats type of event attracting more than 3,000 music hounds. On a different note, the annual San Luis Obispo Mozart Festival, which receives widespread support throughout this arts-appreciative community, offers a weeklong series of concerts at the Cohan during its late July and early August run. In addition to its Cohan center concerts the festival also performs inside the Mission San Luis Obispo in a series of chamber music performances and offers its audiences the innovative Music in the Vines concerts at a regional vineyard. San Luis Obispo Little Theatre, which has engaged local audiences for more than 60 years, presents its September to April season of nearly a dozen community theatre productions in the City Playhouse in downtown San Luis Obispo.

Venues

University Art Gallery
Dexter Hall / CalPoly Campus, San Luis Obispo, CA 93406
805.756.6038 / www.artdesign.libart.calpoly.edu
▲ Offers monthly exhibits of local, national, and international artists.

Arts Space Obispo/SLO Creamery
570 Higuera Street, San Luis Obispo, CA 93406
805.544.9251 / www.sloartscouncil.org
▲ Exhibition and performance venue with artist studios.

San Luis Obispo Art Center
1010 Broad Street, San Luis Obispo, CA 93406
805.543.8562 / www.sloartcenter.org
▲ This downtown exhibition space in Mission Plaza offers year-round shows by local artists.

Hands Gallery
777 Higuera Street, San Luis Obispo, CA 93406
805.543.1921 / www.handsgallery.com
▲ Represents local and national artists working in contemporary fine crafts.

San Luis Obispo Little Theatre
888 Morro Street, San Luis Obispo, CA 93406
805.786.2440 / www.slolittletheatre.org
▲ Community theatre presenting a long season of Broadway productions.

San Luis Obispo Mozart Festival
805.781.3009 / www.mozartfestival.com
▲ Summer performances in a variety of local venues.

Steynberg Gallery
1531 Monterey Street, San Luis Obispo, CA 93406
805.547.0278 / www.steynberggallery.com
▲ Representing an intriguing roster of contemporary artists in uptown San Luis Obispo.

Events

Art After Dark
Downtown San Luis Obispo
805.544.9251 / www.sloartscouncil.org
▲ First Friday of every month with downtown galleries open from 6 to 9 PM.

Downtown Farmers' Market
Higuera Street between Nipomo Street and Osos Street
805.541.0286 / www.downtownslo.com
▲ More than 120 vendors are regulars at this Thursday evening gathering.

San Luis Obispo Poetry Festival

San Luis Obispo Art Center, San Luis Obispo, CA 93406

805.547.1318 / www.languageofthesoul.org

▲ November's Language of the Soul festival features local and national talents.

Open Studios Art Tour

ARTS Obispo, San Luis Obispo, CA 93406

805.544.9251 / www.sloartscouncil.org

▲ More than 250 artists take part in this three-weekend event.

Slumber

Embassy Suites Hotel

333 Madonna Road, San Luis Obispo, CA 93405

805.549.0800 / www.embassysuites1.hilton.com

▲ Pool, fitness center, and a convenient location off Highway 101.

Madonna Inn

100 Madonna Road, San Luis Obispo, CA 93405

805.543.3000 / www.madonnainn.com

▲ Historic, eclectic, one-of-a-kind hotel with nearly 50 years of history as a San Luis Obispo institution. More than 100 guest rooms, a popular steakhouse, on-site wine shop, fitness center, pastry shop, and huge swimming pool.

Garden Street Inn Bed & Breakfast

1212 Garden Street, San Luis Obispo, CA 93401

805.545.9802 / www.gardenstreetinn.com

▲ Nine rooms, four suites, and Victorian charm in an authentic 1887 residence in the heart of downtown San Luis Obispo.

The Sanitarium

1716 Osos Street, San Luis Obispo, CA 93401

805.544.4124 / www.thesanitariumspa.com

▲ This art-filled, historic home with seven guest rooms features soaking tubs, neighborhood quiet, and absolutely no padded walls.

Coachman Inn

1001 Olive Street, San Luis Obispo, CA 93401

805.544.0400 / www.centralcoast.com

▲ This affordable motel is located a short walk from downtown San Luis Obispo.

Sustenance

Art Cafe & Bakery
570 Higuera Street, San Luis Obispo, CA 93406
805.548.8570 / www.artcafeandbakery.com
▲ Biscotti, tofu omelets, flapjacks, and local art on the walls.

Big Sky Cafe
1121 Broad Street, San Luis Obispo, CA 93406
805.545.5401 / www.bigskycafe.com
▲ Known for its consistent quality, local ingredients, local wines, and regional art.

Cafe Roma
1020 Railroad Avenue, San Luis Obispo, CA 93406
805.541.6800 / www.caferomaslo.com
▲ Northern Italian cuisine in a setting filled with local art.

Linnea's Cafe
1110 Garden Street, San Luis Obispo, CA 93406
805.541.5888 / www.linneas.com
▲ Poetry readings, local art, great coffee, and famous desserts.

Award-winning painter Elizabeth Tolley has been a prominent member of the Central Coast's arts community throughout her professional career. A member of both the California Art Club and the Oil Painters of America, in 1993 she cofounded the San Luis Obispo Outdoor Painters group.

"My life revolves around making paintings, though I'll venture off into teaching workshops and last year I had my first book published (Oil Painter's Solution Book: Landscapes, North Light Books). I've painted this area since coming here to attend CalPoly in the early 1970s and have seen the impact of growth. It's been a great place to work as an artist, starting with design projects that helped build my name recognition . . . art festivals and nonprofits, mainly. But I'm definitely a product of this community.

"I find that in San Luis Obispo an artist who reaches a certain level of achievement is seen by the community as being in the business of art and is respected for their contributions. This is the sort of art market that's a difficult place for art galleries to stay in business.

There are a few exceptions up the coast in Cambria, but San Luis Obispo experiences turnover in its galleries, which demonstrates why the art center is considered so important as a place to show local artists' work.

"The art center serves this community in many ways that have been good for the artists here, especially through programs that have brought exhibitions by artists from outside this area into San Luis Obispo. In my work I find that my love for this area, for this land, has allowed me to reach people from around the country. And even if I break away from being active in the community for extended periods of time, San Luis Obispo is always there for me when I need it."

A s executive director of the San Luis Obispo Art Center Karen Kile oversees a centrally located and year-round exhibition and education facility that's ready to embark on a campaign to expand its operations to meet its fast-growing community's needs.

"I think we're at the hub of most of the cultural activity taking place in the county. We collaborate with every organization and business that are willing to work with us, and our efforts on visual arts exhibitions and education are guiding the community's growing awareness of how strong an arts center we've turned into. We're fortunate to have the expertise of the fine arts faculty of the university to draw upon as a resource for our own exhibitions and programs, and their impact has been critically important to most of the arts organizations in the area.

"Having the energy of 16,000 students in town has allowed the art center to extend itself on several levels, but especially in respect to our evening activities and music programming. We are also home to a large and growing community of professional, experienced artists who have moved into the area in recent years. Even though for the most part they're not coming to the art center to exhibit their work, what they are doing is lending their presence and expertise to some of the many things going on around here. They will teach occasional workshops, or others will work individually with artists to help them find ways to resolve technical issues in their art work."

Santa Barbara

Whoever came up with the concept that one of life's most fundamental gateways to success is "location, location, location" must have been born and raised in Santa Barbara. That's because nearly everything about this community of 95,000 full-time residents is so astonishingly picture perfect, from its miles of white sand beaches to the smooth incline of its densely populated neighborhoods. La Cumbre Peak, at 3,995 feet, the tallest point in the Santa Ynez Mountains, divides the North County communities of Solvang, Santa Maria, and Los Olivos from the South County communities of Santa Barbara, Montecito, Goleta, and Carpinteria.

Unlike most places its size Santa Barbara isn't accessed through a high speed ribbon of smog-shrouded freeways. In fact, all of the functional routes in and out of Santa Barbara are a transportation planner's nightmare, from the quaint but teensy Santa Barbara Airport's passenger terminal (though its air connections are excellent) to the historic 1902 grandeur of the beautifully restored, Spanish Mission Revival–style Southern Pacific Railroad depot. As for the road access in and out of here there's the winding route of the Pacific Coast Highway, an efficient and relatively unobtrusive presence separating

While the contemporary art exhibition calendar of the University Art Museum at the University of California Santa Barbara balances a demand for student and faculty shows with exhibitions of work by notable artists from outside the Santa Barbara region, it nonetheless always finds room to display parts of its 750,000-piece Architecture & Design Collection, which tracks the evolution of everything from California drive-in movie theatres to the preservation of Santa Barbara's Mission Revival residences.

Considered by many to be the definitive expression of Spanish Mission Revival architecture, the Mission Santa Barbara was established in 1786 by Padre Junipero Serra.

the beach and Stearns Wharf from State Street's retail core. In many ways the access points to and from Santa Barbara serve as reminders that even though the sprawl of LA lies just 90 miles to the south there's a dramatic shift in the attitudes characterizing this Art Town's spirit.

A good starting point for getting in touch with the community's art vibe is the Santa Barbara Museum of Art, whose Spanish Mission Revival edifice at the heart of State Street's busiest intersection affords this art-collecting institution a central role in the cultural lives of Santa Barbara's residents and visitors. The museum has proven to be up to that challenge, as evidenced through an energetic exhibitions program addressing this diverse community's multitude of interests. Curatorial attention is also paid to the museum's significant permanent collection, which includes works by David Alfaro Siqueiros, Anish Kapoor, Diego Rivera, Carrie Mae Weems, Larry Bell, Milton Avery, and Pablo Picasso. The museum's education programs serve adults and children through a packed slate of free events, while its summer-long social networking programs provide a setting whose themed events have proven a hit with the community's emerging generation of art lovers.

Another touchstone of the community's creativity is found on the historic grounds of Mission Santa Barbara, which was founded in 1786 by Father Junipero Serra. In late May the Mission's parking lot is transformed into a beehive of art activity through the annual staging of the I Madonnari Festival, the nation's most prominent celebration of Italian-style street painting. This three-day event attracts a national and local group of artists who partner with Santa Barbara sponsoring business and nonprofit organizations in a juried competition for prizes. The festival, which raises funds for youth art programs in the Santa Barbara area, was started in 1987 by arts organizer Kathy Koury and has evolved into a major draw whose 25,000 annual visitors stare in awe at the works of art drawn onto the parking lot's asphalt by more than 400 participating artists.

Santa Barbara's signature style of architecture, a sublime combination of white stucco exteriors topped by red tile roofs, is referred to as Spanish Mission Revival. The Santa Barbara Mission is frequently singled out as one of the most significant surviving examples of this

The annual I Madonnari Festival on the grounds of Mission Santa Barbara leave evidence of its skillful artists hands long after the event's crowds are gone.

vernacular. Its widespread influence in Santa Barbara's residential and commercial neighborhoods is the result of wisely conceived urban planning initiated in 1927 by Pearl Chase. Her decades of overseeing the city's Plans and Plantings Committee was memorialized in the naming of Chase Palm Park, which extends along both sides of East Cabrillo Boulevard from the 1,950-foot-long Stearns Wharf and its nearly 4 acres of deck space, south to East Beach. The park is the location of another of this community's many expressions of creativity, the weekly, year-round Santa Barbara Arts & Crafts Show, whose Sunday (and occasional Saturday) staging on the ocean side of Chase Palm Park is where many visitors first come into contact with the Santa Barbara region's accomplished style of creativity. Nearly 250 artists and craftspeople exhibit their work in open air booths from

Downtown Santa Barbara's elegant streets are laced with narrow walkways such as El Paseo, home to restaurants and art galleries.

10 AM to 5 PM (fewer show up on overcast days), carrying on a local arts tradition started in 1965.

Santa Barbara would appear to have the right combination of talent and resources necessary to develop a museum focused exclusively on international contemporary art. The region's cutting-edge sensibility is trained on the exhibition space of Santa Barbara Contemporary Arts Forum (CAF) on the upstairs level of State Street's Paseo Nuevo Center, a short distance from the art museum. Since its 1976 founding CAF has provided artists from Santa Barbara and elsewhere with an important venue for exhibitions, installations, film, music, and performance art. Santa Barbara Art Association's more than 500 member artists exhibit their work at the Gallery 113 inside La Arcada, while OMMA Center for Contemporary Art uses its State Street exhibition space to present work with a decidedly innovative edge. Commercial art galleries in Santa Barbara have their work cut out for them in this competitive marketplace, and while gallery comings and goings are not especially surprising there are several long-standing exceptions to the rule. Waterhouse Gallery, which represents realist painters and sculptors, occupies a conspicuous space on the State Street edge of La Arcada. The nearby San Marcos Building on East Anapamu Street houses Artamo Gallery, a highly regarded contemporary art space representing an international roster of painters and sculptors. Sullivan Goss–An American Gallery has since 1985 represented a wide range of paintings, drawings, etchings, and sculpture in a wonderful setting directly across East Anapamu Street from the Santa Barbara Museum of Art. The gallery shares its space with the Arts & Letters Cafe, whose courtyard dining spot is a bistro-style lunch favorite with artists, art lovers, and art students. From late June through August the cafe's courtyard is transformed into the setting for Opera Under the Stars, whose Saturday evening performances are wrapped around two dinner seatings.

Because of its determinedly proactive stance on preserving the architecture of its past, Santa Barbara is today in the enviable position of offering performing arts venues of all sizes serving the needs of the community's music, theatre, and dance organizations. Center Stage Theater, which presents a diverse schedule that includes the performances of Iridian Dance, Ballet Santa Barbara, Janusphere Dance Company, Genesis West Theatre, and the Santa Barbara Theatre, is a 150-seat "black box" venue on the upper level of Paseo Nuevo Center, directly across the courtyard from Santa Barbara Contemporary Arts Forum's exhibition space. Ensemble Theatre Company, which uses the Alhecama Theater for its innovative season series of new and recent plays, is the sort of professional stage organization that takes risks with the unusually adventuresome material presented on its stage.

The recently restored Granada Theater, a presence on State Street since 1924, is home to the Santa Barbara Symphony's season, while the nearby Arlington Theatre, whose interior recalls the appearance of Santa Barbara in the 1800s, hosts numerous concerts and film events, as well as the touring orchestra performances presented by CAMA, the Community Arts Music Association. Santa Barbara Chamber Orchestra, which has logged 30 years on the local art scene, uses the Lobero Theater for its season concert series, while Speaking of Stories, another Lobero Theater presenter, offers Santa Barbara's literary crowd a season of theatrical interpretations of works by leading authors.

Venues

Santa Barbara Museum of Art
1130 State Street, Santa Barbara, CA 93101
805.963.4364 / www.sbmuseart.org
Admission $9 / Closed Monday
▲ Santa Barbara's centrally located art museum is ground zero for the region's creative community.

Santa Barbara Contemporary Art Forum
653 State Street, Santa Barbara, CA 93101
805.966.5373 / www.sbcaf.org
Free / Closed Monday
▲ This stalwart presence on the contemporary art scene delivers provocative exhibitions, installations, performances, and film throughout the year.

UCSB University Art Museum
552 University Road, Santa Barbara, CA 93106
805.893.2951 / www.uam.ucsb.edu
Closed Monday and Tuesday

▲ UCSB's 18,000 students and the general public enjoy access to the museum's 8,500-piece permanent collection and its year-round changing exhibitions.

Artamo Gallery
11 West Anapamu Street, Santa Barbara, CA 93101
805.568.1400 / www.artamo.com
Closed Monday and Tuesday
▲ Representing an intriguing roster of local and national contemporary art talents.

Waterhouse Gallery
114 State Street, Santa Barbara, CA 93101
805.962.8885 / www.waterhousegallery.com
▲ Santa Barbara's leading gallery for traditional realism and impressionism.

Sullivan Goss–An American Gallery
7 East Anapamu Street, Santa Barbara, CA 93101
805.730.1460 / www.sullivangoss.com
▲ From Georgia O'Keeffe, Marsden Hartley, and Joseph Fleck to Douglas Kent Hall, Ida Kohlmeyer, and Gary Fagin, this gallery covers all the art bases . . . and serves a killer double cafe mocha, to boot.

OMMA Center for Contemporary Art
1221 State Street, Santa Barbara, CA 93101
805.895.4141 / www.omma.us
▲ Art book publisher and festival organizer with an experimental art space.

Gallery 113
1114 State Street, Santa Barbara, CA 93101
805.965.6611 / www.sbartassoc.org
▲ Member-operated gallery of the Santa Barbara Art Association.

Events

Summer Solstice Celebration
Alameda Park, Santa Barbara, CA 93101
805.965.3396 / www.solsticeparade.com
▲ The longest day of the year is marked with a mardi gras–style parade down State Street and a weekend-long arts festival.

Santa Barbara Arts & Crafts Show
Chase Palm Park, Santa Barbara, CA 93101
805.897.1982 / www.sbaacs.com
▲ On a sunny Sunday as many as 250 artists spread out along the park's lawns for this outdoor art fair. Also held on the Saturday of holiday weekends.

Santa Barbara Certified Farmers Market
State Street and Santa Barbara Street, Santa Barbara, CA 93101
805.962.5354 / www.sbfarmersmarket.org
▲ Tuesday afternoons and Saturday mornings lure locals and visitors to this, one of the state's most highly regarded fresh produce markets.

Slumber

West Beach Inn
306 West Cabrillo Boulevard, Santa Barbara, CA 93101
805.963.4277 / www.coasthotels.com
▲ Ideal location across the street from Stearns Wharf, with free wi-fi and a pool.

Holiday Inn Express Hotel Virginia
17 West Hailey Street, Santa Barbara, CA 93101
805.963.9757 / www.hotelvirginia.com
▲ Built in 1917 and now restored to its historic beauty, this 61-room retreat is located just off State Street's collection of galleries and restaurants.

Colonial Beach Inn
206 Castillo Street, Santa Barbara, CA 93101
805.963.4317 / www.colonialbeachinn.com
▲ Located two streets from the beach and Stearns Wharf, with 23 rooms, a pool, and Charleston-style design flourishes.

Sustenance
La Super Rica Taqueria
622 N. Milpas Street, Santa Barbara, CA 93101
805.963.4940
Closed Wednesday
▲ Legendary outpost for authentic Mexican foods and well worth waiting in the inevitable line.

Daily Grind Coffee & Tea Station
2001 De La Vina Street, Santa Barbara, CA 93101
805-687-4966
▲ Free wi-fi and superb lattes are just two blocks west of State
Street in this laid back, locals' favorite.

Spudnuts
3629 State Street, Santa Barbara, CA 93105
805.569.3719 /
▲ This multilocation Southern California donut store exerts
hypnotic powers over American-style pastry lovers.

Ahi Sushi
3631 State Street, Santa Barbara, CA 93105
805.687.6942 / www.ahisushi.net
▲ Friendly, spotlessly clean, awesome quality, and affordable.

As director of the Santa Barbara Museum of Art, Larry J. Feinberg has broadened both the museum's exhibitions programs and its community outreach initiatives to tomorrow's art leaders. Prior to assuming his post at the museum Mr. Feinberg served at the Art Institute of Chicago.

"Coming to Santa Barbara from Chicago was a surprisingly easy transition that was made easier by this community's lively social life and very active intellectual life. Our museum offers the community an encyclopedic collection spanning 5,000 years of human history with superb classical pieces right through the contemporary, impressionism, and strong Asian collection. Our collection of works of art on paper by major figures will soon be exhibited in its own dedicated gallery space.

"There's a certain old world grandeur to the museum, with its classical facade and arches, to its interior spaces that flow from one majestic space to another. We have very important works of art that haven't been exhibited often enough, and we are working on developing a rotating, constantly changing series of exhibitions to bring more attention to these pieces.

"We are very community oriented and work to serve the children of Santa Barbara, especially disadvantaged children. And we've had great success with our 'Nights' program, which serves as a series of cultural gathering events for people in their early career years, along with a new program to draw people further into the museum through

social events such as lectures by experts in areas of the museum's collection. Increasingly we are striving for more intergenerational participation in this museum's relationship to the community. Our goal is to do all this while building the museum's reputation as a nationally and internationally significant presence in the art world."

As recreation programs manager for the City of Santa Barbara Parks and Recreation Department, Judith C. McCaffrey oversees the Santa Barbara Arts & Crafts Show, one of the nation's premier, weekly outdoors art events. From its modest beginnings in 1965 on a downtown Santa Barbara plaza, it's now staged underneath the palm trees lining Santa Barbara's beachfront. The event showcases nearly 250 artists.

"The Santa Barbara Arts & Crafts Show brings a lot of people into Santa Barbara for their first visit here, and it provides repeat visitors with something they can plan their stays around once they're already here. In our 43rd year we certainly qualify as an important local tradition, and one that remains important to the artists. The premise of the show is that we allow people to become exhibiting artists at the beginning of their careers and give them the opportunity to develop their skills, build a group of collectors of their work, and be a way for artists who are residents of Santa Barbara to sustain their careers.

"Our rules are designed to allow for direct interaction from the artist to the buyer, and we are strict about there being artist-made work only in each artists' booth. By staying handcrafted, staying unique, and staying local we've been able to stand up to the test of time. Over the last 10 or so years the show has changed in that we now have an artist's attendance requirement, so the people who are in the show are dedicated to both their art and to the community."

Santa Cruz

K nown as one of the birthplaces of California's surfing culture and home to its own Surfing Museum, the city of Santa Cruz has a south-facing location at the northern tip of Monterey Bay. With its oceanfront boardwalk, a reliably early jump on summer weather, expansive beaches, and a large population of college students it makes sense that this community of 56,000 full-time residents has also been called the northern fringe of Southern California. Continue 75 miles north of here along the Pacific Coast Highway 1 and the dim sum palaces of San Francisco will be at the beck and call of your chopsticks, with spectacular sights such as the Pigeon Point Lighthouse and Half Moon Bay passed along the way. Santa Cruz is the type of place where traditions of individuality dovetail with an admiration for creativity, setting the stage for this exceedingly artistic community's profusion of artists, actors, galleries, theatre companies, coffee shops, festivals, and studio tours. To be enveloped in Santa Cruz's creativity is akin to taking a journey through an arts amusement park.

While the most popular starting point for many Santa Cruz visits has historically been its century-old Beach Boardwalk and the 1924 Giant Dipper roller coaster, there's another way to sample the community's historic past. That approach would start with a visit to Mission Santa Cruz and its peaceful neighborhood. Operated as a state park, the mission building is actually a reconstructed replica of the original 1791 church. No matter which starting point suits you best, a warm weather inevitability is that the beaches will exert their magnetic charm, most likely sooner than later.

For families there's Main Beach, which lies to the south of the Santa Cruz Wharf and has lifeguards from April through September. The

Downtown Santa Cruz's streets are an inviting setting for restaurants, public works of art, bookstores, and coffee bars.

wharf serves as one of the region's prime locations for events such as the Annual Clam Chowder Cookoff, Art on the Wharf in July, and the Polynesian Festival in August. Main Beach hosts the popular Bands on the Beach series of free July and August concerts. A laid back environment is what you'll find at the 2-mile ribbon of Seacliff State Beach in nearby Aptos, as well as along the 3 miles of Sunset Beach, a 20-minute drive south of Santa Cruz. The pretty village of Capitola, which lies between Santa Cruz and Seacliff State Beach, is known for its Labor Day weekend Capitola Art & Wine Festival, an event featuring more than 200 artists and up to two dozen wineries, all within reach of the aroma emanating from the culinary shrine of Pizza My Heart.

Sandwiched between the metropolis to its north and the concentration of Carmel's galleries an hour's drive south, the Santa Cruz arts community developed its audience and identified its niche in the regional economy not by imitating other models but by striking out on its own path, emphasizing the diversity of its enterprising arts culture. While visual artists share the spotlight during Santa Cruz's numerous outdoor art festivals and well-attended studio tours, the community's talent-laden performing arts sector delivers sophisticated and dynamic productions in theatre, music, and dance throughout the

A wide range of programs throughout Santa Cruz serve all sectors of the community's population.

year. A wealth of local nonprofit organizations, working alongside an arts-supportive city and county government, played key roles in realizing the creative community's ambitions.

Downtown Santa Cruz's two leading visual arts organizations, the Museum of Art & History and the Santa Cruz Institute of Contemporary Art, provide the community with a range of exhibitions and programs focused on international, regional, and local artists. On the UCSC campus the Senson Art Gallery showcases topical art and work dealing with current art movements, while the Museum of Art & History's (MAH) exhibitions emphasize artists as well as art issues impacting the local and statewide art scenes. During mid-July the MAH stages its annual Plein Air Affaire, attracting many of the region's leading landscape painters for a two-day brush with California's impressionist traditions. The Santa Cruz Institute of Contemporary Art (SCICA) is one of the many local arts organizations behind development of the Tannery Art Center. A project combining affordable live/work studio space with working studios, art organization offices, and a performing arts center, occupancy of the center's first phase of 100 housing units will take place in 2009. Working in partnership with Minneapolis-based Artspace Projects, the art center is projected to become the anchor of an arts district around the Tannery's San Lorenzo River location and provide an important venue for the Santa Cruz creative community. SCICA is also the guiding force behind the Attic, a 5,000-square-foot exhibition, performance, and cafe space, and the Hide Gallery, whose younger artists create work with an urban edge.

From the local artist exhibitions at the Santa Cruz Mountains Art Center in Ben Lomond to the steady stream of plays, concerts, readings, and taiko drumming workshops offered at the Mello Center for the Performing Arts in Watsonville, creative expression in all of its variations is hard to miss in Santa Cruz County. One of the most intriguing ways to catch a sense of the Santa Cruz arts vibe is through one of the multipurpose arts facilities in pedestrian-friendly downtown. The 418 Project, a multidisciplinary and multiethnic arts organization, uses its Front Street facility for visual art shows, dance training, affordable health care alternatives, poetry readings, and the Jumping Monkey Cafe's authentic cuisine of India. The Attic takes a similar approach in operating its Pacific Avenue facility, serving as a stage for salsa and rumba bands, a high-profile gallery for local artists, a cafe and teahouse, and a meeting place for visual artists. E3 Playhouse, also on Front Street, foregoes visual art shows in pursuing its interests in Latin dance, modern jazz, calypso, and world beat, alongside the E3 Playhouse Cafe's bistro menu. Local businesses provide visual artists with alternative exhibition venues, with places such as Lighthouse Bank on Mission Street and Bad Ass Coffee on Pacific Avenue rotating shows monthly.

Santa Cruz Improv Festival, which uses downtown's Santa Cruz County Actors theatre to present its monthlong, July roster of comedy shows, also offers a series of workshops that aim to bring out the stand-up comedian hiding in many of us. Top comedy pros from prestigious organizations such as Chicago's famed Second City are among the festival's instructors.

After the the setting sun rolls off the edge of Santa Cruz Wharf, downtown's streetlights signal the nightly metamorphosis that turns sidewalks and side streets into an entertainment district. Kuumbwa Jazz Center's location on Cedar Street is one of northern California's leading venues for touring jazz stars, while local jazz legends are featured at Hoffman's Bakery Cafe, Severino's Grill, and Bocci's Cellar. Touring rockers perform at the Catalyst on Pacific Avenue, Moe's Alley on

The coastline's dramatic beauty lies just a few miles north of Santa Cruz at Pigeon Point State Historic Park.

Commercial Way, and on the stage of the Rio Theater, a 685-seat shrine to Streamline design values. Romantics and conversationalists gravitate toward volume-modulated live music venues such as the Cava Wine Bar in Capitola and Mangiamo's on Almar Avenue.

Art Towns are typically not in Santa Cruz's position of having overlapping fine arts departments at two local institutions of higher learning. Both UCSC and Cabrillo College support visual and performing arts departments through stable and significant commitments to education and presentation. Cabrillo College Theatre is one of the area's busiest facilities, serving as the home of Cabrillo Stage's season of summer stock musical theatre, a series of joint efforts between the college's Theatre Arts Department and Pisces Moon Productions, and the concerts and recitals offered by the college's music department. UCSC's 528-seat Mainstage Theatre offers a season of Arts & Lectures from October through April, as well as academic year seasons of recitals, concerts, readings, and plays in the 231-seat UCSC Second Stage. Downtown's two largest performance venues are the Civic Auditorium, which is home to the Santa Cruz County Symphony, and the restored art deco Theatre Del Mar, a 500-seat, 1926 movie palace that each May serves as the focal point of the Santa Cruz Film Festival. The Civic Auditorium also serves as the late July to mid-August home of the

Cabrillo Festival of Contemporary Music, which has established an international reputation for its string of ASCAP accolades for Adventuresome Programming of Contemporary Music. The festival spreads itself around the community through its concerts at venues such as the Kennolyn's Hilltop Hacienda and Mission San Juan Bautista. Summer's other big-name event, Shakespeare Santa Cruz, uses UCSC's campus venues for its season of four productions. Two plays are performed amongst redwood trees in the 600-seat Sinsheimer-Stanley Festival Glen outdoor amphitheatre, while the Mainstage Theatre hosts the other two plays. The festival's productions, which start in mid-July and continue through August, are enormously popular, a reflection of more than 25 years of of presenting classics in updated and innovative ways.

Venues

Museum of Art & History
705 Front Street, Santa Cruz, CA 95060
831.429.1964 / www.santacruzmah.org
▲ Downtown institution with a fast-changing schedule of exhibitions and strong connections to the local art scene.

Santa Cruz Institute of Contemporary Arts
1040 River Street, Santa Cruz, CA 95060
831.454.8200 / www.scica.org
▲ Moving Santa Cruz's contemporary art scene forward on multiple levels including infrastructure development, festivals, exhibitions, and performance.

The 418 Project
418 Front Street, Santa Cruz, CA 95060
831.466.9770 / www.the418.org
▲ With its dance classes, performances, exhibitions, cafe and art instruction, 418 has become central to Santa Cruz's creative community.

University of California Santa Cruz
1156 High Street, Santa Cruz, CA 95064
831.459.2159 / www.ucsc.edu
▲ Visual art exhibitions at the Senson Gallery, performances in drama and music in the Mainstage Theatre, plus recitals, experimental works, and lectures.

Pisces Moon Productions
Various Venues, Santa Cruz, CA 95060
831.429.2339 / www.piscesmoon.org
▲ Compelling productions of contemporary theatre.

Santa Cruz County Actors Theatre
1001 Center Street, Santa Cruz, CA 95060
418.427.4008 / www.sccat.org
▲ Contemporary theatre productions with local talent, and a summer Improv Festival.

Events

Shakespeare Santa Cruz
1156 High Street, Santa Cruz, CA 95064
831.459.2121 / www.shakespearesantacruz.org
▲ Staging its summer productions on the UCSC campus, using an outdoor amphitheatre as well as the Mainstage Theater.

River Arts Festival
San Lorenzo Park, Santa Cruz, CA 95060
831.427.8212 / www.riverartsfestival.com
▲ Seventy-five artist booths, temporary installations of public art, and a gelato competition make this mid-May event a highlight on the community's cultural calendar.

Open Studios Art Tour
2400 Chanticleer, Santa Cruz, CA 95060
831.475.9600 / www.ccscc.org
▲ Three October weekends showcasing more than 300 artists throughout Santa Cruz County.

Slumber

Capitola Hotel
210 Esplanade, Capitola, CA 95010
831.476.1278 / www.capitolahotel.com
▲ Comfortable, nine-room inn with free wi-fi fronting onto Capitola City Beach. This friendly and affordable boutique hotel is an incredible bargain for a surf, sun, and sand weekend.

Adobe on Green
103 Green Street, Santa Cruz, CA 95060
831.469.9866 / www.adobeongreen.com

▲ Classic, historic home with lots of Mission-style charm on a quiet street.

Hampton Inn
1505 Ocean Street, Santa Cruz, CA 95060
831.457.8000 / www.thesantacruzlodging.com
▲ Offers special package deals to the "World Famous Mystery Spot," just three miles from the front desk.

Sustenance

Hoffman's Bakery Cafe
1102 Pacific Avenue, Santa Cruz, CA 95060
831.420.0135 / www.hoffmansbakery.net
▲ Live music, outdoor dining, European pastries, and brunch on weekends make Hoffman's a local favorite.

Tavernetta Limoncello
503 Water Street, Santa Cruz, CA 95060
831.427.0998 / www.tavernettalimoncello.com
▲ Foodies think nothing of driving Highway 17's twists and turns . . . provided chef Giovanni Maio's pasta is waiting for them in this highly rated Santa Cruz restaurant.

Bad Ass Coffee
1207 Pacific Avenue, Santa Cruz, CA 95060
813.460.1007 / www.scbadasscoffee.com
▲ Local art, Kona Coast coffee, and friendly smiles.

The Center Street Grill
1001 Center Street, Santa Cruz, CA 95060
813.423.4745 / www.thecenterstreetgrill.com
▲ California cuisine blends in nicely with classic Greek dishes in this half-Athens/half–Santa Cruz restaurant.

Since assuming the position of executive director of the Museum of Art & History in 2003, Paul Figueroa has overseen the operations of a multidisciplinary institution located in downtown Santa Cruz. The institution's broad focus on fine arts, education, and historic artifacts combine to lend the museum a year-round flow of visitors.

"I relocated from Charleston, South Carolina, to the West Coast to take over this landmark facility in downtown Santa Cruz. We're the county's leading place for people to gather to experience local art, culture, and history in the setting of a 15,000 square foot structure that was built to accommodate the needs of what once were two separate groups.

"Bringing the art museum and the history museum together allowed for the creation of a center that could combine certain functions and thereby free up resources to expand all of the center's exhibitions and programs. Our permanent collection of art is growing to include greater numbers of contemporary artists from the Santa Cruz area, as well as to broaden its representation of artists from the Bay Area and the Central Coast. We've pursued the opportunity to acquire a collection of Santa Cruz studio ceramics, and there are a number of very well-known ceramics artists who are either living here or once had their home and studio here."

As executive director of the Cultural Council of Santa Cruz County, Dr. Alberto Rafols applies the steady hands of his concert pianist past to a multitiered arts organization whose reach includes the successful Open Studios Art Tour, distributing funding to arts groups, and administration of the SPECTRA artists residency program in public schools.

"My background in arts administration includes positions in Dallas, Portland, and Seattle, all of which prepared me for the incredible diversity of individuals and art forms that we have in Santa Cruz. Here we have first-rate jazz, year-round world music, a superb symphony orchestra, and fantastic concerts by touring artists. Having a strong music scene enabled me to easily connect with the community's creative spirit. Santa Cruz is a unique community filled with people who have made conscious decisions about their desires to live nontypical lifestyles. Many of the people living here pursue some form of creative expression through the arts, so they are very tolerant of all forms of expression and truly enjoy being part of an artistic community.

"The cultural council is very challenged to keep pace with the expanding range of art needs in a community like this, especially in a

state whose level of financial support for the arts leaves something to be desired. Our strategic planning process allows us to look into how the community values the work that the cultural council engages in, and which directions we can guide ourselves toward in the continuing effort to adjust our expertise in meeting the changing needs of Santa Cruz."

Santa Monica

This beachside community of 88,000 residents stands out as one of the state's most visited Art Towns for many reasons, not the least of which is its proximity to one of the nation's best stretches of prime people-watching terrain: the broad pathways connecting Santa Monica to its neighboring community of Venice Beach. Since the entire point of sauntering along a pathway (be it on foot, bicycle, board, blades, or wheelchair) is to take a relaxing break from the need to buckle up and drive, another of Santa Monica's attributes is its stature as one of the few places around Los Angeles where the sensible thing to do is leave the car parked and just walk around the community's attractive streets, taking in the sights and local culture. In fact, the culture and sights framing Santa Monica's art scene are so plentiful that taking it all in requires determined effort.

While many of Santa Monica's residences have been carefully restored to their original beauty, parts of the community also are home to dramatic expressions of new forms of contemporary American architecture whose origins can be traced to the drafting tables of Santa Monica's sizable population of architects and designers.

Ocean breezes usually keep nearby LA's smog problem at bay, though Santa Monica's air quality is generally as pristine as that enjoyed in other coastal Art Towns. The seasonal blankets of coastal clouds known hereabouts as the May Gray and the June Gloom, both of which turn Santa Monica's atmosphere into a fog-shrouded, mist-covered, Londonesque etherealness, are a more pressing matter to local residents. Incorporated in the late 1800s, at one point Santa Monica was supposed to become a commercial port serving as the terminus for transcontinental trains. But Long Beach and San Pedro used some backroom political muscle to grab the deal away from Santa Monica, whose promoters then became stuck with the Santa Monica Pier, a 1600-foot wood behemoth built in 1909 as an inducement to railroad moguls weighing the attributes of Santa Monica and its competitors. Eventually Santa Monica decided to develop the pier for other purposes, opening the door to private investment that backed construction of the Looff's Pier Hippodrome, the La Monica Ballroom, and the Blue Streak Racer roller coaster. Only the hippodrome survives today, serving as the home of an ornate, fully functional and carefully restored 1922 Philadelphia Toboggan Company carousel.

Bergamot Station's loading docks and warehouses have been converted into Los Angeles's leading setting for contemporary art galleries.

The legacy of Santa Monica's historic past is also found in the architecture of its residential neighborhoods and commercial shopping districts. Among the best of the latter is the compact corridor along Abbot Kinney Boulevard in neighboring Venice, (where a dozen or so galleries conduct business), and the larger commercial artery of Main Street in Santa Monica, where nearly 13 blocks of retail stretches from Dogtown's Navy Street north to Pico Boulevard. Though the emphasis along Main Street is primarily on clothing, interior furnishings, restaurants, and bars, several art galleries have established themselves here over the years, including the sophisticated environs of Angles Gallery, the contemporary art space of Applegate Gallery, and the M. Hanks Gallery with its outstanding roster of African American artists.

North of Pico Boulevard there's another vibrant, pedestrian-focused retail cluster along the Third Street Promenade, which does double duty as home to a community of professional street buskers performing their routines on the area's busy weekends. Galleries in the Promenade district include the contemporary realism stalwart of Terrence Rogers Fine

Abbott-Kinney, a once quiet neighborhood, has evolved into a magnet for art galleries and locally-owned businesses.

Art, the artwork of music stars such as Grace Slick, Paul Stanley, Ringo Starr, and Ron Wood represented by Gallery 319, and the California contemporary artists exhibited at Hamilton Galleries.

While the galleries along both Main Street and the Third Street Promenade conduct their business inside the settings of commercial districts whose focus swings wide enough to accommodate everything from independently owned bookstores to Pinkberry yogurt shops, an entirely different dynamic is in place at Bergamot Station, one of the contemporary art world's most influential gallery districts. Located three miles east of the hubbub of Main Street, Third Street Promenade, and the Santa Monica Pier, the 8-acre grounds of this former Red Line trolley switching yard and appliance factory were redefined by artist and visionary developer Wayne Blank as an ideally industrialized setting for the display of contemporary art. His plans were realized in 1994 when Bergamot Station opened with a dozen or so galleries clustered along the fringes of several asphalt-paved acres of parking, delivering to art-savvy Angelinos one of their most treasured talismans, a supply of free, safe, and convenient parking. Today the site's galleries number over 30, and include some of the most influential art dealers in the contemporary art world's top tiers. Among the multitude of Bergamot Station's irresistible concentration of art spaces are Mark Moore Gallery, Rose Gallery, Tarryn Teresa Gallery, Kay Richards Gallery, Shoshana Wayne Gallery, Patrick Painter Gallery, and Rosamund Felsen Gallery.

Bergamot Station's concentration of art galleries proved to be the logical site to serve as the home of the Santa Monica Museum of Art (SMMA), which stands out in Southern California's crowded arts marketplace for its status as a noncollecting art museum with a keen sense of how art trends will impact the Southern California arts community. Instead, SMMA focuses its resources on the curating of a dynamic slate of changing exhibitions in its main gallery and two project rooms, spotlighting the full range of international contemporary art talent from the emerging to the established. Since opening at Bergamot Station in 1998 the museum has become a driving force behind Santa Monica's steady rise in the contemporary art world, proving to be an attuned counterpoint to art-exhibiting institutions structured along more traditional lines. Its innovative Emerging Artists Family Workshops provide just one of the multitude of vehicles structured as educational outreach and linking artists featured in the museum's exhibition program with the area's young people and their parents. The museum's Discussion Series presents leading art world authorities and talents in free public programs for open-ended conversations about art and art issues.

With its wealth of galleries and a respected art museum it's entirely understandable why the promoters of contemporary art fairs have brought their international extravaganzas into this Art Town's whirlwind of creativity. "Art LA, the New Los Angeles International Contemporary Art Fair, occupies the Santa Monica Civic Auditorium for a two-day event in late January attracting nearly 75 exhibiting galleries from New York City to London, Auckland, Mexico City, Berlin, and elsewhere. In late February the Santa Monica Arts Festival occupies the same venue with its more artist-driven showcase of more than 200 talents, while throughout the year the auditorium serves as a preferred site for shows focused on books, fine crafts, tribal arts, jewelry, and more.

Santa Monica is also home to one of the West Coast's most energetic and original theatre scenes. South of Pico in a converted Venice neighborhood storefront the Pacific Resident Theatre offers both a main stage season of original works alongside rarely-performed classics, as well as a series of co-op productions in which the theatre's member actors, director's, and playwrights rehearse, workshop, and fine-tune productions destined for the main

The forever-entertaining cast of artists and strollers along Venice Beach is one of Southern California's best free shows.

stage. Santa Monica Theatre Guild's Morgan-Wixson Theatre, which is located on Pico Boulevard, continues the Guild's 60-plus years of achievement through its year-round production of Broadway hits and newer works, while the Powerhouse Theatre on 2nd Street offers a decidedly less mainstream experience through its diverse range of Latenite productions, Storytelling workshops, New Works plays, and weekend matinee performances of childrens' stage classics. On the north side of Pico the Santa Monica Playhouse stages youth theatre productions, while the Westside Electric mixes theatre and comedy. City Garage, one of LA's most closely watched venues for new plays, is known for its international perspectives and experimental edge.

Venues

Santa Monica Museum of Art
2525 Michigan Avenue, Santa Monica, CA 90404
310.586.6488 / www.smmoa.org
$5 Donation / Closed Sunday and Monday
▲ Influential exhibition facility in Bergamot Station presenting leading contemporary artists.

Angles Gallery
2230 Main Street, Santa Monica, CA 90405
310.396.5019 / www.anglesgallery.com
Closed Sunday and Monday
▲ Sleek contemporary art space with two gallery rooms primarily featuring American artists.

Terrence Rogers Fine Art
1231 Fifth Street, Santa Monica, CA 90401
310.394.4999 / www.trogart.com
▲ Represents an outstanding group of contemporary realist painters.

Shoshana Wayne Gallery
2525 Michigan Avenue, Santa Monica, CA 90404
310.453.7535 / www.shoshanawayne.com
Closed Sunday and Monday
▲ Bergamot Station's original art space represents artists such as Kiki Smith, Dinh Q Le, Victor Estrada, Irit Batsry, and Shirley Tse.

The Powerhouse Theatre
3116 2nd Street, Santa Monica, CA 90405
310.396.3680 / www.powerhousetheatre.com

▲ Once regarded as a neighborhood eyesore, the old generating station that's now home to the Powerhouse Theatre hums with activity.

City Garage
1340 1/2 4th St., Santa Monica, CA 90404
310.319.9939 / www.citygarage.org
▲ Ensemble stage company founded by Charles Duncombe and Frederique Michel known for presenting edgy, experimental work.

Pacific Resident Theatre
707 Venice Boulevard, Venice, CA 90291
310.822.8392 / www.pacificresidenttheatre.com
▲ Co-op theatre run by actors, playwrights, and directors known for its in-progress presentations.

Events

Art LA
Santa Monica Civic Auditorium, Santa Monica, CA 90404
323.937.4659 / www.artfairsinc.com
▲ This January art fair features international art dealers from across the globe.

Santa Monica Arts Festival
Santa Monica Civic Auditorium, Santa Monica, CA 90404
805.461.6700 / www.americanartfestivale.com
▲ Features more than 200 artists and craftspeople from across the continent.

Slumber

The Hotel California
1670 Ocean Avenue, Santa Monica, CA 90404
866.571.0000 / www.hotelca.com
▲ Cool Rooms / Warm People is the motto of this beachside hotel next to the Santa Monica Pier. Check-out times are, however, something the management has tightened up over the years. Reasonable rates, long-term stay policies, free wi-fi, and an international clientele.

Shutters Hotel on the Beach
One Pico Boulevard, Santa Monica, CA 90404
310.458.0030 / www.shuttersonthebeach.com

▲ Stylish beachfront lodgings with a pool, spa, and fitness room, located just steps away from all of Santa Monica's best attractions. One of Shutters most attractive features is its outstanding collection of contemporary art, which includes work by William Wegman, Richard Diebenkorn, Claes Oldenburg, David Hockney, Robert Motherwell, and Roy Lichtenstein.

Ambrose Hotel
1255 20th Street, Santa Monica, CA 90404
310.315.1555 / www.ambrosehotel.com
▲ Deirdre Wallace's 77-room, Euro-style boutique hotel is located a short jaunt from Santa Monica's beach but is within a few blocks of the contemporary art action at Bergamot Station. Fitness facility, free wi-fi, koi pond, hybrid car rentals, and a commitment to environmentally-conscious practices.

Loews Santa Monica Beach Hotel
1700 Ocean Avenue, Santa Monica, CA 90401
310.458.6700 / www.loewshotels.com
▲ With its 342 oceanside rooms, Ocean Spa & Fitness Center, Ocean & Vine restaurant, high speed Internet, and celebrity guests, it's little wonder why this hotel is Santa Monica's most impressive.

Holiday Inn Santa Monica Beach Hotel
120 Colorado Avenue, Santa Monica, CA 90401
310.393.7145 / www.ichotelsgroup.com
▲ Located on the ocean and adjacent to Santa Monica Pier, this 132-room hotel offers free wi-fi, and a heated outdoor pool.

Sustenance

i Cugini
1501 Ocean Avenue, Santa Monica, CA 90401
310.451.4595 / www.icugini.com
▲ Inspired by the seafood restaurants of Italy's Amalfi Coast, the Sunday Jazz Brunch is one of LA's best.

Finn McCool's Irish Pub & Restaurant
2702 Main Street, Santa Monica, CA 90404
310.452.1734
▲ Never underestimate the power a Guinness has when it comes to defeating the June Gloom.

Hama Sushi Restaurant
213 Windward Avenue, Venice, CA 90291

310.396.8783 / www.hamasushi.com
▲ Great sushi on the traffic circle just off Venice Beach. Don't miss the dancing sushi chefs banging out "Hotel California" at quittin' time.

O ne of the most active California artists working in public art, Blue McRight is known for efforts such as her works of "Light Sculpture" for large spaces, and her "On the Lawn" series of oil on panel paintings commenting on America's obsession with their front yards. Her "Impossible Lawn Chair," a 9-foot long chaise lounge with astroturf surfaces, was installed as part of the Art on the Outside exhibition along Santa Monica Boulevard.

"Since I moved to the area in 1985, opportunities to both participate in and view a wide variety of exhibitions have greatly increased as the number of galleries and noncommercial venues has surged. As a result the attendance at art events in Santa Monica has also grown tremendously, enabling artists to present their work to a much larger audience. Although artist-run spaces like the 18th Street Arts Complex play an important role, the nexus of this growth is the Bergamot Station Art Center and Santa Monica Museum of Art, which provide an incredible resource for local artists.

"The large number of galleries (at Bergamot Station) provides opportunities for both local and out of town artists to participate in and view a wide range of exhibitions. Santa Monica Museum of Art contributes to this yet does even more: the museum works directly with local artists through exhibitions (for example, I created an installation for a 2005 Project Gallery show), annual events like INCOGNITO give hundreds of artists and collectors a chance to connect, in-depth educational programming features artists interacting directly with people of all ages, and lectures, performances, and films enhance the Museum visitor's experience.

"The excellent art schools in the Los Angeles area contribute to a large pool of young emerging artists and gallerists in Santa Monica, while there are also many older more established artists, gallerists, curators, and arts administrators working here as well. In my opinion, representation of women and minorities is steadily increasing but there is still room for improvement. Santa Monica's art scene will no doubt continue to expand in the future. I'd like to see increasing interaction and exchange with other SoCal, national, and international cultural institutions as well as increased opportunities for women and minority artists. More affordable studio space would be great, too!"

L isa Melandri is deputy director for exhibitions and programs for the Santa Monica Museum of Art.

"As the anchor tenant of the Bergamot Station Art Center, a must-see cultural destination, SMMoA has chosen to offer exhibitions and programs at a variety of times and days to best serve the different audiences that visit. We have effectively maximized what we offer so that there is always a great reason to stop by. In addition, whenever possible, the Museum arranges its exhibitions and education programs to dovetail with like offerings at adjacent Bergamot galleries.

"In addition to its main gallery, SMMoA has two Project Rooms that often feature the works of emerging and midcareer artists, including artists from Santa Monica, such as midcareer artist Blue McRight. Often this is the first museum exhibition for these artists, garnering them critical, public, and media attention. Our education program features workshops run by a wide range of emerging and mid-career artists, many of them local. In addition, the Museum's annual signature fundraiser, INCOGNITO: An Exhibition and Art Sale, includes hundreds of local, national, and international artists, from the well-known to the emerging.

"The essence of SMMoA's successful growth as an arts institution is premised on its ability to serve a wide range of audiences, national, international, and its very important local constituencies through vibrant exhibitions and programs. This tripartite audience model may well be an example of best practices that other institutions could follow. The Museum's public programming seeks both to increase access and understanding of the visual arts, but also, in keeping with SMMoA's mission, to connect art with a wide swath of disciplines: literature, the environment, politics, to name a few. In this way, SMMoA seeks to give all those who visit the Museum fresh and new perspectives, not only on art, but on the world.

"To continue to grow and be on the cutting-edge of the burgeoning Santa Monica art scene, SMMoA would like nothing better than to continue to increase the cultural cooperation it currently engages in with other Santa Monica and Southland groups. One of the important touchstones for the many projects and initiatives that the Museum undertakes is that we act in concert and community with other local institutions, from the performing arts, to service organizations, to business groups."

Sebastopol

Northern California's striking beauty has occasionally been overwhelmed by a variant of development whose "Wonderful Wine Country" theme verges on the overbearing. But in the western reaches of Sonoma County a slowed-down lifestyle and an agricultural heritage have managed to either elude developers' sights or fought off their advances . . . and most likely benefited from a little bit of both . . . in preserving places like Sebastopol. With its compact business district bisected by the apple-honoring Gravenstein Highway (CA-116) and the Luther Burbank Memorial Highway (CA-12) celebrating America's greatest horticulturalist, this community of 7,800 residents retains the distinct flavor of its ties to the region's abundance of vineyards and family farms. Hiding, however, just an inch or so below that camouflage of overalls, work boots, and rich topsoil is a local and regional art scene of substantial size, diversity, and achievement whose impact plays no small role in West Sonoma County's quality of life.

By the time Luther Burbank established his 15-acre Gold Ridge Farm just west of Sebastopol's center in 1885, the community was already known as the nation's applesauce capitol. Orchards dedicated to raising Gravenstein apples were then, and to this day remain, central to the local economy, and Burbank's farm is now overseen by the county's Historical Society. Nearly everything planted in this fertile ground seems to thrive in Sebastopol's year-round moderate climate. The 13 miles of rolling hillsides separating it from neighboring Bodega Bay usually wring out the Pacific's coastal fog and replace its impenetrable mist with rays of sunshine, allowing for not only the development of more than a half-dozen local vineyards and wineries but also the region's

Walkable, friendly, and diverse, the downtown sidewalks of Sebastopol are an ideal place to spend a lazy afternoon.

flourishing organic produce industry. From April through December the area's agriculture pros gather on Sunday afternoons in Sebastapol's Downtown Plaza to take part in one of the county's top farmer's markets. When it's not overrun with mounds of apples, piles of cherries, and rivers of spinach, downtown's Plaza serves as the center of Sebastopol's public life, with its stage used for summer's Plaza Performance Series of free Thursday evening concerts, its fountain as a favored meeting place, and its landscaped grounds as an exhibition venue for the community's Art in Public Places initiative.

Another aspect of Sebastopol's culture takes place on the shaded grounds of Ives Park, which is not only the site of Ives Pool but also the summer home of the annual Sebastopol Shakespeare Festival. This extension of the Sonoma County Repertory Theater has presented a season of two outdoor productions covering at least one of Shakespeare's classics since 1993, with performances beginning after the July 4 holiday and continuing through late August. Throughout most of the year's warmer months Ives Park is the venue of choice for everything from a Roma Festival of gypsy music in early March, to the three-day Celtic Festival in September and summer's annual gumbo-flavored Cajun Festival. Originally known as the Main Street Theatre, the Rep presents a year-round mainstage season of five productions in its storefront theatre, which occupies the northwest corner of the busiest intersection in town. In addition to its professional theatre productions the Rep also organizes a full-scale educational outreach program that includes but isn't limited to a student Shakespeare company that gets its own night under the Ives Park spotlights, Summer Theatre Day Camps for young people ages 6 to 18, Young Actors Conservatory programs in acting and production, and a Student Rep Company staging its own productions. The Rep, whose yearly audiences exceed 10,000 for its stage productions and 5,000 for its youth presentations, also offers playwrights opportunities to test new scripts through its New Dramatic Works readings series. Sebastopol's other theatre company, the Independent Eye, operates in the Fringe Theatre tradition in that it foregoes the burden of operating from a year-round playhouse in favor of maintaining the ability to engage in productions ranging from collaborations with other theatre companies (including Sonoma County Repertory Theatre) to self-produced plays performed in local as well as out of town venues. The company's thought-provoking plays take a wide angle look at life from both personal and societal perspectives.

The Sebastopol Center for the Arts (SCA) follows a multidisciplinary approach in its stewardship of several components of the local art scene. On the visual arts front SCA uses the two exhibition spaces inside its 10,000 square foot of warehouse-style space for changing exhibitions of both themed monthly shows (the majority are juried) and a rotating slate of one-artist shows in its Gallery II, which serves as a short-term rental space. Education initiatives in visual arts, literary arts, and music attract adults and young learners to SCA, as do its concerts, readings and spoken word performances. SCA's impact is also evident in events the center organizes and presents, such as the biannual Sebastopol Film Festival, whose three days of screenings take place in early March. The annual "Sculpture Jam" is an outdoor, weekend-long October gathering of more than a dozen local sculptors on the Downtown Plaza, each working in her or his chosen media to create public art. Another of SCA's efforts is the annual Benefit Auction's May celebration of local art, wines, and culinary arts.

The father of American horticulture needed to come up with some fast cash when he decided to break away from his family's farm near Boston and head West, a journey that eventually landed him in Sebastopol. So in the early 1870s he sold his rights to reproducing a certain variety of potato to a seed company for $150, hopped a train and never looked back. Roll Forward 140 years and that same potato has turned out to be known as the Burbank Russet and is the french fry choice of fast food purveyors from McDonalds to In 'n Out.

The annual Sculpture Jam organized by the Sebastopol Center for the Arts attracts some of Northern California's top creative talents during its early October staging.

There's a substantial presence of visual artists at many local events including April's annual Apple Blossom Festival, a Sebastopol tradition since 1910 that fills Ives Park with music stages, food vendors, wine tents, and a sea of 125 artists' booths. In August, after spring's blossoms have matured into Gravensteins, the majestic oaks of Ragle Ranch Regional Park's 157-acres attract a similar number of artists during the annual Apple Fair. While many of downtown's businesses keep their doors open late for the monthly First Thursdays ARTwalk, an ideal forum for connecting with most of the area's artists takes place across the two October weekends of ARTrails, a self-guided, open studios tour coordinated throughout Sonoma County. More than 100 artists in West Sonoma County alone open their work environments to any and all comers during the tour. Two June weekends mark the annual staging of Art at the Source, another open studios tour. Like ARTrails, Art at the Source is a self-guided tour attracting more than 100 participating West Sonoma County artists.

The west county communities surrounding Sebastopol are hotbeds of creativity in their own right, though none have a comparable depth of performing arts presentations, visual arts exhibitions, and outdoor festivals. Bodega Bay is home to galleries such as the Ren Brown Collection and its wide variety of contemporary Japanese ceramics, baskets, and prints, Local Color Gallery's diverse group of local artists working in different media, and the Bodega Bay Heritage Gallery's top-notch inventory of realist and impressionist paintings by well-known 19th and 20th century artists. California's impressionist painting tradition is also celebrated a short distance north of Bodega Bay at the Christopher Queen Galleries in tiny Duncan Mills, while a group of 45 local artists is represented in the array of paintings, gourds, woven horsehair baskets, leather gloves, and glass sculptures in the Artisans' Co-op on the Bodega Highway between Bodega Bay and Sebastopol. The region's twice-yearly open studio tours tend to knock the legs out from underneath commercial galleries by filling the local art market's needs as well as capturing large chunks of what's generated by nearby San Francisco's art collectors, resulting in Sebastopol's changing palette of art galleries. Artisana Functional Art represents a number of the region's top jewelers at its North Main Street location, while Sebastopol Galleries, an artist-owned space on North Main Street, exhibits the work of 13 local talents working in ceramics, oil painting, bronze, and photography.

Venues

Sebastopol Center for the Arts

6780 Depot Street, Sebastopol, CA 95472
707.829.4797 / www.sebarts.org
▲ This busy art center uses its 10,000 square feet of industrial space for an extensive education, exhibition, and performance calendar that parallels its organizing of community art festivals.

Sonoma County Repertory Theatre

104 North Main St., Sebastopol, CA 95472
707.823.0177 / www.the-rep.com
▲ Its downtown digs might not offer the Rep enough seating and rehearsal space, but that hasn't prevented it from programming as though it had a 20,000 square foot performing arts center at its disposal, offering extensive and comprehensive education and performance initiatives, including Sebastopol's annual Shakespeare in the Park.

Gold Ridge Farm

7781 Bodega Avenue, Sebastopol, CA 95472
707.829.6711 / www.wschs-grf.pon.net
▲ This 15-acre shrine to the legacy of Luther Burbank, the father of American horticulture, stages its annual open house during April's Sebastopol Apple Blossom Festival.

Sebastopol Gallery

150 North Main Street, Sebastopol, CA 95472
707.829.7200 / www.sebastopol-gallery.com
▲ Artist-owned and operated, this downtown art space exhibits the creations of its 13 member artists.

Artisans' Co-op Gallery
17135-A Bodega Highway, Sebastopol, CA 95472
707.876.9830 / www.artisansco-op.com
▲ Nearly 50 fine artists and fine craftspeople from across the far reaches of West Sonoma County are represented through this artist owned and operated space on the road connecting Sebastopol and Bodega Bay.

Artisana Functional Art
146 North Main Street, Sebastopol, CA 95472
707.829.3036 / www.artisanafunctionalart.com
▲ This downtown Sebastopol art gallery represents local and regional talents in fine crafts, jewelry, and home accessories.

Events

Sebastopol Apple Blossom Festival
Ives Park, Sebastopol, CA 95472
707.823.3032 / www.sebastopol.org
▲ April's kickoff to summer features a parade, quilt show, pie eating contests, and an outdoor art fair.

Sebastopol Farmers Market
Downtown Plaza, Sebastopol, CA 95472
707.522.9305 /
▲ Sebastopol's farmers gather from 10 AM to 1:30 PM on Sundays from April through December.

Sculpture Jam
Sebastopol Downtown Plaza, Sebastopol, CA 95472
707.829.4797 / www.sculpturejam.org
▲ This October event turns Downtown Plaza into an outdoor sculpture studio and results in sculpture installations throughout downtown.

Slumber

The Sebastopol Inn
6751 Sebastopol Avenue, Sebastopol, CA 95472
800.653.1082 / www.sebastopolinn.com
▲ Also the home of Coffee Catz Coffeehouse, this centrally located hotel features gardens, free wi-fi, and a hot tub.

Casa Carolina
7740 Nora Avenue, Sebastopol, CA 95472
707.823.3543 / www.casacarolina.us
▲ Quiet bed and breakfast inn on the outskirts of Sebastopol.

Pearlessence Vineyard Inn
4097 Hessel Road, Sebastopol, CA 95472
707.823.5092 / www.pearlessenceinn.com
▲ Three-room inn with large rooms and spacious grounds.

Bodega Bay Lodge & Spa
103 Coast Highway 1, Bodega Bay, CA 94923
707.875.3525 / www.bodegabaylodge.com
▲ This rustic, 84-room retreat offers spectacular ocean views, a swimming pool, fitness center, and an afternoon wine tasting.

Holiday Inn Express Hotel & Suites
1101 Gravenstein Highway South, Sebastopol, CA 95472
707.829.6677 / www.winecountryhi.com
▲ Convenient to all of Sebastopol's offerings, this affordably priced hotel has free wi-fi, a fitness center, and fireplace.

Sustenance

GTO's Seafood House
234 South Main Street, Sebastopol, CA 95472
707.824.9922 / www.gtoseafoodhouse.com
▲ Gene and Tess Ostopowicz might have put their Jazzfest days behind them, but thankfully they haven't forgotten how to mix a perfect Hurricane.

French Garden Restaurant & Brasserie
8050 Bodega Avenue, Sebastopol, CA 95472
707.824.2030 / www.frenchgardenrestaurant.com
▲ Sebastopol's leading restaurant combines local farm freshness with new approaches to French cuisine with consistent excellence.

California Cider Company / Ace-in-the-Hole
3100 Gravenstein Highway North, Sebastopol, CA 95472
707.829.1101 / www.acecider.com
▲ Wonderful pub serving memorable ciders and a full restaurant menu.

A s executive director of the Sebastopol Center for the Arts, Linda Galletta oversees an organization serving more than 13,000 residents of west Sonoma County annually through year-round exhibitions, performances, and events.

"We're a very cooperative and supportive organization in terms of serving the artists and arts organizations in this part of the county. From enhancing the local arts environment to developing the arts audiences of the future, our doors are always open. There's an opportunity, for instance, for the city to redevelop the warehouse district that's home to our art center and a growing number of artists' studios. I think that providing a more user-friendly approach to making this area a walkable extension of Sebastopol's downtown is just one of the ways we can serve as a resource center for members of the community who may or may not come through our doors for exhibitions or programs.

"Sebastopol recently passed a percent-for-the-arts initiative that will fund public works of art throughout the community, and will help to build upon the already prominent displays of sculptures in the downtown area. We sponsor an annual sculpture jam in the first week of October that results in sculpture installed around town for either one or two years. The city has worked closely with us in terms of finding suitable sites to install the sculpture and even assist in the process of installing them on the sites. Their support has been very appreciated."

B ruce Shapiro found his calling in art at a point in life where he was working as an MD in Minneapolis. Trading his stethoscope and scalpel for a plasma cutter and Bridgeport mill he now lives on a rural property near Sebastopol.

"I'd been doing my work back in Minneapolis until my wife and I discovered this perfect home near Sebastopol. It was one of those trips where we were passing through and just started looking at real estate. The combined attributes of being close to the ocean, having 5 acres of fruit trees on the property, and being located in the kind of climate where I could work outside, year-round, were what convinced us that we needed to be here. I'm more than 50 percent located in Sebastopol, though parts of my studio are still back in Minneapolis.

"I wasn't aware of the arts community that was already in Sebastopol when I first got here, so finding out that there's a number *of accomplished artists living here has been a pleasant surprise. The type of technological-based art that I create isn't typical of the kind of art most people associate with Sonoma county, though just in the short time I've been here I've noticed that several artists working in technology have bought homes here.*

"Shortly after we bought our place I was invited to show my work at the Sebastopol Arts Center, so there's been a genuine interest in my work in this community."

Tahoe City

From the northwest shore of Lake Tahoe, life takes on a picture-perfect quality. To its east there's the 191 square miles of azure hued waters known as the legendary Lake of the Sky. To stand on the lakeshore's edge and watch a summer sunrise illuminate its mirror-smooth surface is to understand why Lake Tahoe's original residents, the Washoe Tribe, considered it a sacred place. But turn 180 degrees from that same spot on the lakeshore and the other side of picture-perfection towers into view in the form of the Sierra Nevada range. This 400-mile mountain mass passes Lake Tahoe's western shores in the form of snow-covered giants such as 8,878-foot Twin Peaks, 8,473-foot Stanford Rock, and 8,885-foot Squaw Peak. With some of the continent's best skiing just steps away from its back porch and one of North America's most spectacular bodies of water lapping up against its front porch, there's little wonder why living in and around Tahoe City has made crystal-clear sense to this community's 1,800 full-time residents.

Legend has it that it Lt. John Fremont's soldiers were first guided through these mountains by Kit Carson. Years later the Comstock Lode's discovery in nearby Virginia City and the American River gold discovery of 1848 led to the founding of boom towns such as Truckee, whose snowy streets became the setting for the shooting of *The Little Tramp*, Charlie Chaplin's 1924 film classic. Located just 10 miles north of Tahoe City, Truckee has moved beyond its Gold Rush heritage to become home to a growing number of art galleries and restaurants, with long-range plans to redevelop its railyards into an arts, entertainment, and residential district roughly along the same lines as what Santa Cruz has set out to accomplish through its Tannery Art Center project. Lake Tahoe's waters flow into the Truckee River from behind the Lake Tahoe Dam to the south of Tahoe City. The dam's crest at a 6,233 foot elevation ensures that the trophy-sized cutthroat trout that live in the Truckee River draw fly fishermen throughout much of the year.

The cultural scene along north Lake Tahoe extends from the Tahoe Maritime Museum in the community of Homewood to Sand Harbor State Park on the Nevada side of Lake Tahoe's Northshore. Between those points is the Tahoe City home of North Tahoe Arts, the region's leading arts center and home to an exhibition space whose monthly exhibits not only showcase the work of Lake Tahoe's fine craftsmen, painters, photographers, sculptors, and jewelers but also extend to include impor-

The dramatic beauty of Lake Tahoe unfolds behind the Sand Harbor stage of the Lake Tahoe Shakespeare Festival.

tant artists from Nevada and California. In addition to its summer YouthART camp for school-age kids the center also organizes the popular Seasons of Martis Plein Air Painting Competition, a weeklong event in which a juried group of artists ventures out to several of the region's premier painting sites to create work destined to be auctioned at a fundraising gala. Nearly a dozen unconventional venues such as bank lobbies, cafes, and medical offices serve as rotating, bimonthly venues for NTA's Art in Public Places exhibitions featuring for-sale work from local painters and photographers. Some of the same artists whose creations are exhibited through the Art in Public Places program are represented in the center's ARTisan Shop, an art gallery displaying creations from across creative media. The two July weekends of ARTour provide visitors and local art lovers with six days of opportunity to visit the workshops and studios of artists throughout Truckee, Incline Village, and Tahoe City.

Ethos Gallery, located in the Village at Northstar, is a contemporary art space exhibiting the work of mainly California but also national painters and sculptors. Its companion art space, Spirits in Stone, specializes in contemporary art from Africa. Vista Gallery's emphasis extends toward a range of expressions including vintage photography, contemporary photography by talents such as Robert Desmond and Wyatt Ogilvy, Ron Hagerty's welded sculpture, and Gene Purcell's paintings. Gallery Keoki in the Village at Squaw Valley showcases the work of photographer Keoki Flagg as well as paintings and fine crafts by artists from throughout the nation. The region's most established exhibition venue is Lakeside Gallery in Kings Beach. Serving as both an art gallery and an education center hosting art workshops, Lakeside Gallery's instructors include national figures such as Howard Rees, Joyce Ortner, and David Mallory. Tahoe City's Boatworks Mall is where James Harold Gallery exhibits the more than 50 artists it represents. Carmel Gallery in Truckee, exhibits the work of its photographer owners Olof and Elizabeth Carmel, two global gadabouts who for years have reached their wide base of collectors from a historic Truckee residence. Another Truckee art space, White Buffalo Gallery, sells work by a variety of Native American jewelers, weavers, and potters, while Riverside Studios in Truckee's Brickelltown district serves as an alternative exhibition venue for work by local artists.

One of the more recent success stories on the region's performing arts front has to do with the Truckee Community Chorus, a 65-member group whose performances in school auditoriums have slowly but steadily built a local audience for classics from Vivaldi, Schubert, Britten, and Bizet. The Diablo Valley College Philharmonic Orchestra joins with the Truckee Community Chorus in some of its more ambitious productions.

Sand Harbor State Park, located on the Nevada side of North Lake Tahoe, is the summer home of the Lake Tahoe Shakespeare Festival. This nearly 40-year old festival performs in an open amphitheatre with the lakeshore itself serving as the backdrop to productions taking place on its Warren Edward Trepp Stage. The festival's July and August plays take place during the evening, with the short season somehow accommodating three productions, two of which are classics from the Bard, with the third being an original play featuring the festival's Shakespearean actors in contemporary roles. On its community outreach side the festival stages more than a dozen free performances for students and offers a weeklong theatre camp. Another lakeshore setting, Tahoe City's Commons Beach, serves as the venue for a series of free Sunday afternoon concerts from late June through Labor Day weekend. During that same time period Commons Beach turns into the community's open-air cinema for Movies at the Beach, whose offerings are quite family-appropriate. Independence Day's fireworks are best viewed from Commons Beach, while the town's annual Heart & Solstice Festival spreads its classic car show, wine tasting, and farmers' market

The historic building that's home to North Lake Tahoe Arts serves an enormous territory with workshops, exhibitions, and expertise.

throughout the community. River Ranch Lodge, located a few miles from the center of Tahoe City on the road leading to Truckee, serves not only as the headquarters of June's annual Truckee Duckee Derbee but also becomes the area's top venue for outdoor concerts from mid-June through Labor Day weekend when Renegade Productions turns on the funk, rock, and world beat talents.

When Truckee fully opens its new community and cultural center in late 2009 the local art scene will gain a much-needed asset in the form of a new performing arts venue. The primary beneficiaries will be Truckee's existing performing arts groups such as Innerrhythms Dance Theatre, the region's foremost dance company. Innerrhythms works across the range of Truckee's performing arts taste by presenting programs as diverse as African Dance Workshops to a Summer Intensive for experienced dancers to a Summer Fun Dance Camp and a Tahoe Young Dancers Workshop. The annual Truckee Renaissance Faire set up its ingenious array of Medieval-style tents, stages, artists' booths, and warrior encampments in mid-September on the grounds of Truckee River Regional Park. The Shyre lasts only two days, which is barely enough time for the faire's jousting, jesting, belly dancing, and witchcraft shows.

Venues

North Tahoe Arts
380 North Lake Boulevard, Tahoe City, CA 96145
530.581.2787 / www.northtahoearts.com

▲ From its modest quarters in the Community Center building this focused and efficient organization serves as the binding agent for many parts of the region's far-flung creative scene. Worth a visit just to check out the shows in its changing gallery and its ARTisan Shop.

Riverside Studios
10374 Donner Pass Road, Truckee, CA 96161
530.587.3789 / www.riversideartstudios.com
▲ This Brickelltown building is home to several of the area's best artists. Be sure to stop in for its monthly First Fridays openings.

Truckee Community Chorus
530.582.8488 / www.truckeecommunitychorus.com
▲ Who would have guessed, at the founding of this homespun performing arts group in 2002, that Music Director Chris Nelson could convince Truckee residents that singing was too cool for words.

Ethos Gallery
5001 Northstar Drive, Truckee, CA 96161
530.562.0860 / www.ethosgallery.com
▲ Representing talents such as painters Teri Blodgett, Linda G. Fisher, Michael Holland, and Catheryn Austin, this gallery at the base of Northstar ski area is complemented by the contemporary African art exhibited at Spirits in Stone, whose Shona masters include Edias Muromba, Henry Munyaradzi, and Creto Simon.

Vista Gallery
7081 North Lake Boulevard, Tahoe Vista, CA 96148
530.546.7794 / www.vistagallery.com
▲ Artist Gordon Taylor's one-of-a-kind art space is a must-see stop on any first-time visitor's Lake Tahoe itinerary.

Events

ARTour
North Tahoe Arts, Tahoe City, CA 96145
530.581.2787 / www.northtahoearts.com
▲ Scheduled across two weekends in mid-July, this self-guided exploration of the studios of dozens of the region's painters, fine craftsmen, sculptors, and jewelers begins with a kickoff gala at North Tahoe Arts on the Wednesday prior to the tour's opening weekend.

Truckee Renaissance Faire
Truckee River Regional Park, Truckee, CA 96161
530.587.3946 / www.truckeerenfaire.org
▲ This annual gathering of Lords, Ladies, Knights, Wizards, and assorted hangers-on turns out large crowds on a late summer weekend.

Lake Tahoe Shakespeare Festival
Sand Harbor State Park, Incline Village, NV 89451
800.747.4697 / www.laketahoeshakespeare.com
▲ The perfect way to spend a midsummer evening by the lake.

Slumber

Sunnyside Steakhouse & Lodge
1850 West Lake Boulevard, Tahoe City, CA 96145
530.583.7200 / www.sunnysidetahoe.com
▲ With 23 guest rooms on the lake this historic lodge offers classic Lake Tahoe style, along with fabulous dining on the deck of its steakhouse restaurant.

Lake of the Sky Motor Inn
955 North Lake Boulevard, Tahoe City, CA 96145
530.583.3305 / www.lakeoftheskyinn.com
▲ This convenient and affordable motel has a heated pool and a picnic area.

Pepper Tree Inn
645 North Lake Boulevard, Tahoe City, CA 96145
530.583.3711 / www.peppertreetahoe.com
▲ A heated swimming pool and large guest rooms plus affordable rates.

Tamarack Lodge
2311 North Lake Boulevard, Tahoe City, CA 96145
530.583.3350 / www.tamaracktahoe.com
▲ This getaway on 4 acres of seclusion has free wi-fi, an outdoor fireplace, horseshoe pits, a ping pong table, and bocce court.

River Ranch Restaurant & Lodge
2285 River Road, Tahoe City, CA 96145
530.583.4264 / www.riverranchlodge.com
▲ For nearly 40 years this rustic hideaway on the Truckee River has been a favorite of Lake Tahoe visitors. Raft in, bike in, or drive in, and settle into one of the lodge's 19 guest rooms. Chef Julia

Walter's solid approach to seafoods, salads, and steaks makes dining at the River Ranch Bar a Tahoe treat.

Sustenance

Dragonfly
10118 Donner Pass Road, Truckee, CA 96161
530.587.0557 / www.dragonflycuisine.com
▲ Chef Billy McCullough's winning formula combines a sushi bar with regional microbrews, a touch of Thai style, and creative combinations of farm-fresh ingredients.

Jake's on the Lake
780 North Lake Boulevard, Tahoe City, CA 96145
530.583.0188 / www.jakestahoe.com
▲ With its killer views, local brews, and friendly attitudes, Jake's is everyone's lakeside favorite.

Tahoe House Bakery & Gourmet
625 West Lake Boulevard, Tahoe City, CA 96145
530.583.1377 / www.tahoe-house.com
▲ Best place on the lake for fresh baked breads, key lime pies, and a roast beef on rye.

A s executive director of the Lake Tahoe Shakespeare Festival, Catherine Atack brings to her position a range of nontraditional credentials that include stints in public relations firms as well as regional tourism agencies. When it comes to overseeing this successful performing arts organization, Atack understands how the Bard fits into Tahoe's bigger picture.

"I became executive director in December 2003 and since then we've increased attendance in our outdoor theatre by approximately 26 percent. We've also brought more of our production functions in-house, which gives us start-to-finish control over everything from national auditioning for our 25 roles to all of the design expertise required for the three plays we present in our summer season.

"Shakespeare's work represents the very best in literary craft from a very different time, and it remains relevant because it deals with human nature, which is timeless. Our emotional reactions to the world around us haven't changed since the time of Shakespeare's writing, so the message still applies, though centuries later.

"We've made community outreach an increasingly important part of our mission through initiatives such as our own in-school "interACT" program, which allows us to collaborate with the Reno-based Nevada Shakespeare Company. We take seasoned theatre professionals as well as educators to different schools where we will work with students for the purpose of not only developing audiences for Shakespeare's work but to also identify those students who can be moved into acting roles. So today we actually have several young actors in our main stage productions who got their start through the "interACT" program."

Photographer Olof Carmel is co-owner with photographer Elizabeth Carmel of the Carmel Gallery of Photography & Art, which is located in the community of Truckee, California. Together, this married couple not only pursue their quests for capturing the Tahoe region's year-round beauty, they also own and operate one of the region's leading fine art galleries. This interview was conducted with Olof Carmel.

"Truckee is a historic mountain community in the heart of the beautiful Sierra Nevada Mountains. It is very close to the most beautiful lake in the world, Lake Tahoe. Many artists are inspired by the mountain scenery and the dramatically changing seasons. Our small town atmosphere has the sense of community that artists love. Truckee has recently started a downtown art stroll on summer Thursday evenings and is starting to work with a major art show promoter to develop more art events. Elizabeth and I are expanding our little art gallery to a 2,600 square foot space that will also feature a collection of Asian antiques and artifacts.

"Our local government is working with Truckee's arts and culture commission to determine what the most pressing needs are from the perspective of our working artists. One of the goals of that effort is the possibility of developing locally-focused venues for the express purpose of exhibiting art that's created here. Ideally, that space would be able to exhibit work both indoors and outdoors.

"The 'Railyard Project' that's being built now will provide a new alternative to downtown Truckee. When it's finished the arts community will have access to new galleries and performance venues, which in turn will improve our standing as an Art Town."

Ventura

The foothills of 4,900-foot Santa Paula Peak frame Ventura's eastern horizon, while its west flank opens up to views of the Channel Islands, whose rugged terrain is a protected wilderness. Ventura County's landscape, which includes mountains and ocean beaches, has proven as perfectly suited for agriculture as it is for industry. Citrus farming powers a substantial share of the region's economy, tracing its roots to the local founding of what today has evolved into the 6,500-member Sunkist growers cooperative. In the late 19th century oil drilling in nearby Santa Paula led to Union Oil's corporate emergence. Though the wildcatters and most of their rigs are long gone, oil's impact endures in the form of several drilling platforms visible from Ventura's sandy beachfront.

This coastal community of 105,000 residents is living proof that every now and again it pays to have been passing time on life's sidelines. In Ventura's case riding the bench meant observing from a distance many of the mistakes made during the nearly two decades of Southern California's late 20th century development boom. The downtown streets of Ventura's business district went largely untouched by grandiose development initiatives, leaving the community's pedestrian-friendly grid of streets, neighborhood parks, and small-scale retail clusters intact. Unlike nearby Santa Barbara, which benefited from the presence of its large university, as well as its year-round influx of high spending tourists, Ventura had to survive on its wits. For decades the promise of transformative development proved elusive, with the result being that by the mid-1990s its downtown started looking like it had registered a broadside hit.

When it's occupied in early 2010, the WAV (Working Artists Ventura) complex will provide an affordable, ideal living and creating environment for artists and their families in downtown Ventura.

But what many saw as economic inertia for a community founded as Mission San Buenaventura (Spanish translation: good fortune), a dedicated group of Ventura artists, urban planners, elected officials, and creative visionaries interpreted as an ideal opportunity to try something new. They understood that having a stable and strong regional economy surrounding a distressed downtown was counterproductive to the area's quality of life and its prospects for transformative growth. Their vision of the road back for downtown Ventura's economy hitched its wagon to the arts, which up to that point was present but hardly prominent in terms of the community's identity. In lining up broad-based support for their plans they also successfully guided a mosaic of funding initiatives in support of their arts-leveraged downtown revitalization plan through public and private sources. What followed portrayed the community in positive ways on both government and commercial fronts, and Ventura began referring to itself as California's New Art City. Encouraged by the campaign's early successes, county and city agencies increased their support for downtown's art-related initiatives. For Ventura's artists there was general support for the welcome mat being unrolled in their direction, and a creativity migration into downtown's cultural district began to take

Nuvi Mehta conducts while Corey Cerovsek performs at the Ventura Music Festival. (Photo © Linda F. Peterson Photography)

hold. Padre Junipero Serra's Mission San Buenaventura was seeing its hopes for better fortunes come true.

For artists the 75-mile distance separating Ventura from Los Angeles translates into affordable residential, studio, and live/work possibilities. But while the Ventura Highway's congestion is a daunting obstacle for daily commuters it also places the downtown Ventura arts district within range of weekend, road-tripping urbanites. It's been their response to Ventura's energetic schedule of gallery walks, outdoor art fairs, exhibition opening receptions, and artist demonstrations that's provided the foot traffic sustaining downtown's dozen or so commercial, noncommercial, and alternative art exhibiting venues. Among the highest profile events is Arts & Crafts by the Sea, a year-round Saturday outdoor show organized by the San Buenaventura Artists' Union and taking place along the California Street Plaza adjacent to Ventura's waterfront.

Downtown Ventura's galleries, events, theatres, and artists will likely experience the rippling benefits from the opening in 2009 of an innovative, purpose-built, mixed-use structure serving as affordable live / work space for artists. Working Artists Ventura (WAV), the project's official title, is also intended to provide a nurturing environment that will spur an arts-centric form of intelligent development throughout the community. WAV will add to Ventura's downtown a dynamic mix of 54 units of affordable live/work artists space, 15 units of housing for recently homeless families and individuals, 13 condos to be sold at prevailing market rates, retail space for street level businesses engaged in the arts, and a community theatre / gallery space. Located two blocks from Mission San Buenaventura and just a short bicycle ride to the surfer's favorites of Promenade Park and San Buenaventura State Beach, the facility will set the tone for the next phases of downtown's revitalization efforts.

Just a few streets north of WAV, the creative community of Art City Studios clusters an established group of resident and visiting artists creating three-dimensional work onto a site dedicated to the fabrication and exhibition of sculpture in stone, wood, and metal. Its Micro Gallery Showroom and sculpture garden on Dubbers Street is a great place to find work by nearly two dozen Ventura artists, including that of Paul Lindhard, who for more than 20 years has been a driving force on the community's art scene. Another of the must-see art venues taking part in the monthly First Fridays Ventura downtown art tours is Bell Arts Factory, located in a former mattress warehouse on North Ventura Avenue. More than 20 artists maintain studio spaces within the 20,000 square foot facility, which also hosts after-school and weekend art education programs for Ventura youth. The building's Under the Sun Gallery represents work by several of the Bell Arts Factory artists in addition to a range of regional and national talents.

From mid-July through mid-September the courtyard of Olivas Adobe, a 160 year old hacienda that's part of Rancho San Miguel on the southern outskirts of Ventura, is home to a Saturday evening Music Under the Stars series showcasing a range of Ventura music talents, and culminating with a silent movie accompanied by a live orchestra.

Rubicon Theatre Company, one of Ventura's most prominent performing arts organizations, presents its offerings of original and compelling Broadway productions in the Laurel Theater. Its classic design provides Rubicon with an intimate, 200-seat environment for efforts such as its Rubicon International Theatre Festival. This multisite and multiproduction event's staging takes place across a 10-day July time frame. Considered part of the leading edge of Los Angeles's theatre community, during its decade of productions Rubicon Theatre Company has originated a full component of adult and youth education programs in addition to programs presenting Shakespeare and cabaret music. Among its numerous accolades are Ovation Awards, Robby

Awards, Indy Awards, and an NAACP Theatre Award. New West Symphony, the area's leading classical music organization, presents its season of symphonies, student concerts, and emerging artist concerts in two venues, the Thousand Oaks Civic Arts Plaza, and Oxnard's Performing Arts Center. The late April through mid-May staging of the Ventura Music Festival uses several Ventura venues for its concerts. The festival has established itself as an internationally-focused presentation of some of the most prominent talents expanding the boundaries of orchestral, chamber, and virtuoso performance. Outside of its festival season the organization provides a compelling range of touring artist concerts as well as education programs in local schools.

Held three times each year, ArtWalk Ventura presents a spring, summer, and autumn weekend combining visual art with music and performance at more than 50 venues scattered both indoors and outdoors throughout the downtown arts district. A free shuttle service circles among the ArtWalk's venues, staying in service well into the evening hours. An early December Sunday features the Holiday Street Fair and its gathering of artists on downtown's streets, while Ventura's largest community arts event takes place across the span of July 4, when the morning's annual Pushem-Pullem Parade is followed by a 300-artist street fair along Main Street, attracting nearly 50,000 art lovers into town.

Venues

Museum of Ventura County
100 E. Main Street, Ventura, CA 93001
805.653.0323 / www.venturamuseum.org
$4 admission / Closed Monday
▲ Once its 18,000 square foot expansion is completed Ventura's cozy museum will greatly expand its capacity to exhibit local and regional artists.

San Buenaventura Artists' Union Gallery
330 S. California Street Plaza, Ventura, CA 93001
805.643.3012 / www.venturaartistsunion.org
Closed Monday to Wednesday
▲ Great venue to find contemporary art by local talents, plus poetry on Tuesday nights.

Buenaventura Art Association's Buenaventura Gallery
700 E. Santa Clara Street, Ventura, CA 93001
805.648.1235 / www.buenaventuragallery.org

Closed Sunday and Monday
▲ More than 100 local artists belong to this member-run space.

Under the Sun Gallery
432 N. Ventura Avenue, Ventura, CA 93001
805.804.6433 / www.underthesungallery.com
Closed Monday
▲ Part of the Bell Arts Factory complex, representing mostly international work.

Bell Arts Factory
432 N. Ventura Avenue, Ventura, CA 93001
805.643.7489 / www.bellartsfactory.com
▲ More than 20 artists studios keep this complex busy 24/7.

Art City Studios
197 Dubbers Street, Ventura, CA 93001
805.648.1690 / www.artcitystudios.com
▲ Working studios complex for nearly two dozen sculptors working in stone, metal, and wood. Plus an art gallery and sculpture gallery.

Red Brick Gallery
328 E. Main Street, Ventura, CA 93001
805.643.6400 / www.redbrickart.com
Closed Tuesday
▲ Representing more than 30 local and regional artists in all media.

Rubicon Theatre Company
1006 E. Main Street, Ventura, CA 93001
805.667.2912 / www.rubicontheatre.org
▲ Leading theatre presence with year-round productions and a festival of new, international plays.

Events

Music Under the Stars
Olivas Adobe Historical Park, Ventura, CA 93003
805.658.4728 / www.olivasadobe.org
▲ Midsummer concerts on the grounds of a historic hacienda.

First Fridays Ventura
City of Ventura Cultural Affairs Division
805.658.4793 / www.cityofventura.net

▲ More than a dozen downtown arts district galleries keep their doors open late for this monthly, self-guided event.

4th of July Street Fair
City of Ventura Cultural Affairs Division
805.654.7830 / www.cityofventura.net
▲ More than 50,000 attend this daylong event featuring 300 artists on Main Street.

Slumber

The Clocktower Inn on Mission Park
181 E. Santa Clara Street, Ventura, CA 93001
805.652.0141 / www.clocktowerinn.com
▲ With its wonderful location in the heart of downtown next to Mission San Buenaventura, this popular inn is built around a restored 1940s firehouse.

Four Points by Sheraton—Ventura Harbor
1050 Schooner Drive, Ventura, CA 93001
805.658.1212 / www.starwoodhotels.com
▲ Frank Lloyd Wright design sets this full service, 106-room hotel on the Ventura waterfront apart from its competition.

The Victorian Rose
896 E. Main Street, Ventura, CA 93001
805.641.1888 / www.victorian-rose.com
▲ Spectacular, 110-year old former church with five rooms and a convenient downtown location.

Country Inn & Suites
298 S. Chestnut Street, Ventura, CA 93001
805.653.1434 / www.countryinns.com
▲ Located just two blocks from the Ventura Pier, this comfortable, 120-room hotel features a swimming pool and free wi-fi.

The Pierpoint Inn
550 San Jon Road, Ventura, CA 93001
805.643.6144 / www.pierpointinn.com
▲ Built in the early 1900s as a luxury getaway for wealthy Los Angelenos, the Pierpoint Inn is a treasure of architectural diversity and resort-style comfort. Its 77 guest rooms are located on a coastal bluff whose spectacular views take in Ventura's natural splendor. Swimming pool, day spa, gardens, Austen's restaurant, and traditional California elegance.

Sustenance

My Florist Cafe & Bakery
76 S. Oak Street, Ventura, CA 93001
805.653.0011 / www.myfloristcafe.com
▲ David Lacey expanded his popular downtown Phoenix dining
spot to Ventura's downtown arts district, bringing great salads,
affordable wines, and good vibes.

J's Tapas
204 E. Main Street, Ventura, CA 93001
805.648.4853 / wwwjonathansatperanos.com
▲ Popular downtown restaurant with live music on weekends.

The SideCar Restaurant
3029 E. Main Street, Ventura, CA 93001
805.653.7433 / www.thesidecarrestaurant.com
▲ Chef Tim Kilcoyne's menu emphasizes local ingredients and the
restored beauty of a 1910 Pullman train car.

When Joshua Addison opened the downtown Ventura arts complex known as the Bell Arts Factory in 2004 the community gained access to 20,000 square feet of mixed-use space supporting everything from a Youth Arts Program to a gallery space for visiting artists and a Community Room where local arts organizations could hold meetings. But perhaps most important the facility also provided low-cost work space in the form of 27 Artist Studios dedicated to making sure that Ventura's working artists continue creating.

"The Bell Arts Factory had since 1937 been a factory making mattresses, with my family taking over the business in the 1950s. About four years ago, after the place stopped making mattresses, we needed a new use for the building and decided to join the broad civic initiative to closely work with the arts community. Fortunately we already had a 20,000 square-foot building with high ceilings perfect for art creation, exhibition, and performance.

'We had made studio spaces available on a rolling basis, opening parts of the building as renovations proceeded. The local artists picked up on these spaces immediately, which was partly the result of the extensive community outreach efforts we put together like becoming part of the monthly downtown Art Walk as early as we could. We also encouraged day use of the facility by various Ventura artists, which

easily filled the space with poets, painters, performers, drummers, and sculptors.

"Our mission has always been to generate the kind of value to both ourselves and to the resident artists that couldn't only be measured in monetary terms. There's a need in the neighborhood where we are located to help turn around the perceptions of the area as less than desirable, and the Bell Arts Factory has been a major step forward in that direction."

———————————•———————————

As the most prominent Ventura creator of public works of art, the talented MB "Universe" Hanrahan relocated to Southern California after completing her MBA degree studies at Humboldt State University in the Art Town of Arcata, California. Today her paintings, murals, sculptures, and art cars have helped define Ventura as a community where the arts and artists are key components in this Art Town's future.

"My art form, which manifests as many art forms, is generally participatory and employs materials and methods in effective but unusual ways. It pushes the envelope of the institution involved and is completed by the participation of an audience. Ventura's always been the kind of place where artists enjoy living but it used to be a more tolerant and less bureaucratic place than it is today. Like in a lot of places that have a number of artists there's been a degree of gentrification and compartmentalizing of the local art scene in recent years.

"Many of the artists here have a commitment to improving this community through the practice of "artification," and it's that sort of bohemian charm that sometimes gets tossed to the wayside in the bigger picture of someone's march toward progress. As government tightens its regulations in a gentrifying community there's a tendency for artists to feel more pressure to make ends meet, which in turn causes them to turn to making art that's more middle of the road and less about art than it is about making a living. I'm not really interested in making paintings of the pier because to me as a full-time artist there's no sense in being stuck to the middle of the road."

Index

261